ADAPTIVE WISDOMS

LEAD FROM THE SKIN IN

NLP MASTERY FOR LEADERS
VOLUME 1

PAUL O'NEILL

Copyright © 2025 by Paul O'Neill

All rights reserved.

No part of this book may be reproduced in any form or by any electronic or mechanical means, including information storage and retrieval systems, without written permission from the author, except for the use of brief quotations in a book review.

For Mark—

Who lit up our lives with a grin that rewrote the rules

A laugh that pulled others in

And a spirit that made even ordinary days feel like adventures.

Though time keeps moving, your presence is stitched into everything bright—a song lyric, a summer breeze, a moment of mischief I know you'd have loved.

This is for you, wee man—not in mourning, but in thanks.

You taught me joy. You taught me guts. You taught me how short and brilliant life can be. Still missed. Still here.

Always, always celebrated.

RECOMMENDATIONS

"It's rare that I would use such a word but it's extremely well-earned in Paul's case: he is a visionary. His ability to make the complex simple, to get to the heart of an issue and to recommend an effective solution is outstanding. His vitality and energy is infectious"

Emma Jensen, Head of Go-To-Market, OPTUS

"Through the lens of research in neuroscience, Paul can forge interventions that promote resilience. His type of coaching allowed me to be better equipped to cope with stress and adversity, at my level, but also recognising the signs in other people and helped me being a better manager"

Jessica Scalzo, Variety Improvement Manager at COSTA

"Paul is one of the energizing and gifted leaders I know. He is also one of the most skilled NLP practitioners I have had the good fortune to meet"

Tim Dalmau, CEO at Dalmau Consulting

"As a leader, Paul has a unique quality rarely seen in today's leaders and that is: the ability to find and bring out 'the best' in people"

Tony Enache, CFO at Farm Pride Foods.

"Paul offers a refreshing take on leadership and workplace change strategies. He provides time efficient tailored insights and solutions to support and equip leaders to develop, reframe perspectives and shift the status quo to deliver positive outcomes suited to today's dynamic work environment"

Elizabeth Brockbank, Environmental Manager at ALCOA

"Paul demonstrated a balanced consultative senior management approach that could quickly interpret and translate detailed plans and how they could consolidate into overall strategies for KPI success"

Peter Sheehan, Director GM, Western Sydney Airport.

"Paul is an excellent trainer who has transformed my life. His amazing skills, dedicated care and consistent emotional intelligence has opened a new world for me to view"

Philip Hoang, Data Engineer at CBHS

"Paul has been an invaluable asset to both myself personally and in my business strategies. Paul and his unique skill set have aided constant changes in the business and personal arena that mean I achieved positive rather than negative outcomes personally and financially"

Ben Kavich, Director at Workhorse Group of Companies

"My life was just like 'work-retire-die'. But this has changed dramatically after I had couple of sessions with Paul. With his help, I can recognise myself, again. I learned to love myself and make myself a priority, again. Paul's training has not only changed my life, it changed my whole family's life"

Iris Huangfu, Accountant, Sydney, Australia

"Paul's intervention and guidance was a game changer. It's not easy to put into words the impact that his NLP practice had as it wasn't singular nor limited to just myself or to that point in time. Personally, I was brought back to a feeling of inner strength and reminded, not through words or description, but through creating an experience, that I can be in control of how I feel and create calm from within my own skin"

V. Madsen, Perth, Australia.

"I would like to thank Paul for transforming my life. He helped me find a completely different mindset, which you will find will help you discover the keys to the life that you deserve, too. As a female going through the beginnings of divorce, it has not been easy. But I have now gained a deep sense of security and confidence. And I have the excitement of a wonderful new future"

L. Diaz, Sydney, NSW.

"Paul is a fantastic hypnotist who has helped me with a lot of my deep personal issues, both for work and my private life. Every time, he works his magic. Truly, he is simply the best!"

A. Gonzales, Registered Nurse, Sydney, Australia.

"The tools / techniques I learnt through my time with Paul will stay with me a lifetime, and why wouldn't I want that when I'm feeling like I'm floating in champagne bubbles"

Jacqueline D., Palates Instructor, Queensland, Australia

CONTENTS

Preface	xi
Introduction	xv

PART ONE
SHIFTING YOUR SUBJECTIVE

Introduction to Part I	3
1. Mapping the World	7
2. Sensing & Reality	24
3. Changing Your Mind	40
4. Controlling Your Emotions	51
5. Complete Turn Arounds	62
6. Daily Disciplines	70
Leadership Lessons from Part I	89
Conclusion to Part I	93
Technique Summaries I	103

PART TWO
NON-VERBAL LEADERSHIP

Introduction to Part II	145
7. Non-Verbal Awareness	149
8. The Geometry of Presence	157
9. Rapport & Permission	168
10. Non-Verbal Acuity	183
11. Group Dynamics	194
12. Containing the Mood-Wreckers	214
13. Disarming the Verbal Hijacker	229
Leadership Lessons from Part II	243
Conclusion to Part II	249
Technique Summaries II	257

Afterword	311
Notes	315
Bibliography	331
Index	335
Acknowledgments	339
About the Author	341
Also by Paul O'Neill	343

PREFACE

This isn't the first book I've written for leaders—but it was the first one I started. It likely won't be the last. But it may be the one I've contemplated longest. The one I've mulled over most. Because it felt the most quietly urgent.

Not because it's filled with big claims or easy breakthroughs. But because it begins where most leadership texts do not: beneath the surface. Beneath the voice. Beneath the frameworks, agendas, and carefully practised scripts.

It starts where your leadership actually happens—in the quiet, fast, pattern-rich landscape of your own nervous system.

That's why I went back and completed *The Iron Laws* first. To describe the ground beneath every strategy, every signal, and every NLP skill you're about to learn or practise.

This book doesn't teach you how to lead. It describes the reality inside which leadership always occurs.

I've spent much of my professional life alongside leaders in high-stakes moments: restructures, crises, start-ups, shutdowns. Environments where clarity matters and timing is everything. And again and again, I've seen the same tension arise—not between Strategy A and Strategy B, but between *reaction and response*. Not between the right words and the wrong ones, but between *being present... and being hijacked*.

There are plenty of books about what to say, what to do, what to measure. Fewer about how to *be*. Fewer still that show how our *inner condition*—our state—is the foundation beneath every word and every decision.

That's why I wrote *Adaptive Wisdoms*. And why—despite being the last volume I finished—it had to be the first in the NLP Mastery for Leaders trilogy. Because if we don't begin with how we're wired—if we don't understand how stress, instinct, and perception shape our leadership before we even speak—then everything else is decoration.

Let me be clear: this book is not about becoming calm for calm's sake. Nor is it about resilience in the performative sense of that word—toughing it out, gritting your teeth, soldiering on. It's about reclaiming access to yourself *in the moments that matter*. When the pressure rises. When trust thins. When the old pattern takes hold.

It's about knowing what to do with the signal in your chest *before* it becomes a reaction in the room. This is the work of leaders who aren't content to appear confident—they want to be grounded. Who don't just want to communicate—they want to *resonate*. Leaders who are done performing presence—and are ready to *inhabit* it.

The trilogy as a whole—*NLP Mastery for Leaders*—emerged from my Business Practitioner of NLP program. But this isn't a transcript. It's a deep distillation, adapted for the leadership landscape of now: more complex, more volatile, more emotionally loaded than ever.

This volume—finished last, placed first—focuses on the *'Neuro'* of NLP. The part we share with all adaptive mammals: the capacity to feel, react, stabilise, and reset. And so, we begin with the system that always speaks first:

> the human body

You won't find 'hacks' here. You won't find bravado. What you'll find is a kind of apprenticeship—into the textures of breath, the patterns of tension, the architecture of state.

This is leadership not as performance, but as *presence*. Not as posturing, but as *signal*. Not as charisma, but as *coherence*. It's a quieter power. But once you've felt it, you won't want to lead any other way.

So wherever you're reading this—from a corner office or a kitchen table, a boardroom or a bootstrapped start-up—know this: you're not just holding a book. You're holding a set of practices. And a set of possibilities. You don't need to change who you are. But you may find a steadier way to be who you are—under pressure, without collapse.

That's the work. That's the promise. And that's why this is where we begin.

Paul O'Neill

April 2025

INTRODUCTION

In the umpteen operational start-ups, business restructures, turnarounds and closures I've either led directly or supported as a consultant, guide, or coach, one leadership maxim has proven itself again and again. I've put my own twist on it:

People might follow your strategy.

But they always follow your state.

Because we possess this unique human gift of speech, we often forget something more fundamental—that we are, first and always, primate mammals. Our leadership doesn't begin when we talk to our teams. It begins the moment we enter the room.

Long before anyone hears your words, they've read your walk, your stillness, your silence. Long before they hear your script, they're reading you.

In moments of high pressure, people don't look to abstract strategy. They don't want a clever reframe. They're looking for something solid. Something stable. Something embodied. And very often, that something... is you.

This book begins at that moment—before words are spoken, before plans are drafted—when the state of the leader is about to become the state of the team. It begins where breath tightens, faces set, and futures are felt before they're thought through. That's where this work begins. Not with slides or slogans. *With state.*

Because if you've led for any length of time, you've felt it—that gathering pressure in the room. The unreadable silence just before the pitch. The moment the air changes and suddenly everyone's looking at you. Your nervous system registers it before your intellect catches up. That slight narrowing of breath. That weight behind the eyes. It's subtle. But it's real.

And if you can't manage your state, you can't hold the room. That's not a criticism. That's biology. But it's also something more hopeful: it's trainable.

Most leadership development is built backwards. It starts in the head —with frameworks, deliverables, and policy—and hopes the body will come along for the ride. But influence doesn't work that way. Leadership doesn't trickle down. It pulses outward.

Which brings us to a field you may have heard something about— sometimes with curiosity, sometimes with caution: *Neuro-Linguistic Programming,* or NLP.

A LITTLE HISTORY: In the early 1970s, a mathematician named Richard Bandler and a linguist named John Grinder set out to answer a deceptively simple question:

INTRODUCTION

> *What exactly do great communicators do that makes them effective?*

Not what they say they do. What they actually do—in tone, timing, structure, and story. They began by modelling therapists like Milton Erickson, Virginia Satir, and Fritz Perls—extraordinary practitioners whose results often outpaced explanation.

What they discovered was quietly radical: beneath every feeling, every belief, every change, was a structure. A sequence of sensory experience. A map of patterns. And when you adjusted the structure, everything else shifted with it—fast. In short, they cracked the code of subjective experience.

Over time, NLP evolved into a powerful—if sometimes controversial—toolbox for influence and change. Some took it too far. Treated it like magic. Misapplied it with bravado. Sold certainty where only curiosity belonged. Fair criticisms, to a point.

But the core of NLP remains *revolutionary*:

> A way for understanding how people construct meaning—and how they can reconstruct it.

The early developers of NLP didn't work alone. Their models were grounded in the lived brilliance of people like Milton Erickson, whose hypnotic precision guided the unconscious without force; Virginia Satir, who revealed how communication patterns shape families and organisations alike; and Fritz Perls, who brought raw, present-moment awareness into the therapy room.

Each of these figures left behind a legacy of practical wisdom—not theories, but behaviours that could be observed, mapped, and taught. From this modelling came more than techniques—it birthed a way of thinking: if you could decode the structure of excellence, you could replicate it.

This is the quiet revolution at the heart of NLP. And while some practitioners veered into showmanship or pseudo-certainty, the original spirit of NLP remains simple and profound: *pay attention to what works—and how—and make that teachable.*

In the decades since, NLP has found its way into diverse fields—from coaching and education to leadership and peak performance. Practitioners like Robert Dilts expanded its models into innovation and strategic leadership; Michael Grinder brought non-verbal mastery into classrooms and boardrooms; Paul McKenna and Michael Breen translated its principles for the mainstream; Tony Robbins catapulted its essence into the world of personal transformation.

Each brought a different lens—but the core remained:

> *Decode what works, and make it usable.*

This book is not a 'greatest hits' compilation of NLP techniques. It's something more precise. More principled. More attuned to the *leadership challenges of our time.*

Because let's face it: business isn't getting simpler. It's getting stranger. Faster. More emotionally charged. More culturally complex. You're expected to inspire trust, manage ambiguity, and hold your team together—not just during performance reviews, but in crises, pivots, restructures, and existential disruptions.

You're expected to lead across domains—not just strategy and metrics, but stress and meaning. Not just planning and performance, but psychology, story, and state.

- What do you do when the logic runs out—but people are still watching?
- How do you stay anchored when the waves hit and everyone's looking at you?

That's what this book is for.

It begins with the body—your own. Your breath, your presence, your nervous system's invisible baseline. Not to make you robotic. Not to strip out emotion. But to make you available again—to the moment, to your choices, to others. *To your better self.*

Then we move into language. Not tired leadership clichés, but real language. Words that land. Stories that shift perception. Questions that uncover what's hidden. Structures of speech that build bridges between inner experience and shared understanding.

Finally, we move outwards—into programming. Not in the technical sense, but in the cultural one. Influence at scale. The kind of leadership that doesn't just win arguments—it shifts operating systems. Creates alignment. Unlocks resilience. Builds the strange, quiet magic of teams that move as one.

This isn't about turning you into someone else. It's about turning you into *more of you*. With precision. With presence. With power that doesn't overpower.

Here's what to expect.

Each volume builds on the last:

- *Adaptive Wisdoms* (this volume) lays the groundwork—calm, composure, choice. It explores the 'Neuro' of NLP: the parts that unite us with all other primates and, more broadly, all mammals.

- *Logic & Language* builds problem-solving and influence—insight, story, meaning, momentum. At its heart are logic-based language models, and thus, the *Linguistic* aspect of NLP.

• *Moving as One* scales to the organisational level—so your impact isn't limited to the room you're in. It captures the *Programming* side of NLP applied to groups and living systems.

These volumes aren't about delivering NLP as a toolkit. They describe the *conditions* under which NLP thrives. Because NLP is the study of *subjective experience*. And subjective experience is the bedrock of leadership and influence.

You'll find tools here. Exercises. Techniques. Models. Frameworks. But more than that, you'll find a way of *seeing*. A way of *being*. A blueprint for working with yourself, not against yourself. For leading from a state that *invites* trust—not just demands results.

You don't need to be perfect. You need to be *available*. And trained. This book begins that training.

So if you've ever felt the pressure mount—and your breath shorten—know this:

You're not broken. You're reading signals that were never meant to be read alone.

Stress isn't the problem. It's everywhere in nature—like wind or rain.

And your state? It's built to respond. That's what it does.

The real problem is thinking you can't influence it. Or that you can't influence the state of others.

Lastly, I've written a prequel to this trilogy:

The Iron Laws

This 'Volume o' doesn't teach NLP at all—beyond the occasional reference. It exists because, in every training I've attended or delivered, one pattern has repeated: a wide variation in how participants understand the objective realities that shape human behaviour.

That diversity isn't just expected—it's welcomed. In general NLP practitioner programs, people come from every walk of life, bringing rich, plural perspectives. That's part of the field's strength.

But when NLP is applied in more specific contexts—whether therapy, sales, leadership, or golf—a flattening of that variability becomes not just desirable, but essential for high-performance outcomes. Precision matters. Shared ground becomes non-negotiable.

This curated prequel offers that shared ground—a common foundation in the neurological, socio-psychological, and systemic constraints within which leadership and influence must operate.

- Not as theory, but as *constraint*.
- Not as dogma, but as *orientation*.

So you can better *observe, frame, decide—and lead*.

Welcome to Volume I: the *'Neuro'* workshop. In print.

PART ONE
SHIFTING YOUR SUBJECTIVE

INTRODUCTION TO PART I
THE WEAVE BENEATH THE INSTINCT

The room is hushed but heavy. A decision hangs in the air—unspoken, urgent, thick with consequences. Around the boardroom table, pens are tapped, throats cleared, glances darted. In these moments, it is not the cleverest plan that leads. It is the nervous system that moves first: a hand tightened on a pen, a gaze sharpened into warning, a breath held too long. Strategy may come later. But the body always speaks first[1].

You are not alone in this. Every leader carries the same hidden weight—the legacy of a body designed to read threat before thought, to brace before reason catches up.[2] It is a superb system for survival. But left unseen, it can also steer meetings, decisions, and futures down paths no one consciously chose.

This part of the book is about something most leadership manuals never touch: the living, breathing architecture underneath your instincts[3]. The fine structures that govern what you notice, how you feel, and whether you lead with presence or react from panic. Not the plans you write when the world is calm—but the currents you ride when it is not.

If you stay with this work, you will find something rare. Not the illusion of control over chaos—but a precision of navigation through it. The ability to feel the first tug of tension, the first tilt of internal gravity, and still choose your course. The instincts you have are not flaws. They are foundations. This part of the journey is about reading them. And, where necessary, rewriting them.

Most people move through the world as passengers inside their own systems. The heart races, the jaw tightens, the words spill—or don't—and they are left puzzling over what went wrong. They imagine that they are simply 'bad at stress', 'not natural under pressure', or 'wired this way'. They are wrong.

There is wiring, yes. But wiring is not fate. Wiring is structure. And structure can be read, understood, and—crucially—shaped[4].

This part of the book offers no empty slogans. No chants to 'just think positive' or 'stay calm' in the teeth of turbulence. What it offers instead is a set of lenses, tools, and practices designed to do something harder but truer: give you real agency over the machinery that moves you.

You will not eliminate pressure. Nor should you try. But you will learn to shift the way pressure moves through you. You will learn to listen earlier, to intervene cleaner, to recover faster[5]. And from there, leadership becomes less about wrestling the day into submission—and more about dancing it with unexpected grace.

Across the coming chapters, you will meet a series of practices that may seem deceptively small.

- Surfacing submodalities—those fine sensory distinctions that quietly steer whether you step forward or pull back[6].
- Anchoring deliberate states—linking chosen emotional strengths to specific physical cues.

- Reversing the spin of emotion—teaching the body to soften, not sharpen, under strain.
- Embedding daily rhythms of return—so that resilience is not a desperate act of salvage, but a natural state, ready at hand.

None of these tools is cosmetic. They do not live at the level of slogans or surface behaviours. They cut deeper—into the patterns of attention, sensation, and meaning that shape every choice you make. Each tool you learn here is a strand in a larger weave: a new architecture of leadership from the inside out.

It would be tempting, at this point, to imagine this work as a technical upgrade—like replacing worn parts in a machine. It is not. It is more like learning the currents of a wild river you once thought random. It is more like becoming literate in a language your body has been speaking all along, but which you are only now learning to hear with clarity[7].

The truth is, no script can prepare you for every meeting, every crisis, every sharp turn life throws. But there is a kind of preparation that outlasts scripts: the preparation of the nervous system itself. The training of awareness, adjustment, and return.

You cannot control the river. But you can learn to read its signs—to know when it rises, when it eddies, when it threatens to pull. And you can train yourself to respond, not with brittle control, but with grounded agility. This is the craft of true resilience.

Picture a craftsman working with wood. The grain runs a certain way; tension lies hidden under the surface. An inexperienced hand forces the tool, snapping the timber. A skilled hand feels the whisper of resistance, adjusts the angle, finds the flow. Leadership is no different[8].

The challenges ahead will not announce themselves with labels. They will come disguised—as awkward conversations, as unspoken tensions in a room, as the quiet coiling of your own gut before you even know why.

This section of the book is your apprenticeship in feeling those grains. In working with them, not against them. In learning that your instincts are not chains—but wood, supple and strong, ready to be shaped with wisdom. You have already taken the first steps. You are ready for more.

What follows is not a lesson in managing behaviour[9]. It is a field guide to mastering presence. Let get stuck in.

ONE
MAPPING THE WORLD
WHAT YOUR BODY BUILDS BEFORE YOU SPEAK

No two people share precisely the same experiences
Richard Bandler

THE LIGHT FLICKERS. A shadow moves across the lab bench. In an instant, the mouse freezes—muscles locked, breath stalled, whiskers trembling like antennae. It does not think. It does not decide. It simply *knows*. The world has shifted, and it must not move until the pattern makes sense again. Its safety depends on it.

Now shift scenes. A senior manager sits alone in a high-stakes meeting. The room hums with polite tension, but something unseen curls beneath the surface. A stakeholder narrows their eyes. The manager feels it—not consciously, not yet—but a subtle pressure tightens the chest. Breath shallows. Posture stiffens. A dozen threads of social context, past betrayals, old doubts, and subtle cues weave together into a felt signal: *Hold back. Watch. Wait.*

In both cases—mouse and manager—there was no time for language. No 'why'. No inner monologue forming reasons or narratives. What occurred was not a thought but a shift. A *map*, updated in real time, from within the nervous system. Not the territory. The map. A representation of the world built not from facts, but from filtered impressions—sensory fragments fastened by biology and sharpened by experience.

This map is not unique to humans[1]. It belongs to the broader fraternity of mammals. Every creature with a spinal cord and a social structure runs this same playbook: scan the environment, sense the shift, prepare the body. The mouse does not need to name the hawk. The human does not need to name the threat. Both detect. Both decide. Both act—or withhold—on instinct wrapped in structure.

What follows in this chapter is not a discussion about thought, but about what comes *before* thought. Before language, before logic, before even conscious awareness[2]. This is about how mammals construct reality—not as it is, but as it is felt. Not with certainty, but with speed. What we call the NLP Communication Model is, at its core, a mammalian survival tool: a way of turning sensation into orientation, context into meaning, without uttering a single word.[3]

And that matters. Because if our most important reactions occur before reason, then leadership begins *not* with what we say—but with what we sense. Not with how we explain the room, but how we first *read* it

Universal Model

Before there is understanding, there is orientation. Before there is reason, there is response. Long before a creature has words to say what's happening, it already knows — in the deepest, most practical sense — how to act.

Step into the forest again. A rustle in the underbrush. The bird takes flight. The fox pivots. The deer freezes. None of these reactions are 'chosen' in the human sense. But neither are they random. Each is grounded in something very old, very fast, and remarkably structured.

This is where our internal world begins — not with thoughts, but with *maps*.

Every living system that moves, competes, survives, builds a representation of its environment[4]. It cannot function otherwise. That representation — or map — is not a mirror. It is selective. It is shaped by what the nervous system can detect, by what matters to survival, and by what has mattered before.

Mammals, in particular, construct these maps in strikingly similar ways. A bat, a wolf, a horse, a human — all rely on sensory input to filter what's relevant and discard what's not. They don't process the full flood of reality. That would be paralysing[5]. Instead, they sample: a flicker of movement, a sudden temperature drop, a shift in tone. From that, a picture forms — not of the world as it is, but of the world as it *feels*, right now.

This process is not conscious. It happens fast, automatically, and according to the logic of the body. In NLP, this is captured by what's often called the communication model — though that label may be misleading, because this isn't really about conversation. It's about *construction*.

Here's how it unfolds. First, raw sensory input enters through our five primary channels: what we see, hear, feel, smell, and taste. These impressions are vast, overwhelming in their richness. So the system simplifies. It deletes what it deems irrelevant. It distorts certain signals to fit expectations. It generalises others, drawing shortcuts from previous experience. The result is a kind of internal compression — a representation that is good enough to act on, even if it isn't perfectly accurate.

That representation then triggers a state — emotional, physiological, embodied. The breath shifts. The muscles prime. The stomach clenches, or the shoulders drop. From state comes behaviour. Action. Speech. Stillness. Withdrawal. Advancement.

At no point does the organism need to name what's happening. The mouse does not need to say 'predator' to move. Nor do we need to say 'resentment' to feel its pull. These reactions live below the level of language — structured, efficient, deeply intelligent[6].

What's striking is that humans are not exempt from this process. We are subject to it. Our ability to talk about our experience does not precede our experience; it follows it. The body acts first. The story comes later. This means that much of our so-called decision-making is actually post-hoc explanation. We rationalise what we've already sensed and done[7].

That's not a flaw. It's a feature of being mammalian.

Where humans *do* differ — and where we'll travel in later volumes — is in our capacity to *notice* and *work with* this internal mapping process. We can observe it, interrupt it, even revise it. But we cannot avoid it. Every moment, we are filtering, framing, and forming a picture of reality — and that picture determines how we feel, what we do, and whether we thrive or flounder in a given moment.

So when we talk about awareness in leadership, we are not talking about being clever, or eloquent, or emotionally fluent. We are talking about something far more primal: the ability to perceive the moment accurately enough to respond rather than react. And that begins not with the outer world, but with the *map* your body has drawn inside you — often before you've realised it's even there.

The model is not merely a framework. It is a reality. You are constructing your experience even as you read these words. The question is not whether the map exists — but whether you know what's shaping it, and whether you trust yourself to read it before it runs the show.

. . .

Species-Specific Subjectivity

Stand next to a dog at dusk, and you may believe you're both sensing the same moment — watching the same garden, hearing the same breeze, breathing the same air. But that's an illusion born of proximity, not perception. While you glance at the shifting shadows or glance at your phone, the dog is reading scent trails left hours before, decoding chemical whispers in the grass that your nose could not register if it tried. You're not sharing an experience. You're sharing a location.

Every animal lives in a world sculpted by its nervous system. Not a shared objective world, but a species-specific one — a lived reality filtered through what its body can detect, process, and use[8]. A bat hears in sonar. A snake sees in temperature. A horse senses microtremors through the ground. Each builds a map not of *the* world, but of *its* world — shaped by what matters most to its survival, attention, and social needs.

And so it is with humans.

We like to believe our perception is neutral — that we observe reality as it is, then draw conclusions from the facts. But this is fiction. We don't see the world as it is. We see it as our system allows us to. And like every other mammal, that system is shaped by both shared biology and individual experience.

Consider the architecture: our inner ear is a mammalian design, evolved not for conscious analysis, but for the rapid detection of changes in tone and vibration — cues of threat, belonging, or deception. Our vagus nerve, which plays a central role in regulating heart rate, digestion, and social connection, is myelinated — a feature we share with mice, not reptiles[9]. These aren't trivial details. They're evidence that our core wiring is mammalian through and through. Complex, yes. But not unique.

What *is* distinctive about humans is not the presence of internal maps — other mammals have those too — but our capacity to reflect on them. To question the picture[10]. To notice that what we're reacting to might not be 'real' in the objective sense, but a projection shaped by past fears, inherited reflexes, or misread cues.

This power of reflection is both a gift and a liability. It allows us to break free from automatic patterns — but it also tempts us to override instincts entirely, to talk ourselves out of what our body knows. The art lies in recognising that our subjective map is real, but partial — that it deserves attention, but not blind obedience.

Subjectivity is not a flaw. It is a fact. All creatures live by it. The only question is whether we become aware of our version — and what we choose to do with that awareness.

In this light, leadership becomes less about having the answers and more about sensing the terrain — not just intellectually, but biologically. Because the leaders who learn to read their own species-specific subjectivity, and to distinguish it from what's actually unfolding, hold an advantage no algorithm can replicate. They don't merely navigate complexity. They *inhabit* it — fully, consciously, and with a clarity grounded in the body as much as the mind.

The Filters: Why We Never See 'Reality'

Imagine walking through a crowded street with a friend. Same route, same time of day. Yet at the end of the walk, your memories diverge. You remember the music from the café, the rhythm of passing footsteps. Your friend remembers the faces in the windows, the scuff on a child's shoe, the smell of roast garlic from the corner deli. You were both there. But you were never in the same world.

This is not just a matter of attention. It is a matter of filtration[11]. No living creature processes the full stream of information coming in. To do so would be overwhelming, and worse — fatal. Nature is economical. She teaches every system to ignore the irrelevant, exaggerate the meaningful, and compress the rest into patterns that can guide fast action[12].

In NLP, we describe this as *delete, distort* and *generalise*[13]. But these aren't flaws in cognition. They are biological necessities.

Deletion comes first. Most of the sensory data entering your system is ignored completely. Your skin is touching your clothes right now — were you aware of that until this sentence pointed to it? Every moment, your body deletes vast quantities of sensory input. Not out of negligence, but out of necessity.

Then comes distortion. The edges of reality are bent to fit expectation. A glance that lingers just a moment too long is read as judgement. A silence in the meeting is interpreted as disapproval, when it might just be thoughtfulness. We see patterns even where there are none — not because we're irrational, but because the nervous system is wired to predict threat, not just reflect truth[14].

And finally, generalisation. One mistake becomes a rule. One betrayal becomes a warning label stamped on every similar face. These shortcuts save time, reduce risk, and help the system decide — but they also flatten nuance, replacing the richness of the world with templates. They are efficient. But they are not always accurate.

Every creature uses these filters. A lion generalises the rustle of a bush into a possible prey. A horse distorts a fluttering flag into a threat. A rat deletes the static hum of its lab enclosure to focus on the faint crackle of a food wrapper. These are not cognitive errors. They are survival strategies, sculpted over time.

What makes humans vulnerable is not that we filter — but that we forget we're filtering. We confuse the map for the territory. We mistake the sensations we've retained and the meanings we've constructed for objective reality[15]. And once we do that, we react not to the situation as it is, but to the version we've assembled — often hastily and unconsciously.

Leadership, then, demands not just awareness, but *meta*-awareness. The ability to step back and ask, 'What might I be missing? What am I assuming? What have I already decided without knowing it?' These questions don't make us indecisive. They make us accurate. They slow the rush from perception to action just long enough to allow choice.

In complexity, where no map is perfect and the landscape keeps shifting, the best leaders are not those with the strongest opinions, but those with the most flexible perceptions. They know the filters are working. They just refuse to let the filters work *them*.

The world is not what it is. It's what we perceive — and what we're willing to question.

VAKOG: The Five Input Channels

Step into a memory. Any memory — sharp or vague. Perhaps it's the scent of a childhood kitchen, the flicker of a gaze across a crowded room, or the feeling of a steering wheel beneath tense hands. Don't analyse it. Just find it. Let it come alive.

Now ask: how do you know it happened?

Not the fact of it — the *experience* of it. What do you see, hear, feel? Does a voice echo? A light shift? Does your chest tighten or your skin prickle as the moment returns? This is not memory as concept. It's memory as sensation. The nervous system doesn't archive ideas. It records *impressions* — and it does so through five core channels: sight, sound, touch, smell, and taste. Visual. Auditory. Kinaesthetic. Olfactory. Gustatory. VAKOG[16].

Every mammal builds its world through these five gateways. But not all channels are created equal — not by nature, and not by context. A hawk hunts through visual acuity, a bloodhound lives in the world of scent, a dolphin listens with its whole body. Each species leans on the senses it has honed over millennia. The rest are there — but quieter, peripheral.

Humans, too, are biased perceivers[17]. We tend to assume our version of reality is clear and comprehensive, but really, we're running a complex filter system shaped by both evolutionary tuning and personal history. Some people live in pictures. They recall faces, colours, layouts, and light. Others hear tone and cadence, the weight of words and the rhythm between them. Still others feel everything — the temperature of a room, the tensing of a jaw, the way emotions settle into the limbs like weather. And some live more in the internal theatre of thoughts — an inner voice narrating, criticising, advising, or echoing the words of others long gone.

These sensory preferences are not personality traits. They are *orientations*[18] — routes through which experience flows and meaning is made. And they can shift. The man who walks into a negotiation with a strong visual strategy may, under pressure, collapse into visceral tension. The athlete who listens to the crowd may, in a moment of fatigue, lose touch with her own kinaesthetic signals. What dominates changes with state. But the channels remain constant.

What's crucial to understand is that VAKOG is not a communications model in the conventional sense. It's not about how we talk to others. It's about how we build the *reality* we then react to. Sensory input shapes our internal map before any words arrive[19]. If a dog cowers at the sound of thunder, it's not misunderstanding language — it's reacting to a bodily map formed through sound and memory. When a child recoils from the smell of a certain food, or an adult finds their heart racing at the touch of a certain fabric, they are not making a decision. They are responding to input that's already shaped perception.

In this way, VAKOG is the architecture beneath awareness — the scaffolding upon which feelings are built, actions decided, and meaning later added. To know which of these senses your nervous system privileges under pressure is to gain an early foothold in your own self-awareness.

Not to change it. Not yet. But to *notice* it. To say: 'This is how I register the world when it moves quickly. This is how I know what matters when the room goes quiet.'

It's worth pausing here to remember that before we respond to people, we respond to sensation. Before we plan, we *perceive*. And it is through these five windows — what we see, hear, feel, smell, and taste — that the world gets in.

The task is not to be sensory all the time. That would be exhausting. The task is to become *sensory enough* — to track the cues that shape your state, influence your actions, and colour the map you're walking on. Because if the map is wrong, every step becomes a risk. But if the map is clear — even just clear *enough* — then agency returns. And with it, the quiet confidence that you are responding to something real, not a distortion born from unattended sensation.

How Maps Shape Movement

A sudden change in temperature. The flick of an eye across the room. The clipped tone in an email. You don't need to think about it. You already *feel* it. Something in the environment has shifted—and so have you.

Your shoulders rise slightly. Your breath shortens. Your focus narrows. Perhaps nothing has even happened, not yet. But your system is already moving. The body has read something important. It has registered the map — and begun its response[20].

This is the quiet truth behind all human behaviour: *we don't act from reality itself*. We act from how we've mapped that reality inside us. That map, built from raw sensory impressions, doesn't stay in the mind. It cascades down into the body, shifting chemistry, posture, and readiness. Sensation becomes state. State becomes action.

And that transition happens fast — often invisibly.

Consider the leader walking into a tense room. Perhaps there's been friction in the team. No one says anything yet, but the air is taut. A breath is held too long. A laptop closes too quickly. The leader doesn't need a briefing. Her gut is already speaking. The skin tightens. The face steels. The voice drops half a note. She's not consciously calculating. She's responding — not to data, but to atmosphere. To the map drawn in her body a split-second before thought.

State is not a mood. It is a *readiness profile* — a composite of emotion, posture, muscle tone, breath pattern, and perceptual focus[21]. It shapes how we hear others, how we speak, how we interpret what we're seeing. Two people can face the same situation and respond entirely differently, not because the facts differ, but because their states do.

One sees opportunity. The other sees risk. One softens. The other sharpens. Both are acting from the same map, viewed through different states — each drawn by their own sensory history and emotional filters.

The key insight here is that your *map does not stay still*. It is dynamic, constantly updated by micro-signals: the way a colleague pauses before replying, the faint hum of tension in a room, the way your own breath catches before a decision. These aren't abstractions. They are inputs[22]. The nervous system tracks them, evaluates them, and adjusts your internal state accordingly — long before you've had a chance to explain why.

If that sounds unsettling, it should. Much of what we call 'personality' or 'style' in leadership is actually a pattern of state transitions. And many of those transitions are running unexamined, shaped by old contexts that no longer apply.

But here lies the leverage. Once you realise that movement follows maps, and maps follow sensation, then influence begins not with words, but with *awareness*. Not with trying to control what you do, but with learning to read what you're already feeling — and to trace that feeling back to what you just *took in*.

This is not introspection for its own sake. It is the groundwork of poise. Leaders who can detect state changes in themselves before they spill into tone or body language have options. They can intervene early. Re-centre. Reframe. Change the signal they're sending out before it shapes the room around them.

Because it always does. State isn't private. It leaks. Others pick up on your map through posture, tone, breath, gaze — and adjust their own states accordingly. This is how teams calibrate around leaders, how trust is built or broken in seconds, how tension either snowballs or dissolves without a word.

The internal map becomes an external signal. The external signal becomes collective behaviour. And it all begins with what was sensed — often before anyone in the room knew what was happening.

To lead well, then, is not to override state. It is to work upstream of it. To recognise that what you sense *shapes how you move*, and that the moment you become conscious of that fact, you can begin to choose the direction.

The body doesn't wait. But the mind, once engaged, can guide.

HUMANS *as Reflective Mammals*

Picture a dog on a city pavement. Its nose twitches. Ears flick. Muscles ripple with every shift in wind or movement. It doesn't hesitate, but it doesn't rush either. It reads. Every scent and sound is part of a live map: food, danger, friend, foe, home. The dog doesn't question the map. It *is* the map.

Now picture the human beside it, pausing before a meeting, coffee in hand, scrolling through emails. A colleague walks past with a glance too brief, a nod too stiff. Something twists in the gut. The breath shortens. The mind begins to build a story: *They're annoyed with me. Something's wrong.* And then — if the person is practiced — another voice enters: *Hang on. That might not be true. I didn't sleep much. I could be misreading this. Let's stay open.*

That moment — not the tension, but the *interruption* of the tension — marks the difference.

Humans are mammals, but we are mammals with a mirror. We don't just build maps. We can *see ourselves building them*[23]. That doesn't make us better. But it gives us something rare: the capacity to question our instincts *while* they're unfolding. To put a hand on the tiller mid-course and adjust[24]. No other mammal does this.

We still flinch. We still tense. We still sense atmosphere before logic arrives. But we are also able to *wonder* about those sensations. To ask: 'Is this mine? Is this now? Is this helpful?' That reflective layer, when cultivated, becomes a powerful tool[25] — not for suppressing instinct, but for working alongside it with intelligence.

Of course, not every human uses this ability. Many don't know it exists. They trust the map entirely. They live in a world of quick conclusions, emotional weather systems, and relational misfires. They mistake reaction for reality, certainty for safety. They are not unwise. They are simply unpractised.

But leaders cannot afford this. In complex environments, where relationships, timing, and subtle cues matter, the unexamined map becomes a liability. Without reflection, instinct misfires. Old fears shape new decisions. Trust erodes before a word is spoken.

The alternative isn't cold rationality. It's *warm awareness*. It's being able to feel the pull of a reaction — the spike of defensiveness, the thrill of dominance, the collapse into doubt — and *stay with it*, without immediately obeying it. It's noticing that what felt like a threat might just be an old echo. That what seemed like disrespect might be distraction. That what looked like disloyalty might be uncertainty looking for reassurance.

In those moments, leadership is not about performance. It's about *presence.*

This is why reflective capacity is not a luxury. It's a survival skill for modern leadership. It allows us to ride the wave of our mammalian inheritance *without drowning in it*. To partner with instinct, but not be overruled by it. To lead with empathy, clarity, and agility — even when our inner animal wants to bolt, bark, or bristle.

To be human is to flinch — and to reflect on the flinch. The pause, however brief, is where agency lives[26].

The best leaders don't eliminate their mammalian nature. They *hone* it. They learn to walk with the animal, not behind it — and in doing so, they earn something few ever master: influence that is both natural and deliberate. Trusted because it's felt. Respected because it's chosen.

THE MAPPING ANIMAL

Every animal navigates through maps. Not cartographic ones, but living, moment-to-moment representations of what matters. These maps aren't drawn with ink and legend; they're drawn in breath, muscle, posture, and mood. They begin the moment sensation arrives and continue shifting with every sound, smell, glance, or touch.

You are not exempt. Your nervous system, like a mouse's or a lion's, filters the world through five sensory channels — VAKOG — constructing an internal model shaped not by objectivity, but by relevance[27]. What you delete, distort, and generalise forms the contours of your map. And it is from this internal terrain that your state emerges: how you feel, how you move, how you respond when things go still or strange.

This mapping happens fast. Pre-thought. Pre-verbal. You do not choose it, but you do live by it. And yet — unlike other mammals — you have the rare capacity to *see the map forming*. You can catch the moment when a glance becomes a judgement. When an old fear inserts itself into a new interaction. When your own breath betrays a state that has nothing to do with the room you're in. That capacity, when cultivated, gives rise to a new form of leadership: not reactive, not repressive, but reflective — grounded in biology, yet guided by awareness.

This chapter has not introduced a technique. It has reintroduced you to something older than language: the animal in you that maps, that moves, that reacts — and, if you listen closely enough, that can be taught to collaborate with your more deliberate self.

You are a mapping animal. Every state you enter, every action you take, every relationship you lead is shaped by a world your nervous system has constructed[28]—rapidly, invisibly, and sometimes inaccurately. To lead well, you must first learn to read that map. Then to question it. Then, when needed, to redraw it.

This mapping process is not random. It follows a layered architecture —captured in what NLP calls the *State–Structure–Content* framework.

Content is what appears in consciousness: a composite of external sensory input (VAKOG) and the internally constructed representations that emerge after deletion, distortion, and generalisation. It includes not just raw sensation, but the shifting, interpreted terrain of what the system *thinks* matters—part signal, part memory, part projection.

Structure is the patterned sequence beneath that content. It's how your nervous system strings together sensory information, submodalities, and associations—deciding what rises to awareness and in what order. Structure governs salience. What the system foregrounds, what it sidelines, and how each detail leads to the next.

From this interplay of sensory content and structural filtering, **State** arises: a full-bodied readiness profile of muscle tone, breath, posture, emotion, and attentional focus. State is not just a mood. It is the sum of your organism's preparations: what it's bracing for, leaning toward, or unconsciously avoiding.

But here's the part often missed: you are not mapping in isolation. As a leader, your *own state becomes part of someone else's content.* Your gestures, your gaze, your breath—all are picked up, filtered, and sequenced by the people around you. Before you speak, you've already entered their map.

Which means: to lead well, you must not only master your own mapping—you must become skilful at how you show up in others'.

The chapters that follow will explore exactly how. But the work begins here: not with changing your maps, but recognising that you have them — and that the animal who made them isn't wrong. It's just sometimes working with old coordinates.

Before you plan your next move, pause. Feel the ground beneath you. Listen for the shape of the map you're standing on. Ask: *Is this the terrain — or just my training?*

Because the answer to that question changes everything.

TWO
SENSING & REALITY
THE BUILDING BLOCKS OF EXPERIENCE

> *Changing the submodalities of a memory changes the emotions associated with the memory.*
> **Richard Bandler**

THE FIRE ALARM'S SHRIEKING. You didn't plan to react—you just did. Muscles clench. Breathing tightens. Eyes scan, ears tune, thoughts narrow. You're alert, poised, ready. Not because you thought it through, but because your body did. That's *mobilisation* in action—your nervous system running a playbook millions of years old.

Now picture the same scene, but with a different twist. Smoke billows. Escape routes vanish. There's no way out. Suddenly, your body doesn't rev up—it shuts down. Limbs feel heavy. Vision tunnels. A strange calm descends, eerie and hollow. This, too, is nature at work. It's not passivity. It's a last resort. *Immobilisation.*

Both are ancient reflexes—designed not by your conscious mind, but by your biology. Your brainstem doesn't ask permission. It reads the world, makes a call, and acts before "you" even know. The story you tell yourself afterwards—the justification, the logic, the meaning—is a postscript. Useful, but not causal[1].

This isn't just true in the wild or during emergencies. It happens every day, including in meeting rooms and Zoom calls. Our civilised exteriors do not overwrite our mammalian interiors. As Darwin reminded us, the scaffolding of our instincts is ancient[2]. The flesh may wear a suit, but it's still wired for survival.

Consider David, a Regional Manager leading a critical pitch. On the surface, he's composed. But under pressure, his breath shallows, his jaw tightens, and a flicker of doubt floods his gut. He's not imagining the threat—he's responding to it. His body is doing what it was built to do. Prepare. Mobilise. Survive.

That response, when harnessed well, becomes performance: clarity, urgency, presence. But when misunderstood, it can feel like sabotage —nerves, freeze, tunnel vision.

Here, the tools of NLP offer something rare: not tricks, but a precision language for studying the architecture of your own experience[3]. Our senses—what we see, hear, and feel—are not just information channels. They are access points to the patterns beneath our patterns. Within those sense modalities live what NLP calls *submodalities*: the fine-grain structure of your experience. And within those structures lie your default responses.

To explore this, you don't need a theory. You need attention. Deliberate, quiet attention. You'll be studying your nervous system from the inside. Not a general human pattern, but your specific, embodied coding. Because before you can shift your responses, you need to see how they're built.

How Your Senses Shape Your Reality

As you began surfacing submodalities, you likely noticed something curious. Not every distinction stays neatly in its lane. Sometimes a sight seems to pulse with feeling. Sometimes a sound seems heavy, like it carries physical weight. These crossings aren't mistakes. They're clues.

In psychology, this blending of the senses is called synesthesia[4]. In the more practical world of experience, it's simply how meaning thickens. How life becomes textured. A smell isn't just a smell. It's memory and longing braided into one. A phrase isn't just heard. It's felt, like a blow or a balm.

In the work ahead, it's worth attending to these crossings. Synesthetic moments reveal the hidden architecture of your instinctive coding. When a sound "presses" down or a colour "shouts," your body is telling you how deeply it's reading the world. These fusions aren't anomalies to be corrected. They're guideposts.

Alongside these crossings, you may notice another pattern emerging: a preference. Some people store and retrieve experience mainly through images—seeing the sharp flash of a moment before any words form. Others tune first to sound: the lilt of a voice, the low hum of a mood. Still others lead with sensation—the churn in the gut, the quickening of breath. And some run an internal script—a voice narrating events as they unfold.

These preferences aren't absolutes. They're tendencies. Flexible, shifting, but reliable enough to offer leverage. Knowing your preferred representational system—whether visual, auditory, kinaesthetic, or internal dialogue—is less about pigeonholing yourself, and more about becoming literate in the language your body speaks fastest.

Noticing these preferences sharpens your tools. When you want to shift a state, you'll know whether to adjust an image, modulate an inner voice, or work directly through bodily sensation. You'll be speaking the dialect your nervous system responds to most readily.

And there's one more layer to lay in here, quietly but crucially: the art of *collapsing anchors*. As you build new, deliberate connections between physical cues and empowered states, you'll soon discover that old patterns—unhelpful reactions, lingering fears—can be rewritten too. Not by force, not by denial, but by skilfully bringing two states together—the old and the new—until the nervous system, faced with incompatible codes, lets the old wiring fall away.

We'll come to that soon. For now, your focus remains clear: map your senses. Catch the crossings. Honour your preferences. Forge new anchors.

You are not just studying your experience. You are beginning to edit it. Not by theory. By craft. Let's continue. Find a calm space. Leave distraction behind.

What follows isn't just a technique—it's a conversation with your most ancient self. And like the inscription at Delphi reminds us: *Know thyself.* Not just the thoughts you think. The instincts you live. There is a hidden architecture to every experience you have ever lived.

Each memory, each reaction, each moment of triumph or recoil is not stored as a simple fact, but as a layered tapestry of sensory impressions. The way a moment looks, sounds, and feels inside you is not random. It is patterned. Structured. And the details of that internal structure—what we call the fine distinctions or *submodalities*—are where your real leverage lives.

Submodalities are not abstract. They are specific, concrete details within your senses: the brightness of an image, the direction a sensation spins, the distance of a sound. Your nervous system treats these fine-grain qualities as critical information. It does not wait for your conscious mind to interpret them; it acts.

By learning to detect and—later—adjust these sensory codes, you step beyond mere understanding. You begin to shift the experience itself, at the level where it is formed.

What follows is not theory, but practice. You will not be studying 'human nature' in general, but your own embodied blueprint, in particular.

And with each discovery, you reclaim something vital: the ability to live not just by reaction, but by deliberate design. As the blueprint is already within you. It's time to begin reading it.

"Surfacing Submodalities"[5]

Begin by selecting two instinctual reactions: one that pulls you forward—like desire, hunger, or craving—and one that makes you recoil—such as fear, revulsion, or grief. Jot them down. No need to overthink. Just go with what's strong and familiar in your experience.

Now, take a moment. Close your eyes. Call up a memory that captures that "move towards" impulse at full force. Whether it was lust, a craving for power, or a surge of want so raw it pushed everything else aside—bring that moment to life.

We don't often discuss these urges at the morning staff meeting. But make no mistake—they steer much of your behaviour beneath the surface. They are evolutionary residues of the mammalian brain. And if you want to understand them, you need to feel them as they were: urgent, electric, non-negotiable.

So go there. Not tentatively. Fully. If it's lust, remember the moment you were magnetised. If it's greed, recall that exact sensation of "I must have it!" Don't sanitise the memory. Immerse yourself in it.

You want the level of intensity you'd see in a starving man catching the scent of roasting meat[6]. The kind that hijacks attention and floods the body.

Now replay that memory through your own senses:

- **What did you see?** Look through your own eyes, not from above or outside. Was it bright or dim? A still image or a moving scene? Close-up or distant? Saturated in colour or muted?
- **What did you hear?** Were the sounds loud, rhythmic, piercing, or ambient? Voices? Internal monologue? Was the tone smooth, sharp, seductive, commanding?
- **What did you feel?** Track the energy in your body. Was it rising or swirling? Heavy or electric? Did it pool in your chest, twist in your gut, or pulse behind your eyes? What was your breathing like—rapid and shallow, or long and low?

Amplify the sensations. Make the colours bolder. Turn up the volume. Let your body *remember* fully.

Then, with those details vivid, record the sensory attributes—your VAK submodalities. Use the reference sheets in the *Technique Summary I* section to record them.

Next, do the same for the "move away from" state. Yes, this one might be harder—but that's the point. Pick a moment when you truly felt it: the fear that gripped, the disgust that turned your stomach, the sorrow that weighed you down.

Relive it, not from a safe emotional distance, but from the inside. Let it rise until you feel it in your breath, your muscles, your skin. Like a hunted animal sensing danger—alert, reactive, sharp.

Again, capture the visual, auditory, and kinaesthetic properties. Don't rush. If it's intense enough to be uncomfortable, you're doing it right.

That means your nervous system is engaged—and that's where the pattern lives.

Once you've mapped both experiences, lay the details side by side. Now here's the key: look not for the commonalities, but for the *contrasts*.

Maybe both scenes are dim—that's not the point. But if one image has sharp contrast and the other is washed out, note that. If one voice comes from inside your head and the other from across the room, that's significant. If one feeling spirals upward while the other presses downward—pay attention.

These differences reveal how your mind encodes attraction and avoidance. You are not analysing content—you are decoding the structure of your instinctive experience. And once you see the structure, you can begin to change it.

Now that you've mapped how experience is structured, there's a next, vital step: learning how to link states you want to strengthen to simple, repeatable actions. In other words, how to give your nervous system a handrail—one it can reach for when the ground shakes. This is where *Anchoring* begins.

When pressure strikes, you don't get time to build a plan. You act—or react—based on what your nervous system can access fastest. Anchoring isn't about learning new tricks. It's about planting the right signals in reach before the storm hits[7].

You've already seen how small sensory details can shape an entire emotional experience. Anchoring simply adds precision to this craft: pairing a deliberate physical cue—a touch, a breath, a gesture—with a chosen internal state. Done properly, this connection becomes automatic. It's not superstition. It's skilled neurological engineering.

You've lived this before, even if you never named it. The song that brings back a lost summer. The scent that returns you to childhood. The way a particular doorway tightens your shoulders before your mind realises why. These are natural anchors—laid down without planning. Now, you'll do it deliberately.

Anchoring doesn't erase challenge. It doesn't bubble-wrap you from the world. What it offers is a bridge—back to your centre, back to your clarity—built from within your own experience. It's not performance. It's preparation. Not for someday. For the next breath.

In a moment, you'll build your first deliberate anchor—a small, specific gesture that calls your best self forward when it matters most.

The Craft of Anchoring

> *Anchoring is one of those things that still impresses me today*
> **Richard Bandler**

Long before we had psychology textbooks or brain scans, we knew, intuitively, that certain triggers could call forth powerful internal states. A favourite song that can lift a broken heart. The smell of woodsmoke that floods the mind with memories of childhood winters. A doorway that makes the shoulders tighten before the mind realises why.

These are natural anchors — associations laid down by lived experience, without deliberate intent. The principle behind them is simple but profound: *what is fired together is wired together*. When a physical sensation, an emotion, and a thought occur together strongly enough, they knit into a network. A pathway. A shortcut.

What we are doing now is no different — except this time, we lay the wiring consciously. Anchoring, in this context, is the act of linking a specific physical gesture — such as pressing the thumb and middle finger together — to a vivid, powerful internal state. When done properly, that small gesture can later evoke the emotional state, much like a key sliding into a lock.

It is not magic. It is neurology. Each time you pair a sensation with a state, the neurons strengthen their connection. Done deliberately, practised consistently, the anchor becomes a living bridge — a way to return to calm, clarity, or courage, even when circumstances would otherwise sweep you away.

In a moment, you will build your first anchor deliberately. Not for nostalgia's sake, but for leadership: a way to reconnect to steadiness when pressure mounts, when instincts pull, when the ground trembles underfoot. Anchoring is not a crutch. It is craftsmanship — the deliberate forging of an internal compass, ready to guide you when the ground shakes and the maps blur.

With your first anchor now laid, you haven't just prepared for pressure—you've also begun charting your emotional terrain with a precision most leaders never even glimpse. You've built a kind of inner compass. One that doesn't just register stress, but knows *where* you go under pressure—and how to return.

But self-awareness, as the Greeks warned, isn't always a gift without burden. As Sophocles wrote:

> *"Alas, how terrible is wisdom when it brings no profit to the man that's wise"*

Because life still strikes. A sharp word from someone we love. A missed opportunity. A sleepless week. And suddenly, the clarity you'd cultivated clouds over. The state you'd anchored slips. You find yourself reacting—not leading.

Whether it's a work challenge bleeding into your home life, or personal grief muting your professional edge, the truth is this: even the best of us lose our footing.

What matters is not that we fall from calm — but how swiftly, and how surely, we can find our way back. And that path can be learned.

With your anchor now laid, you have a handrail. But what about when the storm hits so hard the handrail slips from your grasp?

This is where the deeper skill begins: not just to steady yourself in the gale, but to find your way back when the map disappears altogether. A practice I call *Finding Home*.

Not a magical reset button. Not a way to avoid stress altogether (which would be like trying to dodge weather). But rather, a technique that—with practice—lets you *re-centre*. To meet life not from tension or turmoil, but from your natural state: grounded, steady, responsive.

This isn't about perfection. It's about recovery. About remembering the way back when your body forgets

Connect With Yourself

There comes a moment—maybe daily, maybe just Tuesdays—when the world gets too loud and your insides start staging a riot. Your thoughts are doing laps. Your muscles are holding onto stress like it's an unpaid debt. And somewhere in the middle of it, you realise you're no longer driving the bus. You've been hijacked by something with sweaty hands and no sense of direction.

This is when you connect with yourself. Not the calm, composed version you present in meetings, but the deeper current underneath—the one I call your Unconscious Navigator. It doesn't shout. It doesn't need a microphone. But it knows the terrain, and it's got better instincts than the part of you currently fantasising about throwing your laptop into a canal.

So here's what you do.

First, clock it. The stress. The swirl. The bodily static. Just notice it—like you're eavesdropping on your own nervous system. This act alone breaks the spell. It doesn't cure anything, but it stops the acceleration. As if by noticing the storm, you quietly remind yourself that you're not the storm.

Now, drop your attention one inch below your bellybutton. Yes, it's specific. No, it's not magic. Just do it. Pick a colour—any colour—that means 'joy' to you. Neon pink? Gold? Teal? No judgement. Picture that colour glowing softly under your hand, which you'll now place gently over that spot. Hold it there. Not like a soldier saluting, more like someone checking if the kettle's still warm.

Breathe. Three slow, deliberate breaths. Into that colour, into that spot. Let your tummy rise and fall. Not exaggerated. Not performative. Just honest breath. Because it's not the breath that changes you—it's the fact you've come back to where your body lives. To your centre. And in doing so, you start to quiet the parts of you still trying to win an argument from six hours ago.

Then comes the good bit. Pick a memory. A real one. A moment of actual joy—not filtered, not curated for Instagram. Maybe it's someone's laugh. A moment by the sea. A bowl of soup on a day when that was enough. Step into it like it's a room. Look around. What do you see? What can you hear? How does it feel in your body? Let the colours saturate. Let the sound fill out. Let the warmth come back.

You're not just reminiscing. You're reoccupying. You're training your system to re-access what it once knew how to feel, before emails and deadlines taught it otherwise.

And then, while you're there, ask your Unconscious Navigator a question—not out loud, unless you enjoy strange looks. Just quietly, inside. Ask: 'What do I need right now?' Or 'What should I know?' Don't strain for an answer. The good ones usually arrive sideways. A word. A picture. A shrug. Don't be surprised if it says something sensible your conscious mind was too frazzled to hear.

And now—act. Do one small thing in the direction that voice nudged you. Maybe it's standing up. Calling someone. Cancelling something. Or just going for a walk that doesn't involve filling your head with a podcast about productivity.

Because here's the thing: this practice isn't about 'calming down' in the mindfulness-app sense of the phrase. It's about rebuilding the relay between your internal signals and your external actions. It's about remembering that the wiser part of you isn't the loudest—it's just the most reliable.

In a world that never stops shouting, the real power is knowing how to listen when you're quiet. And the miracle isn't that this practice works. It's that it only takes a minute, and you've had the wiring all along.

Finding Home

Let's not kick the door in. Let's knock. Or better yet, sit quietly outside for a moment, listening for signs of life.

Not the world's noise—that's loud enough. But the quiet signals your body's been muttering for days. The stiffness in your jaw. The tight coil behind your eyes. That old flutter in your gut, like it's bracing for something it can't name.

Start there. Pause.

And ask yourself, without flinching: what are the five pressures pushing at you right now?

Don't perform for the question. Don't curate. Just notice. Some of them will arrive dressed in full armour: deadlines, drama, decisions. Others will slink in like mist—vague, low-frequency worries you've learned to ignore out of professional necessity. Name them anyway. Scribble them down if you like. There's alchemy in that simple act. When you bring the unnamed into language, you're doing more than journaling. You're dragging saboteurs into the daylight.

And daylight, inconvenient as it can be, makes it harder for fear to dress up as fact.

Once they're down, don't go full siege mode. We're not trying to conquer them. We're changing your relationship with them. This isn't 'fix it fast' territory. It's closer to 'train your reflexes to stop flinching'. Because the real work isn't bulldozing the pressure. It's building a nervous system that meets it without flaring into panic or slumping into dread.

Start with just one. Pick a single stressor and hold it like you would a spider in a glass: gently, with a firm base and no sudden movements.

Now return—if you can—to that moment earlier, the one where you connected with yourself. Not in a motivational-poster sense. In the sense of a breath taken fully. A body felt from the inside. Recall it. That pause. That inner space. See it, hear it, feel it. Make it vivid. Add texture. Add warmth. Then, press your thumb and middle finger together or your thumb and index finger.

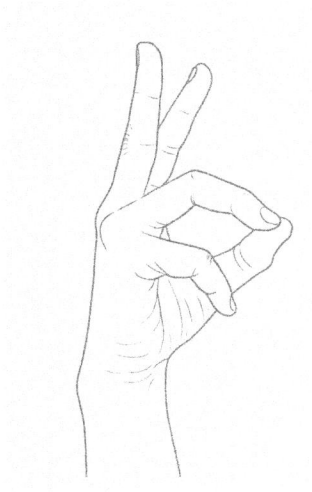

THIS IS YOUR ANCHOR. A small, inconspicuous act that says, 'We're back in safe territory.' As you press, let your breath expand like a lungful of ocean. And watch—there it is. A twitch of a smile. Unforced. Familiar.

Now, summon someone who always cracks you up. A comedian, a friend, a moment of glorious ridiculousness. Let it rise uninvited. Feel how that memory shifts your face, your muscles, your chemistry. That's neuro-associative learning in action. Not a slogan—just biology doing its thing. As that warm hilarity reaches its apex, press the fingers again. Lock it in. Tag the moment.

Then, with calm stitched to your fingertips, bring the stressor back into view. Watch it as if from a safe distance. Not through gritted teeth, but through half-lowered eyelids and a longer-than-usual exhale. See yourself move through it. Not heroically, but cleanly. With poise. Hear the background sounds, feel the floor beneath your feet, and stay with the image of yourself navigating—not evading.

Anchor again. Thumb to finger. Let calm return like a tide, then add a twist. Something goes sideways: a tech glitch, a late train, an arsehole in a tie. But notice—your pulse doesn't sprint. You adapt. Shift. Choose. You're not pretending everything's fine. You're just refusing to let chaos have the mic.

Pause. Scan your body. Something has shifted, hasn't it? Breath? Shoulders? The narration in your head? Even if it's subtle, it counts. You're not chasing peace—you're installing it.

Next stressor. Repeat. There's no leaderboard. No prize for speed. Just a gradual reconfiguring of your default setting—from 'braced' to 'braced-and-breathing'.

What you're doing here isn't mood management. It's subtle neurological carpentry. Quietly rewiring reflexes. In the language of NLP—though we'll keep that backstage for now—you've just performed a manoeuvre known as *collapsing anchors*[8]. Which sounds vaguely aggressive but is, in truth, more judo than boxing.

Instead of wrestling your stress response into submission, you introduced it to calm. Let them sit side by side until the nervous system, being the energy-efficient creature it is, starts to favour the smoother track. That's not magic. It's physics with manners.

You're not scrubbing out history. You're annotating it. Editing instinct with gentleness and repetition until the old grooves grow shallower and new ones take hold.

This isn't about surface calm, either. It's not the spiritual equivalent of holding in a sneeze. You're rewiring the reflexes that govern posture, tone, breath, and presence. You're no longer running your life on muscle memory inherited from stress-addicted ancestors.

We'll come back to this method again. In new coats. With new applications. But this first encounter matters. Because what you've just begun isn't self-soothing. It's self-governing.

Over time, this becomes automatic. The calm you conjured in this exercise shows up uninvited. In meetings. In traffic. On Monday mornings. Stressors still happen. But they find a system that knows how to hold the line.

Take Sharon, for example. Our high-stakes presenter with a heart that leaps into interpretive dance the minute she's handed a clicker. With this practice under her belt, she doesn't see her racing pulse as sabotage anymore. It's fuel. She breathes. Anchors. And walks into the room not to survive it, but to run it.

Even when the audience frosts over. Even when a senior partner offers feedback with all the tact of a chainsaw. Sharon notices the freeze. Names it. Doesn't marry it. She touches base with herself. With someone safe. Re-engages with more poise than panic.

That, right there, is nervous system literacy. And no, it's not just a personal upgrade—it's cultural infrastructure. One conversation at a time, one anchor at a time, we build workplaces and homes where calm is not a luxury but a transferable skill. And to think—we began by doing nothing but noticing.

In the next chapter, we'll explore what it looks like when whole organisations begin to support this shift—creating spaces where calm is contagious, stress is navigated, and human systems thrive.

THREE
CHANGING YOUR MIND
HOW THINKING DIFFERENTLY CHANGES YOU

Dissociation is a technique that involves separating the person from an emotionally charged experience.
Richard Bandler

SHE SAT FROZEN at the end of the meeting room table, watching the conversation unfold like a car crash in slow motion. The meeting had turned—she felt it before she understood it. Something in the body language of the room, the coldness in the phrasing, the unspoken shift in tempo. Words were still being exchanged, but their content had become irrelevant. Influence had drained from her like heat from an open window.

What had begun as a routine investor update had pivoted without warning. One of the partners, leaning back with carefully controlled detachment, had implied—without quite stating—that future support was now contingent. They didn't want more information. They wanted a change in tone. She hadn't prepared for that. She defended, she clarified, she insisted. And with every justification, the oxygen in the room thinned further. She was still speaking, but no one was really listening. The mistake wasn't what she said. It was where she spoke from.

Leadership invites us into high-stakes moments where our instincts shout for attention. But the most decisive shift we can make isn't in our argument—it's in our *angle*. The real power lies not in doubling down, but in stepping outside ourselves. To see clearly what's unfolding, and to decide, deliberately, how to re-enter. Sometimes the best move in the room is to leave it—mentally, momentarily—so we can return with presence instead of panic.

In this chapter, we'll explore two tools that make that shift possible: the ability to change perspective and the ability to detach from overwhelm. They won't make you superhuman. But they will stop you becoming a puppet of your reactions. And in rooms like that, where meaning is not spoken but felt, that difference is everything.

Perceptual Positions

Stand in your own shoes long enough and they'll start to pinch. The problem isn't empathy. Most decent people care. The problem is geometry. Leaders are often trapped in first position—our own perspective, our own motives, our own stress signals looping louder each minute. We speak from the inside of a problem we're trying to influence from the outside. It's no wonder we feel unheard.

But what if you could momentarily borrow someone else's seat? Not symbolically, but perceptually—long enough to feel their weight, see their view, and hear yourself from their side of the table? This is not a metaphor. It is a trainable skill.

In the early days of NLP, long before it became a punchline in cheap sales seminars, Bandler, Grinder and their colleagues mapped the way effective communicators moved between perspectives[1]. They noticed that the best therapists didn't just analyse a client's story.

They inhabited it. Then they stepped back. Then they watched from above. That sequence wasn't a flourish—it was the method. The technique is now known as *perceptual positions*, and it works like this[2].

First position is where most of us live by default. It's the direct experience of self—your own thoughts, feelings, goals, needs. When done well, it brings authenticity. When overused, it breeds tunnel vision. You see only what you want to say, only how it affects you, only what you're trying to get across. Necessary, but insufficient.

Second position shifts you into another person's shoes—not abstractly, but sensorily. You imagine the world from behind their eyes. You feel what they feel. You hear your own words as they would hear them. This isn't agreement. It's alignment. A good negotiator doesn't surrender to the other side. They borrow their logic just long enough to navigate it with clarity. Leaders who skip this step lose the room before they ever open their mouths.

Third position is the neutral observer. The fly on the wall. The corner of the ceiling. It is the act of watching a conversation unfold from a distance, like a film scene. Here, you're not advocating or empathising—you're noticing. Tone. Timing. Power dynamics. Breathing patterns. The micro-adjustments people make when they feel safe, or unsafe. In this position, you become not just a participant but a diagnostician. Detached. Informed. Unemotional but not unfeeling.

There's a fourth position too—rarely taught, often misunderstood. It is the systemic view. The long game. The future echo. You rise above not just the players but the entire frame. You see how the situation fits into the organisation, the culture, the time horizon. It's not a feeling, but a perspective. How does this conflict look three months from now? What patterns have you missed because you were busy chasing symptoms? From this angle, you see trends not tantrums. You begin to think like a strategist.

To the untrained mind, this all sounds fanciful. But try it. Take a recent difficult conversation and replay it from three angles. Yours. Theirs. The ceiling. Now step forward—three months. Ask what mattered and what didn't.

The result isn't enlightenment. It's clarity. Precision. Composure. You begin to realise that influence doesn't come from insisting harder. It comes from choosing the right position from which to speak.

Consider the team leader preparing for a critical conversation with a high-performing employee whose behaviour has started to slip. From first position, he feels annoyed, let down, perhaps intimidated by the employee's technical brilliance. From second position, he senses the employee's confusion—maybe burnout, maybe misalignment. From third, he watches the potential trainwreck: a well-meaning leader framing feedback too late, too vaguely, with the best intentions and the worst delivery. From fourth, he sees a pattern: top talent eroding because the culture rewards output but neglects capacity.

With that insight, he doesn't just say different things—he becomes a different kind of communicator. More grounded. Less reactive. Strategically attuned. This isn't introspection. It's operational awareness.

Perspective-shifting is not about being 'nice'. It's about being useful. It creates space between stimulus and response. And in that space, you stop reacting and start leading. You stop being the problem and start seeing the system. Because when things are tense, it's rarely the person in the room who's wrong. It's the position they're stuck in.

V/K Dissociation

There are moments that stick—not because they mattered, but because they *felt* like they did. A sharp comment in a meeting. A mistake made in public. The moment your mind went blank onstage and the silence lasted longer than it should have. These moments lodge themselves in the body. Long after they've passed, they can still jolt us awake at night, or change the way we walk into a room. This isn't nostalgia. It's residue.

Leaders, no less than anyone else, accumulate these residues. But unlike most people, they must continue to show up—often in the very rooms that triggered the reaction. So the question becomes:

> How do you return to a space without carrying the weight of what happened last time?

And more than that—how do you carry yourself as though it no longer owns you? The answer begins with a small but radical shift: learn to *watch* what once overwhelmed you.

In the early development of NLP, one of the most surprising discoveries was that emotional intensity could be reduced not by logic, or insight, or willpower—but by physically altering the way a memory was visualised[3]. The key, it turned out, lay in the connection between what you *see* internally and what you *feel* as a result. Split the two, and the feeling weakens. Rewire the sequence, and the emotional sting dissipates.

This process became known as visual–kinaesthetic dissociation[4]—or, in plainer language, watching your memories like films instead of reliving them from the inside. Here's what it looks like.

A managing director relives the moment he lost his temper in front of the executive team. He was exhausted, baited, and one cutting remark too far tipped him over the edge. What came out of his mouth wasn't leadership. It was frustration, pride, and raw exposure. And though apologies followed, the moment still lives in him like an unhealed fracture.

Each time he thinks about it, the film doesn't *play*—it *possesses*. He's back inside his own eyes, inside his own chest, re-experiencing the heat, the dry mouth, the crack in his voice. The memory isn't a lesson. It's a trap.

Now imagine something different. He replays the same event, but instead of watching it through his own eyes, he watches himself from across the room. He sees the scene as if on CCTV: him at the table, colleagues around him, the body language before and after the moment. The event has become *visible*, not just visceral. He is no longer the man in the film—he's the viewer.

The result? He begins to notice things. Where his breathing changed. Who flinched. How quickly his posture closed. What no longer surprises him is how it felt—but how clear it becomes, in retrospect, that the room didn't escalate. *He* did.

This is the power of dissociation. Not distance for its own sake, but the ability to move from experience to observation. It offers the leader not detachment, but perspective. Not avoidance, but authorship.

Some memories are too raw to look at directly. V/K dissociation lets you look at them indirectly—through the lens of learning, not the heat of shame. It's a way to reduce the volume on the body's emotional replays without denying what happened.

And crucially, it's fast. A change in visual framing, a shift in inner perspective, and what felt like a minefield becomes, at last, navigable terrain.

In practical terms, you step out of the memory and observe yourself from a safe angle. You see the image shrink in size. You fade the colours. You reduce the volume. It's not magic. It's not memory loss. It's memory *repositioned*. From there, your nervous system begins to loosen its grip. The emotion becomes data. And data, as any good leader knows, is negotiable.

V/K dissociation is not a parlour trick. It's a leadership skill[5]. It allows you to show up again—fully, calmly, and cleanly—without dragging yesterday's mistakes into tomorrow's opportunity. And that, in the thick of pressure and perception, might be the quietest form of courage a leader ever displays.

But there are moments where watching from a distance is not enough. The loop replays not because it's painful—but because it's familiar[6]. Recognisable. Predictable. The system runs the same film because it's not yet been given a better one. And that's where a sharper tool comes in—not to numb the memory, but to replace its opening scene.

THE SWISH PATTERN[7]

It doesn't begin with the crisis. It begins with the coffee. Stale. Bitter. Sitting in a chipped mug in a corridor that never did like you. Or maybe it's the late meeting with no agenda. Or the boss's blink, just a fraction too slow, like they're buffering bad news. Whatever the trigger, your stomach knows before you do. Down it goes. Breath tightens. Shoulders shrink. And that bloody file opens again:

Not Good Enough.

You didn't click it. It opens itself. It always does.

You don't choose this. You react. Like a badly trained dog at the sound of a bell. Fast, reliable, and inconveniently loyal to the worst version of you. This isn't malfunction. This is programming. Just not the kind you've been taught to edit. Until now.

The *Swish Pattern* is not some pixie-dust trick for erasing your past or summoning your future in six easy steps. It won't fix your calendar or your ex or your bank balance. But it *will* do something far more subversive: it'll rewrite the film that flickers across your nervous system in the moment just before you flinch. And in leadership, that frame is everything.

Buried somewhere in your reflexes is a snapshot. A freeze-frame. One that cues your system to brace, shrink, obey. It's not one you consciously chose. But it plays—reliably—just before your mouth dries and your spine curls.

Maybe it's the memory of that meeting. The one where you sounded twelve and looked nine. The moment you forgot your own name while grown-ups discussed budgets and battle plans. Posture like a hostage. Eyes like headlights. That one.

Now, picture this: a different frame. Same moment. But this time, you're there on purpose. Shoulders not tight, just present. Breath, not heroic, just available. You're not performing poise. You *are* it. Because you've seen this pressure before, and it no longer gets your first reaction. It gets your second one—the better one.

That image? It's not fantasy. It's a neural placeholder. A *swap* waiting to happen. And the more you practise replacing the old one with this, the more natural it becomes.

You're not fighting fear. You're giving it a new script. And the body—predictable, obedient, eager-to-please creature that it is—will follow the one it sees rehearsed.

This isn't about pretending to be someone else. It's about cueing your system to remember who you actually are, just in time. So. here's how we do it:

Choose your first image. The flinch one. Small. Still. A snapshot of you mid-mortification. Don't embolden it—let it look faint. Like a bad passport photo left out in the rain. Keep it central, but weak.

Now, load your second image. The version of you that doesn't grovel to the moment. Head up. Jaw soft. Calm—not because things are perfect, but because you're no longer outsourced to the chaos. Picture motion. Fluidity. You're not bracing. You're *moving through*. Not chasing your dignity. Just wearing it, like a well-cut coat.

Now—swish.

Let the old image appear, then rip it away into the distance. Fast. Here a 'swishing' sound as it shrinks out of sight. The bring the the stronger image snapping into place right in front of you. No drama. No fanfare. Just a shift. With a dominant 'swish!'. When you see the stronger picture and feel the stronger feeling.

Then do it again. And again. Five times. Ten. Faster each time, until your reflexes start cueing the new image *before* the old one even gets its coat off. Each time you do it, amplify the feeling. Multiply it. Intensify it through your whole body.

This isn't visualisation for mood boards and moonlight journalling. It's conditioning. Rehearsal. A quiet coup of the body over the past. You're not suppressing the panic. You're outmanoeuvring it. Quietly. Elegantly.

And when it sticks—when the new image becomes the default—something odd happens. Your stomach forgets to drop. Your breath arrives on time. You don't feel like a fraud in your own chair. You feel like the *host of your own state*. You're not pretending to lead. You're leading before the words begin.

So, the next time that twinge arrives—the meeting, the misstep, the corridor of doom—don't wait for the spiral to start. *Swish it*. Replace the signal. Reset the frame. Not a fantasy. Not a performance. A preloaded truth.

You're not changing the world. You're just changing how you show up in it. And sometimes, that's enough to change everything.

Learnings & Understandings

Let's be blunt: composure isn't a mood. It's a craft. People often admire calm under pressure as though it were a temperament, a kind of native grace that some are born with and others must endure the absence of. But those who lead well under fire rarely do so by accident. What looks like unshakeable presence is often built on a layer of invisible rehearsal—techniques embedded long before the storm ever arrived.

This is where the practices in this chapter—perspective-taking and dissociation—earn their weight. Not as abstract ideas, but as *habits of mind*[8]. The goal is not to know them, but to wire them in. To make them available not when it's convenient, but when it's *necessary*.

The test of integration is not whether you can recite the positions or remember the steps. The test is what happens the moment things turn. The email that blindsides you. The team member who snaps. The boardroom goes cold. Do you clench and defend? Or do you step —mentally, even for half a breath—into another vantage point? Do you become the story, or the one who sees the story as it unfolds?

Great communicators and steady leaders aren't born in the moment. They are prepared for it. That preparation doesn't need hours of meditation or dramatic rituals. It needs *usefulness*. Just enough self-regulation to interrupt the body's cascade. Just enough perceptual distance to loosen the grip of shame or fear. Just enough pattern recognition to understand the shape of the room before charging into it.

Here's how it works in practice. You're about to walk into a difficult conversation. Stop. First position: what do I need to say, and why does it matter to me? Second: how might they hear this—and how do I want them to feel when they leave? Third: what would a bystander notice about my posture, my pace, my presence? Fourth: if I get this wrong, what does it cost six months from now? If I get it right, what grows?

Now step in. You're not improvising any more. You're *navigating*.

Later, when the conversation is over and the emotional dust has settled, you sense a residue. Maybe it's the edge in your voice you wish hadn't shown. Maybe it's their silence as they walked away. This is where V/K dissociation becomes the second act of leadership. Instead of mulling it endlessly from the inside, you rerun the film from the outside. You observe without absorbing. You learn without relapsing. You reduce the weight without discarding the value. This isn't detachment. It's respect—for yourself, and for the work.

Leadership is filled with moments that don't go to plan. You will be misunderstood. You will overreact. You will get blindsided. The measure of your influence is not in how often these moments occur, but in how cleanly you can return to form after they do.

The integration of these strategies doesn't ask you to become someone else. It asks you to *return to yourself*, unclouded by yesterday's tension, unshaken by the current crisis. To become not less emotional, but more intentional.

And that's the irony: the more you practise stepping out, the more fully you're able to step in—present, grounded, and ready. Because in the end, it's not about having more control. It's about having more choice.

FOUR
CONTROLLING YOUR EMOTIONS
EMBODIED LEVERS TO CALM

We need to learn to treat our own brain better –
understanding how it works will help us do that
Richard Bandler

THERE'S AN OLD STONE ABBEY, perched atop a cliff as the storm rolls in. Rain lashes sideways against the leaded windows. Trees bend like supplicants. Yet inside, there's a keeper of the flame—someone tending the light that must not go out. The winds rage, but the lantern stays lit. Not because the storm has relented, but because the flame has been protected—and the protector prepared.

Leading in crisis is visceral, resembling this quiet duty. Not the thunderous speeches or strategic forecasts, but the inner steadiness others look to when the world tilts. The essence of it isn't dominance, but containment. Not spectacle, but sanctuary.

In crisis, leadership must become a *light in the black.*

In this metaphor, the candle is your inner clarity, purpose, and presence. But even the strongest candle is vulnerable in the open. The skills we explore in this book—the embodied tools of NLP—are the lantern: the structure that protects the flame from wind, rain, and crisis[1]. Without the lantern, the flame flickers out. But without the flame, the lantern is hollow metal, purposeless.

Gary understood this. As general manager of a manufacturing site under pressure, he watched his top finance lead, Rebecca, freeze during a crisis meeting. Her usual sharpness vanished. She sat stiff, silent, eyes blank. Her body had bolted. Her mind had gone dark. It was not incompetence—it was exposure. A flame, caught in the open.

But what followed was different. Gary didn't shame her. He equipped her. Months later, a restructuring plan triggered that same primal jolt—but this time, Rebecca noticed. And *because* she noticed, she had space to act. She hadn't erased her fear—she had trained her nervous system to build a lantern around it. A learned craft, not a lucky escape. To shelter her clarity. To let her warmth return.

That is what these NLP skills do. They don't eliminate the storm. They don't flatten the terrain. But they do something far more powerful: they keep the light alive when the darkness arrives.

When certainty collapses, they don't follow the plan. They follow the one who can shield their flame. They'll follow you.

"Mountains into Molehills"

Not all storms arrive with thunderclaps. Some settle quietly into the mind —anxieties dressed as memories, fears disguised as foresight[2]. They don't knock on the door. They just move in, rearranging the furniture of your thoughts until it's hard to tell what's real and what's just well-lit fiction.

That's what happened to Sarah. There was no actual threat—no looming danger in the room. But her body didn't get the memo. Her pulse quickened, her breath shallowed, her thoughts narrowed into a tunnel. Why? Because her mind had built a theatre so vivid, her body took it as fact[3]. A scenario composed of shadows and whispers—yet compelling enough to launch her into survival mode.

What helped her step back was not brute will or wishful thinking. It was a small but radical act of re-seeing.

Start here. Bring the worry to mind. Not to wallow in it—but to catch it, just long enough to change your grip. It might come to you as a still image—a face, a headline, a hallway. Or it may spool like old film: grainy, flickering, but emotionally sharp. However it appears, don't judge it. Just notice.

Now imagine stepping out of it. Not fleeing, but shifting. Picture yourself floating a little away—as if you're watching the scene on a screen rather than living inside its script[4]. You can see yourself there, in the middle of it all. But now you're a little offstage, behind the curtain, with more air in your lungs.

With each inch of distance, something changes. The intensity begins to fray at the edges. It's the difference between riding the rollercoaster and watching one from the ground. The rails are the same—but the vertigo fades when you're not strapped in.

Take the colour out. Bleed the scene to monochrome. Without its vivid palette, the emotional grip weakens. The reds no longer shout, the shadows no longer threaten. You're not erasing the image—you're unhooking it from its spotlight[5].

Now, make the whole scene smaller. A tenth of its size, perhaps. Let it shrink like a receding tide, until the moment that loomed like a wave now fits inside the palm of your hand. As it shrinks, so too does its command over your body.

And then—let it fade. Not vanish completely, just soften. Transparent now, like something glimpsed through fogged glass. Still there. Still acknowledged. But no longer sharp enough to cut.

From this vantage, you might find your thoughts returning. Not the frantic kind, but the kind that ask good questions. Do I need to act on this? Is there something here I can learn, adjust, decide?

You don't need to answer right away. The power lies in the pause. In the fact that now—you get to choose.

This isn't about denial. It's about design. You're not escaping your experience; you're redrawing its frame. So the next time the storm rises quietly, you'll have the steadiness to watch it pass, rather than getting swept up in the weather.

And in time, you'll find yourself doing this not just with memories or worries, but in real-time—reframing on the fly, steering your state before the swell crests. Because perspective isn't passive. It's a practice. One that puts you back in the director's chair of your own mind.

"The Past is Over"

> *You need to learn that you are in control of how you think. This includes how you think about your past*
> **Richard Bandler**

Not all anxiety is fiction. Sometimes the surge in your chest, the prickling skin, or the tunnelled hearing isn't sparked by an imagined threat. It's not fantasy—it's memory. And memory, especially the kind forged in high-stakes moments, has a curious way of refusing to stay put.

You might be sipping your morning coffee or walking into a meeting, and then—without warning—you're ambushed by a flash from the past. Not just a scene, but the whole atmosphere: the jolt of adrenaline, the thudding pulse, the world narrowing in on one vivid, unshakable moment. You're not just remembering. You're re-entering.

There's a reason these fragments return so sharply. Our bodies and minds were built for survival, not serenity. When danger loomed—be it sabretooth or speeding car—our internal systems flooded us with the power to respond. Muscles primed, senses sharpened. Adrenaline made the body faster; noradrenaline etched the experience into the brain[6]. These chemicals weren't just preparing us for action. They were engraving a warning label onto time itself: *Remember this. It could save your life.*

But here's the rub. Long after the moment has passed, its echo lingers[7]. The brain doesn't just store what happened—it stores how it felt[8]. So years later, when the memory reappears, it can drag the emotional charge along with it. It's not just history. It's live wire.

And yet, memory isn't a courtroom transcript. It's malleable. Which means it can be edited.

Let's try something different now. Not to forget—but to reframe. To soften the punch without denying the lesson. To keep the wisdom and lose the sting.

Picture this: you're alone in a cinema. One of those plush, hushed spaces where even your thoughts seem to sit down beside you. The screen is blank. The air still. You settle into the seat—safe, undisturbed, and ready.

Now imagine that you can float—not metaphorically, but as if your awareness lifts gently from your body and rises to the projection booth. From behind a pane of soundproof glass, you can see yourself down there: calm, grounded, waiting. You are both the observer and the observed.

On the screen, the memory begins. But not all at once. First, a freeze frame—just before the moment. Not the worst part, but the edge of the cliff. Then another still image—after it's all over. You survived. You endured. You're here.

You let the film roll. Quietly. No judgement. Just the facts, playing out from 'before' to 'after'. And then—stop[9].

Now, imagine running the scene in reverse. Rapidly. Like a tape rewinding. Movements glitch backwards, sounds dissolve, the tension pulls away. You return to the still frame at the start, but lighter. Do it again. And again. Five times. Fast.

Something changes.

You're not erasing the past. You're unhooking its claws. The memory remains—but its grip loosens. You're not at its mercy anymore. You're the editor now.

Yet even after the sharpness of old wounds fades, another kind of challenge persists: the slow, frictional static of daily life. Not a sudden blow, but a steady hum, wearing down resilience grain by grain. This, too, can be rewired—and often, it's the more critical skill to master.

This exercise, though deceptively simple, reflects deep currents in both clinical psychology and the work of pioneers like Richard Bandler. It draws on how memories are not static—how they can be re-coded, gently, deliberately, and with care. Trauma studies call it reconsolidation[10]. You might just call it relief. Whatever name you give it, what matters is this: the past may knock, but you no longer have to answer in fear.

Neuro-Spa

One of the simplest ways to reclaim your composure is also the most overlooked: you practise it. Not in theory, but in motion.

When tension lingers in the background like static—barely loud enough to notice but just enough to wear you down—a well-crafted audio experience can help you reset[11]. Think of it less as an escape, more as a recalibration. A short guided trance, under ten minutes, does just that: it slips beneath the noise and invites your nervous system to breathe differently. To feel safe, focused, and free again.

SCAN THIS QR Code to listen. It began as a favour: a quick, under-ten-minute reset, first crafted in a hotel lobby in Orlando. Later refined and sound-designed, it's now yours to use.

Neuro-Spa

You can listen with your eyes closed or leave them open—it works either way. Try both. Then repeat the exercise a second time. Coming in and out of that altered state, like rehearsing an exit and re-entry, trains your system to shift gears on cue.

That's not just self-care. That's skill-building.

Each repetition conditions the body to release stress before it accumulates. Each pass helps the mind move from idea to action, hesitation to presence. And with enough practice, this shift becomes second nature. Not a concept, but a capability.

This is how freedom begins—not as a breakthrough, but as a quiet habit you learn to trust[12].

APPROACHING a Threshold

> *Imaginary problems require imaginary solutions*
> **Richard Bandler**

No klaxon sounded. No office memo said *Impending Doom*. The earth didn't shake. But something shifted. Quietly, slowly—like a tide inching in beneath the floorboards. Nothing dramatic. Just a few stumbles where once there were strides. A missed target here. A postponed decision there. A project mothballed. A colleague offloaded. No single event to mark the turning, but each one dropping weight, until the air thickened and your outlook with it.

You tell yourself it's a blip. A statistical wobble. Temporary. Probably nothing. But weeks go by, and the silence between explanations starts humming. The narrative, once crisp, begins to curl at the edges. Somewhere between the inbox and the bathroom mirror, a fog takes up residence—not in the world, but behind your eyes.

And that's when it begins: the quiet betrayal of your own mind.

Your thinking, once measured, starts drawing conclusions with crayons. Small delays now feel like omens. Every minor hitch becomes a harbinger. Events don't just happen anymore—they conspire[13]. And the voice inside? It starts drafting headlines:

- Maybe I've lost it.'
- 'Nothing I do seems to work anymore.'
- 'What if this is just how things are now?'

It's not madness. It's misdirection. The mind, ever the overachiever, gets busy drawing up disaster plans. Not because the ship is sinking, but because the forecast looks cloudy. It builds a future out of shadows, sketches worst-case scenarios in permanent ink—and worst of all, it believes its own blueprints.

And the body? Ever loyal, it plays along. Muscles tighten. Sleep frays. Reactions sharpen. Not because something *is* wrong, but because something *might* be. And your nervous system doesn't bother to ask which. It just batons down the hatches.

This is how spirals start—not with a scream, but with a whisper. Not with a fall, but with a forgetting. You forget ease. Forget clarity. Forget that you ever knew how to lead with your shoulders down and your breath intact. And before long, you're a reluctant passenger in a brain that used to be your co-pilot.

But spirals can be interrupted. Not by force, or fanfare, or a midnight epiphany. The real reset is subtler. It begins not with what you *do*, but how you *tell the story* of what's being done to you.

"Control Your Inner Voice"[14]

> *My mantra for silencing the inner dialogue is:*
> *'shut the fuck up, shut the fuck up, shut the fuck up,...'*
> **Richard Bandler**

So, let's go upstream. Past the thoughts, past the tension. Let's find the culprit: the inner voice... the crappy narrator.

You know the one. Not shouting. Just always there. That background commentary that sounds suspiciously like you—but with worse manners. It's the murmur you mistake for truth. Don't fight it. Don't argue. Just listen. Get curious.

- Where does it seem to come from?
- Behind your temples?
- Off to the side?
- Somewhere in the middle of your head, like it's trying to set up a small, underfunded radio station?

Maybe it moves. Maybe it presses. Maybe it hovers. Just notice it. Then, gently, change the format.

Imagine those same lines appearing as subtitles—white text on a black screen. The words are still there, but no longer echoing inside. They've drifted outwards, like fog lifting off the ground.

Now, keep listening—but let the voice come from *out there*. Three metres away. Still droning on, but no longer seated behind your eyes. Still opinionated, still boring—but now someone else's problem.

What shifts?

Exactly.

Without you as host, the voice loses power. You're not silencing it—

you're relocating it. Giving it a visitor's badge instead of a master key. And that change in proximity? That's a change in control.

Now, dial it down.

Like an old radio—just turn the volume gently, incrementally, until it drops to a murmur, then a hum, then nothing. Not silence exactly, but absence. A clearing. And in that cleared space, something ancient stirs—not effort, not hustle. Relief.

The body, no longer bracing, begins to restore. Not through action, but through the exquisite release of *not needing to act*. Your system, so used to scanning for incoming threat, gets to exhale. You've just interrupted the loop—not with logic, but with spatial grace.

And then, a choice appears.

Not a new fairy tale. Not a motivational bumper sticker. Just the chance to write the next sentence differently. A cleaner lens. A closer vantage. A story that's accurate, rather than adhesive.

This isn't self-help fluff. This is signal hygiene. What you just did wasn't metaphor. It was neuromechanical. You moved the locus of attention. You used perception as a lever. And that shift engaged the same circuits that govern stress regulation, sensory integration, and emotional recovery.

You didn't fight the voice. You reframed it—in space, in tone, in power. You taught your system something invaluable: Not every noise is a siren. Not every voice is in charge. And not every thought is worthy of your stage. This—quietly, invisibly—is what I call *the inner game of leadership*. Not a trick. A lens. Not a hack. A discipline. And the more you practise it, the more it practises you. Not just to survive the storm—but to see through it.

FIVE
COMPLETE TURN AROUNDS
REPATTERNING & ELEVATING YOURSELF

*By reversing the spin of a negative emotion,
you can transform it into a positive one*
Richard Bandler

THINKING DOESN'T INITIATE EXPERIENCE, sensing does. Before a leader speaks, before they act, and well before they make any strategic call, something else is already in motion. And it's happening in the body.

Leadership, after all, is more than verbal persuasion or cognitive agility. It is the ability to read—and to influence—the unspoken. The micro-shifts in posture. The tightening in the gut. The flicker of the eyes before an idea is even formed. These are not random quirks of biology. They are patterns. And, more importantly, they are trainable.

The journey from reactivity to resilience doesn't happen all at once—it unfolds in stages. At first, a person may be carried by instinct, responding to situations before they've even registered what's happening. They feel a rush of anger or dread, and then post-rationalise it with some tidy explanation. This is the fog of instinctual ignorance: the feeling precedes the story.

Then comes a moment of pause—a growing ability to detect the early signals. A heat rising. A pressure in the chest. A turning in the stomach. This is instinctual awareness: the first step towards mastering one's state.

But awareness is only the beginning. With practice, leaders begin to map the texture of their inner responses. They notice the subtle ways their perceptions are filtered and framed—how certain images, sounds, or movements inside the mind cue a rush of energy, or shut it down. This is instinctual acuity: the capacity to decode your own nervous system with increasing precision.

And finally, there is a kind of learned elegance—instinctual intelligence—where the body and mind work in sync. Not through suppression or control, but through partnership. Here, the leader can reset their baseline, shift gears, and bring themselves back to calm with an ease that once felt out of reach. They can not only recover their centre but extend that sense of groundedness to those around them.

That's what we're building.

In the last section, we played with internal imagery and sound to soften the sharp edges of stress. These weren't abstract visualisations. They were deliberate neurological interventions—techniques honed in the field of NLP, particularly in the work of Dr Richard Bandler[1]. His approach isn't concerned with what's theoretically interesting. He asks a more pragmatic question: what do people actually do when they get better? Then he turns those behaviours into replicable systems.

Turning **Anxiety Around**[2]

One of the most powerful techniques from his *Neuro-Hypnotic Repatterning* method involves the physical 'feel' of emotion. Not the label—'anxiety', 'anger', or 'panic'—but the actual sensation. Where it lives in the body. How it moves. And crucially: how it can be moved differently because emotions are in motion.

The sensation of anxiety starts somewhere in your body and moves. It may surge upward along the centreline of the body, rising from the base of the torso, curling forward or backward at the top, then dipping and climbing again in a rhythmic cycle. Others report the opposite: a downward pull, like a heavy current descending through the chest or gut, looping underneath, and lifting again.

In some cases, the movement takes a more lateral path—crossing the body's midline from one side to the other. It might rise up the left flank, arc across the shoulders, and fall down the right, before beginning its return.

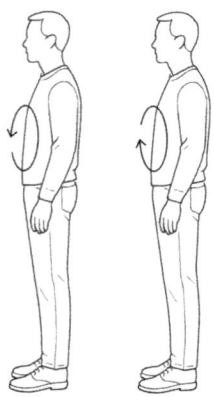

Spinning feeling coming up/down the midline

Or it could spiral lower, descending along one side of the abdomen, then gliding across the hips and rising anew. Another common variant is a flat, circular spin—like a disc turning horizontally through the chest or stomach, sweeping from left to right or right to left in a steady whirl.

Now here's where the method becomes both simple and astonishing: reverse the direction of the spin[3]. Not metaphorically. Literally. Visualise the sensation spinning in the opposite direction. Give it a new colour, a new pace. Green, perhaps.

Slower. Then gradually increase the speed of this reverse motion until something shifts in the body.

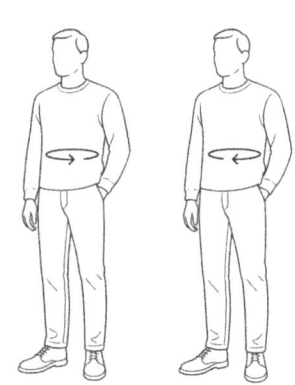

Spinning feeling like a flat disc, on/ crossing the midline

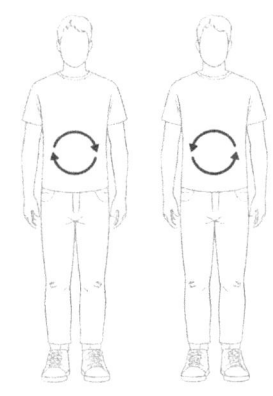

Spinning across the abdominal crossing the midline

That twist, that change, does more than soothe—it re-codes. By adjusting the direction, speed, and texture of an internal feeling, we're not just managing emotion; we're showing the nervous system that there is another way to be.

And with repetition, this becomes more than a technique. It becomes a skill.

To help anchor this feeling of restored calm, we'll pair it with a physical gesture—a light pinch between the thumb and middle finger. This isn't magic. It's neurology. When the mind and body experience peace at the same moment as a specific action, they link. Fire together, wire together.

With time, that link becomes automatic. Pressing your fingers together becomes a kind of shortcut. A way of whispering to your body: 'You're safe now. You can return.'

To deepen this, we add memory. Not abstract nostalgia, but embodied recall. Picture a moment when you felt utterly at peace. Maybe the lilt of water on a quiet shore. Maybe a hammock rocking between trees. Find the texture of that memory and let it wrap around you. Let it spread.

Then loop it.

Each time you revisit this moment, while holding that anchor gesture, you're reinforcing the neurological pathway to calm. And once this pathway is well-trodden, it becomes easier to walk—even when you're under pressure.

Now, recall a moment that used to trigger unease. Nothing overwhelming—just a mild spike of stress. With your calm state spinning and your anchor gesture engaged, see yourself in that situation again. Watch how your body now responds. You've brought in a different baseline. The state has changed. And with it, your response changes too.

This is not about pretending the problem is gone. It's about proving to yourself that your nervous system is not a prisoner of circumstance. It can learn. It can adapt. And so can you.

We'll continue building these capacities. But for now, remember: your state is not fixed. It's flexible. You can spin it, shape it, and strengthen it. The more you practise, the more instinct becomes intelligence. And intelligence—true, embodied intelligence—is what makes leadership trustworthy, even when the world turns upside down[4].

You've built the muscle of turning the spin. Now we deepen it. The next layer is about infusing—not just reversing the momentum of emotion, but threading calm into your system so richly that it becomes your new baseline. This is *Wrapped in Serenity*.

WRAPPED in Serenity[5]

As you spin the god feeling, begin at the back of your mind to remember a time when you felt completely calm, tranquil, and serene. Not just relaxed, but suffused with that rare, full-bodied quiet where everything in you was at ease. No strain. No effort. Just being.

This isn't a flicker of nostalgia—it's a returning. A fully emerged reliving. So go ahead, find your moment.

Perhaps it was a stretch of beach at low tide, the light bending gold across the water, and your mind stretching out just as far. Or maybe it was a winter's afternoon wrapped in a blanket, the rain tapping on the windows and the world asking nothing of you. It doesn't matter where or when—only that you were fully there. Let yourself re-enter that scene. What did it feel like to breathe in that calm? To rest without worry tugging at the edge of your attention?

Let the memory build itself in layers: the air, the light, the textures. What could you hear? Was there warmth or breeze, stillness or sway? Tune into the small details. This is your sanctuary, already stored deep in your nervous system. All you're doing now is opening the door.

For me, it was an island off the coast of Goa. I was younger, with my soon-to-be wife beside me. A hammock swung between two coconut palms, the pale sand cool underfoot, the horizon smeared with sunlight. The sea moved in soft rhythm. Children's laughter echoed faintly in the distance, scattered with the cries of seabirds. The air was thick with salt and promise. I remember closing my eyes and floating—nowhere to go, nothing to fix. The world had let go of its grip, and so had I. That moment still lives in me, as vivid now as it was then.

So find yours. Let the memory wash through you, until it's not just something you see, but something you feel. And as that feeling thickens—like honey warming in the sun—press your thumb and middle finger together on your right hand. Lightly. Intentionally. This is your anchor. A quiet cue linking sensation to state.

Now play gently with the experience. Imagine softening the colours—perhaps they become warmer, more golden, or slightly blurred at the edges. Let the sounds grow more melodic, as if wrapped in cotton. If there's movement, let it slow to the pace of breath. Say to yourself, quietly: 'Soften.' And then again—quieter, gentler. Until even the word dissolves.

Press your thumb and finger again. Let the feeling deepen. The gesture is no longer just physical—it's becoming neurological. Each time you pair it with this state, the association strengthens. Fire it. Wire it. Embed it.

Do this several times. Each repetition is a reinforcement—a groove you're carving into your own nervous system, so that calm becomes a place you can revisit, not a hope you chase. Soon enough, the gesture alone will be enough to trigger the return.

Now, let's add some complexity.

Think of a situation that's previously brought low-level stress—a tense conversation, a deadline looming, a moment where your stomach turned slightly and your thoughts grew sharp. Nothing overwhelming. Just enough to stir discomfort.

As that scene forms, press your fingers together. Spin the calm into it. Let the memory of serenity leak into the stress like ink into water. Picture yourself in that same moment, but this time holding your ground—shoulders easy, breath steady, gaze clear. The scene hasn't changed, but you have.

Let's go further.

Keep the same scenario, but raise the stakes. Maybe you're under pressure. Maybe someone's watching. Maybe time is short. But again, spin the green feeling. Press the anchor. Notice how your body stays open, how your thoughts stay slow. See yourself responding—not reacting—with grace and precision. Calm doesn't make you passive; it makes you powerful.

Now step back and notice the shift. What once felt jagged or draining is now just another moment—one you can meet with composure. That is the mark of practiced calm. Not absence of challenge, but presence of centre.

Keep rehearsing this. The nervous system learns through rhythm and return[6]. Each time you practise, you make calm less conditional. Eventually, it won't matter what the day throws at you—you'll know how to find the signal again. Thumb to finger. Soften. Return.

This is not a parlour trick. It's a disciplined craft. A way to shift your internal state deliberately and on demand. In the world of leadership —where pressure is constant and uncertainty the norm—that's not just useful. It's essential.

This is *Wrapped in Serenity*. Subtle. Embodied. Trainable. A tool not just for you, but for the people who look to you when things get rough.

Because calm isn't a gift. It's a craft. A discipline you forge when the world would rather knock you off balance. It doesn't come from waiting for easy days—it comes from training for hard ones. Now, it's in your hands: small, deliberate, invisible to the world—until the moment it matters most.

SIX
DAILY DISCIPLINES
RHYTHM, RITUAL & RESILIENCE

Brains aren't designed to get results;
they go in directions.
Richard Bandler

BEFORE THINGS GO SIDEWAYS, there's often a whisper. A twitch in the gut. A missed beat in the rhythm of the day. Most people ignore it. Leaders can't afford to. The greatest strength you have isn't how fast you recover—it's how rarely you need to.

This chapter is about anchoring yourself before the waves hit. It's about prevention—not the sterile kind found in policy manuals, but the living, breathing kind that takes shape in small daily rituals. These are the patterns that shore up your state and make breakdowns less likely, less severe, and less contagious to those around you.

Over the years, I've worked with leaders navigating mergers, crises, resignations, restructures—even death. Some buckled. Some bent and bounced back. The ones who fared best weren't simply lucky or genetically calm. They had routines. Habits. Practices so woven into their day they didn't have to think about them. These weren't grand strategies, but micro-decisions made in quiet moments: a breath taken instead of a barked reply; a walk taken before the meeting, not after the meltdown.

Two things are worth remembering as you build your own toolkit:

First, one size doesn't fit all. What steadies one person might agitate another. A cold plunge might sharpen your focus, or it might leave you shivering and grumpy. The only way to know is to try. Your job isn't to find *the* method—it's to find *your* method.

Second, the real magic lies in repetition. Anyone can be calm once. Resilient leadership is built on consistency. It's doing the small things so often that they become part of your operating system. The paradox is that when they're working, you don't notice them. Which is exactly when people stop doing them. Then the pressure builds, the cracks appear, and the old reactive habits take over. The smarter play is this: when it's working, keep going. That's the sign you're onto something.

This isn't about turning into a zen monk or becoming unshakeable. It's about knowing how to return—to clarity, to steadiness, to a state that others can trust and lean into. Because your state sets the tone. Before people hear your words, they feel your presence. Before they follow your ideas, they follow your nervous system.

Let's be blunt: most of us don't fall apart because the storm hits—we fall apart because we never learned to build in the calm.

The 'PACE Protocol' was a solution for a difficulty that I was having keep track during circuitous coaching sessions. I found when I applied it to myself, I got some good results too: the importance is the quality and sequence of the questions and the honesty of my response. Used frequently, the act of asking each question becomes the anchor and the response follows. Over time, the questions become a chain of anchors and responses that become automated, tumbling like dominoes. In NLP, this is known as *'chaining anchors'*[1].

PACE YOURSELF

What if personal resilience wasn't something you had to 'find' in crisis, but something that showed up because you'd rehearsed it long before? That's the promise of PACE. When practiced deliberately, it doesn't just help you recover from strain—it rewires your relationship with it. Over time, you become harder to rattle, quicker to refocus, and far more likely to lead from centre, not reaction.

It begins with the invitation to step into your own day with intention by checking in before your leadership begins:

Have I given myself permission to lead today?

Not permission to dominate, but to be fully present, unapologetically conscious of your role, your influence, and your footing. It's the difference between walking into a room and being in the room.

When challenge strikes—and it will—your body often knows before your mind does. The tight jaw, the shallow breath, the sharp reply. But there's a crucial gap between sensation and action, and that's where choice lives. By noticing what's driving your next move—reflex or reflection—you regain access to your judgement. Ask yourself:

Is this action shaped by panic, or by principle?

That pause isn't dithering—as Viktor Frankl would say, it is the gap between the stimulus and the response[2].

Connection is where this moves from personal resilience to interpersonal leadership. People don't follow plans. They follow presence[3].

And if you're locked in survival mode, you're not available to lead—only to react. So tune in:

Am I available to others right now?

If the answer's no, don't fake it. Reset. Regroup. Because every team inherits the emotional tempo of its leader.

And then, embed. Not once. Not in a seminar. But daily, like breath. The leaders who rise under pressure aren't improvising—they've rehearsed. They've mentally visited tomorrow's stress before it arrives. They've primed the path through uncertainty. So ask:

What challenge can I pre-live today, so I'm ready when it comes?

That's not catastrophising. It's craftsmanship.

To 'PACE Yourself' is not to slow down, but to lead with rhythm. Grounded, calm and focused states aren't made from heroic interventions—it's the quiet mastery of everyday moves. So let's explore how these practices, repeated simply and steadily, give you the edge not just to survive the pressure—but to shape it.

STRING OF PEARLS

At the end of it all, what do we really have? Not the tasks we completed. Not the titles we held. We leave behind what we *carried within*—a lifetime's worth of moments strung together like pearls. A look. A laugh. A walk through dusk. Some gleam brighter than others

—those milestones we'll never forget. Others are smaller, quiet and easily missed. But still, they shine in their own way.

Together, they form something beautiful: *a string of pearls*. A wonderful life, in the end, is made of wonderful experiences. Not necessarily grand or dramatic, but rich in felt meaning. The warmth of a friend's hand when words fell short. The exhilaration of solving something that once baffled you. The stillness of early morning light as the world holds its breath.

These moments don't simply pass—they accumulate. They become the emotional architecture of a life well lived. And the act of remembering them with intention is more than nostalgia; it is a quiet rebellion against the pull of stress, noise, and urgency.

We all need a way back to ourselves. A compass when pressure bends our sense of direction. That's what this practice offers: not escape, but return.

So, begin with what you already own—your lived joys. Create your own string of pearls, a personal treasury of experiences that lift, soothe, and steady you. The time you spoke your truth and were heard. The thrill of setting off on a journey. The scent of rain on warm earth. A small kindness exchanged at just the right time.

But don't stop at remembering. *Relive.* Close your eyes. Let the colours return. Hear the sounds. Feel what it meant to be there, alive and unguarded. Engaging all five senses strengthens the emotional current, turning a flicker of memory into a source of resilience.

Over time, your string becomes not just a record of delight, but a resource for endurance. On anxious mornings, revisit moments of triumph or laughter. When the world feels unkind, summon a memory of deep connection. When self-doubt looms, turn to the pearls that affirm your worth.

Sarah, a senior leader navigating constant pressure, begins each day by holding one such pearl: a memory of hiking alone in the mountains. She remembers the bite of the wind, the crunch of stone underfoot, the widening view as she reached the summit. That memory doesn't solve her day—but it changes how she meets it.

There's research here, too. Positive psychology tells us that actively recalling uplifting experiences rewires the brain to orient toward calm, connection, and inner strength[4]. But this isn't science for the lab. *It's wisdom for living.*

So start now. Gather three pearls from your life—moments that still stir something within you. Write them down. Honour them. Add more over time. Let your string grow, not out of urgency, but out of reverence.

Because when all is said and done, this is what remains. A string of pearls—held together not by time, but by gratitude. And every time you reach for one, you remind yourself:

> This is the life I have lived.
> This is the life I am still living.

Anchor to Launch

The day doesn't wait. It lunges. The moment your eyes open, you're already inside it—caught in a swirl of thoughts, tasks, messages, moods, and other people's needs. That's why the first few minutes matter. Not because they're sacred, but because they're strategic.

What you do upon waking isn't just a habit—it's a signal. To your body. To your mind. To your future self. Begin the day feeling steady, vital, and in touch with something larger than yourself, and chances are, you'll move through its messiness with greater ease. Begin it agitated, distracted, or depleted, and you'll be on the back foot before the kettle's even boiled.

The same holds for your final minutes before sleep. Drift off while agitated or half-scrolling your way into numbness, and your body will struggle to let go. But end the day with a few moments that restore calm, safety, and inner order, and sleep becomes not a collapse but a return.

Of course, routines are no panacea. Even the most seasoned morning person can be derailed by a screaming toddler, a curt email, or a sudden downpour. That's life. Its disruptions don't ask your permission.

But what you can do is create a rhythm—light but durable—that brings you back to centre, again and again. You don't need hours. You need a handful of minutes, well-used. Over time, these moments become ballast—keeping you upright in chaos, tethered in turbulence.

Before we tackle the more jarring shocks—grief, upheaval, major life events—let's get our feet on the ground. This section will show you how to build simple, repeatable morning and evening practices that offer not escape, but edge. A sharper edge. One that's ready for what's next, without being dulled by what's now.

Morning Momentum

How you start your morning matters far more than most people dare admit. It's not about hitting the perfect sequence of productivity hacks. It's about striking the match—something visceral, personal, enlivening—that lights you from within. You don't have to leap into a five-mile run at sunrise. But you *do* need to turn the key. So, the question is simple:

What gets your engine running?

Not what *should*. Not what looks good on a wellness blog. What genuinely stirs you—sensations, scenes, moments you *want* to be part of. Maybe it's the sound of a kettle boiling or the sight of sunlight sneaking across your bedroom floor. Maybe it's remembering the first time someone made you laugh when you thought you'd forgotten how.

Start there. Build yourself a 'charge list'—not a checklist, not a to-do. A list of the things that charge your batteries, plug you back in, pull you forward. Let it be vivid. Let it be irrational. Let it be yours.

"Delight at Dawn"

There are those mornings when your body feels like it's still in bed, even if technically it isn't. If that's you, then don't waste precious effort trying to shame yourself into action. It won't work. Your system doesn't respond well to scolding. What it does respond to is *spark*.

Some find it in music. Others in cold water. I used to summon the memory of my father's voice—commanding, no-nonsense, echoing from another room with a barked 'Move!'. Effective, yes. But as I've learned, energy can be summoned more elegantly.

Try this instead: four seconds in, four to hold, four to let go. Repeat. Box breathing—simple, powerful, deceptively gentle. Like flicking on a switch for your nervous system. Do it three or four times. Then, once the breath has cleared a little space, drop in something energising from your string of pearls.

Let's say it's that moment your team pulled off the impossible. Or that wild run down the mountain slope. Or the look on your child's face when they laughed so hard their cereal nearly escaped the bowl. Call it up—not as a memory, but as a movie. Brighten the colours. Turn up the sound. Step into it fully. Let delight into your body. Feel the pulse pick up. Let your mouth curl into a *big cheeky grin*.

Relive it to the max! Make the sound even crisper and richer. Make the colours larger and more vivid. Spin a wonderful feeling faster and faster and let it spread all over your body. And then, like rolling thunder from somewhere deep and powerful, say inside your mind:

This day is mine!

"Soften at Sunrise"

Then there are the mornings that begin already clenched. Not tired, but taut. Your stomach knows before your mind catches up: there's something on today's horizon that's drawing breath away before the sun has even risen. That's not weakness. That's vigilance. Your system thinks it's protecting you. And in a way, it is. But you can teach it something better.

Try 4-7-8 Breathing: breathe in for a count of *four*, hold for *seven*, exhale for *eight*. This longer out-breath has a way of whispering calm to your insides. Three rounds, maybe four. No need to force it. Just invite the calm in, like an old friend pulling up a chair beside the fire.

Once you've carved out a little calm, bring to mind something that grounds you in your own competence. Not the kind that wins awards. The kind that brings you home to yourself.

It might be a craft or a ritual. Gardening. Whittling. Cooking a flawless omelette. Or the quiet satisfaction of reordering a chaotic inbox. The point isn't glamour. It's certainty. Rehearse that certainty in your mind's eye—rich, full-colour, surround sound. Let the scene open up like a cinema screen. Stretch it wide. Step into it.

Feel what you feel when you're in it: grounded, capable, assured. Let that feeling move through you—not like caffeine, but like roots digging in. Locate that grounded feeling and spin it at a rate and speed that give you centred calm and confidence.

And let your whole body just soften. Let the tension evaporate from you like steam from a coffee cup. And when you're ready, let this thought rise, calm and unshakable:

Today... belongs... to me!

What you do in the first moments of your day doesn't just colour the hours that follow—it sets the tone, the tempo, the texture of your inner weather. You are not just getting out of bed. You are stepping onto the stage of a day that will demand something of you. So it matters—deeply—*how* you enter.

There's a world of difference between mumbling something halfhearted to the mirror and *claiming* your intention with presence. One is a whisper into the void; the other is a signal flare sent straight to your nervous system.

If you tell yourself, 'Today is mine', but sound as though you're apologising for it, your body won't believe you—and neither will the day. But if you say it with the grounded authority of someone who means it—someone who feels it in their chest, hears it in their voice, and can sense the shift as it lands—then the effect is unmistakable. You don't just hear the words. You *become* them. It's not theatre. It's transmission. It's not a step. It's a *stomp*!

Balanced on the Brim

It's not the empty cup that undoes most people—it's the full one. Not full of wisdom, clarity, or insight. But full of noise. Full of things half-swallowed and never let go. Slights that cling. Words you wish you hadn't said. Things they should have seen. The half-meant compliment you twisted into a warning. Stress, frustration, tension—it all accumulates. Slowly, silently. Until the cup tilts.

Leaders don't always see it coming. They pride themselves on being composed. Professional. High-functioning. But no one is immune to overflow. I've seen it countless times. Someone known for being grounded suddenly flares or crumbles. The trigger looks trivial—a meeting gone long, a report delayed, an offhand comment. But it's never just that. That moment is the tip of something long ignored and poorly tended.

The truth is, many of us are walking around with cups too full. And not full of the right things. Not the good stuff that steadies us—those bright moments of laughter, meaning, contribution. But of recycled stress. Echoes of bad conversations. Arguments replayed and re-edited in the mind. It's emotional residue, and it builds. A cluttered emotional attic, stacked high with things we never meant to keep.

We are not meant to carry every moment. Nor are we built to dwell on each wound. That's not resilience—it's emotional hoarding. The body remembers what the mind replays, and each replay comes with a hormonal cost: cortisol, adrenaline, isolation, mistrust. You stop connecting. You start surviving.

And here's the paradox: what feels like coping—pushing through, gritting your teeth—is often the very thing that keeps you from clearing your cup. You become vigilant, brittle, defended. Less curious. Less kind. Your leadership shifts from creating to controlling. From presence to pre-emption.

But the wise don't just protect their energy. They curate it.

They don't let the worst parts of the day set up camp in the best parts of themselves. They empty the cup often—consciously, deliberately. They let the bitter moments pass, instead of stewing in them. And they collect the good ones—the small wins, moments of grace, hard-earned insights. Like pearls on a thread. That's what fills the cup with meaning. That's what steadies the hand.

Because the real art isn't in holding more. It's in knowing what not to hold at all.

The question for any leader is simple: *What's in your cup?*

Because whatever it is—sooner or later—it spills.

Get Rid of It

You wouldn't eat last night's dinner off a filthy plate. Not out of snobbery, but sanity. Nor would you ignore the stench of a full bin in summer, pretending it'll sort itself out. We clear the kitchen not because we're neat freaks, but because mess has consequences. Spills attract ants. Rot invites worse.

Yet somehow, many leaders overlook a mess far closer to home—their own internal residue. The bitter taste of that meeting gone wrong. The lingering odour of disappointment from a decision they regret. The mental clutter of days that didn't go to plan. It builds up, quietly but persistently, like leftovers hidden behind the milk.

Jerry—bright, capable, admired—still finds himself lying in bed, replaying the day's misfires. Not reflecting. Ruminating. It's as if he's pressing his own emotional bruises just to feel them throb. And each time he does, the pain grows a little more familiar. A little more comfortable. That's the trap. Unresolved emotions don't fade with time; they ferment.

This is no vague metaphor. Connection, in physiological terms, is not a luxury. It's a necessity. When we disconnect—when we freeze or bottle or broadcast stress—we suppress the body's in-built capacity to regulate and reset. It's like placing a healing wound back into the fire. And here's the part we often miss: the body is built to recover. But only if we let it.

So, if you've had a rough day—don't just sleep it off. Do the mental equivalent of clearing the kitchen. There's a technique for it. Not mystical. Not dramatic. Just effective. Think of it like rinsing the mental dishes before sleep.

First, call to mind a moment that's been bothering you. The kind that plays on repeat at the worst time of night. Now imagine the memory as a short film. Freeze the frame. Drain the colour. Flicker it between black and white rapidly—five times. Then shrink the image in your mind's eye until it becomes laughably small. Repeat that sequence five times. It takes seconds.

Then—here's the twist—start the film at the end, and play it backwards. Let people walk in reverse, speak in gibberish, even fall back into chairs. This scramble disarms the emotional charge. Do that five times. Faster each time. By the third or fourth pass, the sting has dulled. By the fifth, it's lost its bite.

To anchor this, spin up a good feeling in your body—something you practised earlier with calm induction. Then run the reverse reel again while holding that feeling steady. What you're doing is not denial or avoidance. It's pattern interruption. It's taking back authorship of your own memory stream.

Richard Bandler—whose irreverent genius often concealed deep practical wisdom—designed these tools to help people unhook from the emotional barnacles that cling unnoticed. They work. They've helped veterans and executives alike shed trauma's grip.

And for leaders like you, they're a lifeline. Not just for your own sanity, but for those who take their emotional weather from your sky.

So don't let the rubbish fester. Don't sleep in the stress-stained clothes of the day. Take five minutes. Reset. Clean the slate. Then, and only then, rest.

Because resilience isn't what you're born with. It's what you practise when no one is watching. So, to one more time, repeat:

- Flicker the picture black and white for a five-count.
- Shrink the picture, five times fast.
- Then play the sights, sounds and sensations backwards, five times fast[5].

And for good measure, it the sound of a toilet flushing as the emotions are sent to where they belong.

Deep Refreshing Sleep

You don't *get* to sleep. That's half the problem. Sleep is not something you seize; it's something you allow. Like a guest that arrives when the house is quiet and the lights are low, sleep turns up when you stop trying to impress it[6].

Yet many people lie in bed like hosts at a dinner party gone wrong—overthinking, over-apologising and overcompensating for a guest that never arrives.

Here's the mistake: they bring the noise of the day with them. A passing embarrassment, a difficult conversation, a looming deadline—looping endlessly like a late-night newsreel. Not only does this keep them awake, it trains the body to associate bedtime with threat.

Each night, they lie down and rehearse panic. They run mental marathons while begging for rest. And so the body, bless it, does what it's designed to do when it senses danger: it stays alert.

Tell an insomniac to drink a large caffein-rich can of *Monster* before bed. They'd throw you out of the room. Yet every night, people serve themselves an even more potent cocktail of worry, stress and adrenaline then expect blissful rest. It's nonsense, of course. But it's practiced nonsense. And practice, as you know, makes permanent.

Let's try something else.

Start earlier than you think you need to. The best nights begin with a kind of quiet housekeeping of the heart. You don't need to *solve* the day, but you do need to *put it down*. If something bothered you, take a moment—while still up and about—to name it, face it, and let it be done with. There's no need to invite it to bed.

Then, build what I call your *Bliss List*. This isn't a bucket list or a vision board. It's a small treasury of memory—simple things that have made you feel deeply at ease. A warm mug in your hands on a winter's morning. Laughter that caught you off guard. A kind look. The sound of trees swaying when you had nowhere to be. These are not grand experiences; they are quiet ones. And their quietness is precisely the point.

Write them down. Picture the list in your mind. Then, as you lie in bed, recall each one with the tenderness it deserves. Use your inner voice—but softer, slower. The kind of voice you'd use if you were reading someone to sleep.

While you do this, breathe. But don't just *notice* your breath—befriend it. Start where it is, then gently guide it down into your belly. Let it deepen and slow. After each out-breath, pause briefly, as if to allow the silence a turn to speak. Then begin again. Inhale. Exhale. Pause. And with each pause, imagine your body loosening its grip on the day. Soft jaw. Heavy limbs. Shoulders melting like ice in warm water.

Now, place your attention just below your navel. That's your centre. See a small glow there, like a candle flickering inside you. With each breath, let it grow brighter—spreading warmth, not heat. Feel it reaching through your body like sunrise through a sleeping house.

Return to your Bliss List. Choose one memory and settle into it. Let it open. Let it play. As your body begins to relax, allow your mind to wander—but kindly. If it drifts somewhere unpleasant, gently redirect it to the next item on your list, like changing the station on a radio. No fuss. No failure. Just another chance to re-lax.

And yes, that word is worth breaking apart. Relaxation isn't a one-time act; it's something we return to, over and over. *Re*-laxation. As though softness itself were a skill. And it is.

If you wake in the night—because of noise, a dream, or the call of nature—don't panic. Don't rush back into the day. Simply lie back, curl your toes ever so slightly, and let a sleepy smile pass through your body like a ripple on still water. That's your signal. The lights are low. The guest is welcome again.

So let go. Let your list keep you company. Let the breath lead. Let the body soften. Sleep will arrive when it's ready. And when it does, it will feel like coming home.

Conclusion

You don't wait until the house is ablaze to learn where the fire extinguisher is. Sensible leaders build their resilience before the sirens, before the smoke, before the ceiling cracks. That's the role of the PACE Protocol and its practical twin, *PACE Yourself*—not for rescue, but for readiness.

This isn't mindfulness as mood lighting or self-care as spa day. It's leadership as infrastructure: silent, load-bearing, essential. Like the unseen steel in a suspension bridge, these practices hold tension without giving way. They let you carry the weight—yours and others'—without collapse.

It might seem small, the act of steadying your breath or returning to a touchstone of calm. But these are not anaesthetics. They're investments. Compound interest for the nervous system. Small acts, repeated often, generate disproportionate returns: clarity, elasticity, depth.

And when these acts become habit—not fallback—you don't just manage stress. You model resilience. Culture starts to shift. Your presence becomes the pulse others follow. Psychological safety stops being a slogan and becomes something people can feel. Collaboration firms. Innovation exhales.

In a world veering between frenzy and fatigue, it's tempting to barrel through. But urgency without rhythm becomes erosion. The smarter move is to pace yourself. To lead with intent, not adrenaline. Because presence—like strength—isn't summoned at the cliff's edge. It's forged in quiet, disciplined moments.

So practise before it's urgent. Train before it's turbulent. A breath. A check-in. A tempo you return to when the room wobbles. These are not indulgences. They're strategy. You won't just feel the shift. You'll *become* it—and so will those who follow your lead.

LEADERSHIP LESSONS FROM PART I
PRINCIPLES THAT HOLD UNDER PRESSURE

These lessons aren't abstract theories. They are embodied truths—earned through experience, refined through awareness, and designed to help you lead from the skin in. Each insight reflects a shift in perception, a reframe of instinct, or a tactical upgrade in how you hold yourself under pressure.

Perception & Mapping

1. **You don't respond to reality. You respond to your map of it.**
   - Your behaviour flows from internal sensory representations—not facts or logic. Every decision begins in perception.
2. **Your nervous system edits before you act.**
   - Deletion, distortion, and generalisation aren't flaws. They're survival strategies.
3. **VAKOG defines your reality.**
   - Sensory filtering—what you see, hear, feel, smell, and

taste—creates your internal world. Leadership begins by noticing what you notice.
4. **Subjectivity is not a weakness—it's the medium of influence.**
    - Leaders who understand their filters can adjust them. The rest just project them.
5. **State follows structure. Structure follows sensation.**
    - Change the sequence of how you perceive, and the meaning will follow.

Embodiment & State

1. **Instinct moves first. But awareness can intervene.**
    - Leadership starts the moment you notice the urge—and pause long enough to choose.
2. **A calm leader is not less emotional—they're more literate.**
    - Regulation doesn't mute emotion. It guides it early, from the inside.
3. **You are a mammal with a mirror.**
    - No other species can reflect on its state in real time. This is your evolutionary advantage.
4. **State is a readiness profile—not a mood.**
    - Breath, posture, muscle tone, and attention form your internal weather. That weather drives action.
5. **Recovery is a rhythm, not a rescue.**
    - The goal isn't to stay unshaken. It's to return faster, with less cost.

Tools & Leverage

1. **Submodalities control the intensity of your responses.**
   - Size, brightness, tempo, location—these invisible codes shape what you feel.
2. **Meaning lives in structure, not memory.**
   - The emotional charge of an experience is coded in its form—not its story.
3. **Anchors are neurological handrails.**
   - A touch, breath, or gesture—if practised—can bring you back to steadiness under pressure.
4. **You've been anchored before—just unconsciously.**
   - Now, you're building those pathways on purpose.
5. **You don't change reactions by talking to them.**
   - You change them by recoding the sensory pathways they run on.

Field Notes for the Real World

1. **Before the script comes the shift.**
   - Don't rehearse speeches before you've regulated your state.
2. **State collapse isn't failure—it's feedback.**
   - Don't resent your nervous system. Read it.
3. **The map redraws in microseconds.**
   - One glance, one pause, one breath can change how you feel. Catch it.
4. **You can build memory forward.**
   - Anchoring isn't just for recall. It's for shaping future calm.
5. **Even panic has a pattern.**
   - And once you know the pattern, you can rewire it.
6. **Old states can be gently retired.**
   - Collapsing anchors lets you let go of protective patterns that no longer serve.
7. **Neutral is a superpower.**
   - In chaos, calm neutrality can lead more effectively than positivity.
8. **You are your own co-regulator.**
   - Before you lead others to safety, become a place your own system can trust.

CONCLUSION TO PART I
THE ROAD BEHIND. THE ROAD AHEAD.

The hardest journeys to measure are the ones that happen inside. No flags planted. No headlines shouted. Yet something fundamental has shifted all the same. If you pause and listen—not to the world outside, but to the quieter timbre of your own body—you can sense it. A recalibration. A different kind of gravity, one weighted towards choice rather than compulsion.

This stretch of the road has not been about gathering new theories or adorning yourself with clever techniques. It has been something starker and harder: a return to the raw materials of your experience. The grain of your breath when pressure mounts. The spin of emotion through muscle and mind. The quiet choices hidden in a blink, a breath, a pause.

What you have explored here is not information. It is infrastructure. The hidden struts that uphold not just how you act, but how you experience being *you*. You have read the code written in your senses —the tilt of a memory, the temperature of a fear, the cadence of a desire. You have begun the work that few ever attempt: *mapping the unseen structures that guide your every response.*

At first, it may have seemed almost too simple. Notice the colour of a memory. Attend to the weight of a feeling. But simplicity is often the last thing we master. And in learning to see the subtle architecture of your instincts, you have reclaimed something profound: the space between reaction and response. The first breath of *agency*.

There is no going back from such a shift. Once you have seen the scaffolding, you cannot unsee it. Once you have felt the moment when a tightening breath can be met—and loosened—you carry that capacity forward into every conversation, every decision, every quiet battle of nerves. This work is not about denying your humanity. It is about dignifying it. About stepping into the deep currents that move you, not as a bystander, but as a steward.

The road ahead is different now because you are different. Not in some dramatic, cinematic way. But in the ways that matter most: in the unseen seconds when challenge sharpens and the instinct to survive rises—and you meet it not with blind reflex, but with informed grace.

In the pages that follow, we will turn outward: toward how your presence shapes others, toward the living systems of teams, organisations, and cultures. But this pivot is not a break. It is a widening. The same instincts you have learned to read and recode in yourself are the ones that ripple between people, crafting climates of safety or fear, of stagnation or growth.

You have laid the foundation. You have set the internal gyroscope humming. Now, we move from the personal to the collective—from steadying your own hand to steadying the table where many hands meet. The ground may still tremble. The winds may still whip. But something quiet and fierce has been built within you. And it is ready.

Mapping the Inner Landscape

CONCLUSION TO PART I

For most, the inner world remains an unmapped wilderness. Thoughts flicker. Feelings surge. Behaviour follows, sometimes baffling even to the one acting it out. We name these storms with heavy words—'stress', 'fear', 'ambition'—but the labels do little to illuminate the actual terrain. You, however, have begun to draw a map.

Piece by piece, you've surfaced the elements that make experience vivid and real: the brightness of an image, the pull of a sensation, the lilt or rasp of an internal voice. *Submodalities*. Not grand theories, but fine-grain details—the building blocks of your emotional architecture. You've moved from being a passenger inside your reactions to being an observer, and then a craftsman.

Every time you paused to notice how an urge was coloured, how a memory was weighted, you chipped away at the old blindness. You taught your nervous system a quieter form of literacy. You began to read, in your own body, the hidden script that determines what feels safe, urgent, unbearable, or irresistible.

This was not analysis for its own sake. It was, and is, practical cartography. Because when you can see the contours of your inner world—the steep drops, the hidden paths—you gain choices that were invisible before. You can decide whether to climb, to shelter, to press forward. You can spot where an old reflex would once have swept you away—and instead, stand your ground.

Mapping your instincts this way is not a one-time achievement. It is a living craft. Every day writes new lines. Every setback redraws borders. But the essential shift has already happened: the map is no longer blank. And with each act of noticing, you refine it further.

It is tempting, at this stage, to believe that noticing alone is enough. That if we can name the elements of experience, we have mastered them. But names are only the beginning. True mastery demands movement. The work is not simply to know how your instincts are structured—but to shape them. That shaping is where we now turn.

Building New Pathways

There is an old myth, stubborn and persistent, that change must be wrenching to be real. That growth demands a crisis, a crucible, an unravelling. But real change—the kind that lasts, the kind that alters the fabric of how you meet the world—often begins with something quieter. Something almost imperceptible at first: a new signal laid down within the nervous system.

When you anchored your calm states, you were doing more than rehearsing a trick. You were building a new neural path—brick by brick, breath by breath. You linked vivid emotional states to simple, physical cues, the way a child might tie a thread between two trees to mark the way home. Not because the journey is always easy. But because, in the fog, in the noise, you deserve a way back.

Anchoring works because it respects the economy of your body. When the stakes are high—when stress surges, when emotion hijacks reason—you don't have the luxury of building a fresh plan from scratch. You act—or react—based on the patterns most readily available. Anchoring ensures that some of those patterns lead not into panic or paralysis, but into presence, clarity, steadiness.

In practising the reversal of emotional spins, you went even deeper. You didn't merely patch over distress. You re-coded it at the source. By adjusting the direction, speed, and texture of internal feelings, you taught your body that emotion itself is not a master, but a medium. One that can be tuned, shaped, shifted—not through force, but through skilled engagement.

What once seemed monolithic—anxiety, fear, dread—became pliable. You learnt that a rising churn could be slowed, reversed, softened. That the architecture of a feeling could be as editable as the lighting in a theatre, or the tempo of a song. And that by shifting the structure, you shifted the story the body was telling itself.

This is not about denying pain or past experience. It is about reclaiming agency where you can. It is about knowing, at the most primal level, that you are not simply a product of what happens to you. You are a co-author of what happens next.

Each anchor you set, each reversal you spin, is not a magic trick. It is a small act of sovereignty. A decision that, while the storms may still howl, you will not be a leaf tossed without will or direction. You will know the way home.

But even the strongest anchors and the deftest recalibrations are not enough on their own. What gives these techniques their lasting power is not the act of setting them—but the habit of returning to them. Repetition, in the nervous system, is not dullness. It is declaration. It is how the body learns what is true. And so, we turn to practice—not as penance, but as path.

The Power of Practice

The first time you steady yourself under pressure, it feels extraordinary—like balancing on a tightrope in high winds. You might marvel at your own poise, your unexpected calm. But the truth is, resilience is not defined by one-off moments of triumph. It is forged, quietly and stubbornly, through practice.

Practice is the unseen labour behind the visible art. It is what turns scattered insights into integrated instinct. It is what lays the track for the mind to follow when the wheels threaten to come off.

Every time you repeat an anchoring gesture, revisit a calm memory, or reframe an old surge of fear, you are not simply rehearsing a skill. You are wiring a new future into your flesh. The nervous system is plastic, not fixed. It reshapes itself according to how it is used. And what you repeat, it remembers.

But there is a deeper art to this return—not mechanical repetition, but living engagement. To practise well is not to mindlessly drill. It is to come back, again and again, with fresh curiosity. To treat each anchoring not as a replay of yesterday's move, but as a fresh conversation with today's body, today's mind, today's pressures.

One morning, your anchor might come easily, like stepping onto a familiar path. Another morning, it might feel remote, stubborn, slow to light. Neither is failure. Both are opportunities to hone the craft. To ask: what is different today? What adjustment is needed? What nuance can I hear if I listen closer?

In this way, resilience ceases to be a static thing you 'have' or 'don't have.' It becomes a living relationship with your own nervous system. A dynamic dance between external reality and internal choice.

And over time, a beautiful thing happens. The actions that once required focus, effort, and rehearsal begin to move into the background. They become the default setting—not because you forced them there, but because you walked the path often enough that it wore smooth.

The breath deepens on its own at the first sign of tension. The anchoring gesture comes without thought when nerves stir. The reframe arises naturally when old fears knock. This is how great leaders seem unshakeable—not because they are untouched by emotion, but because they have rehearsed their returns so often, the way home is ingrained in their bones.

You will still feel. You will still falter. But the gap between trigger and response will narrow. The climb back to centre will shorten. You will move through the waves, not be broken by them. And those around you will feel it too.

For resilience is not a private possession. It radiates. It shapes culture, conversation, and collective courage. When you hold steady, others find their footing faster. When you return to calm, others remember that they can too. And in this way, your personal craft becomes something larger than yourself. A source of grounding. *A light in the black.*

CONCLUSION TO PART I

The Map You Have Made

You have not merely read these chapters. You have walked them. Each technique, each practice, each return to calm has been a step across unfamiliar terrain—sometimes steady, sometimes stumbling, but always forward.

At first, the tools of NLP may have seemed like separate islands. Surfacing submodalities. Anchoring calm. Reframing memory. Returning to steadiness. Yet if you look back now, a larger shape begins to emerge. What you have built, piece by piece, is a map. A map not of external territory—but of your own internal landscape.

You now know where the pressure points lie—where the ground tends to give way, where the storms gather first. You know the shortcuts back to steadiness—the handrails, the bridges, the anchoring paths. You know how to spot the old scripts when they stir, whispering fear, urgency, self-doubt—and how to shift the channel before they take over the airwaves.

And most importantly, you know something that few ever do: that none of this is fixed. Experience is not a prison. It is a pattern. And patterns can be softened, reshaped, rewoven with skill and care. This knowledge is not just comforting. It is liberating.

Because if you can change the structure of an old fear, you can change how you lead through a hard meeting. If you can re-anchor yourself mid-pressure, you can shift the tone of an entire room. If you can hold your centre when others lose theirs, you can change not just your experience, but the emotional weather around you.

And if you can do it once, you can do it again. And again. Until resilience stops being an act of will and becomes a way of being. The nervous system you inhabit today is not the one you inhabited yesterday. It has already begun to rewire itself in response to your attention, your practice, your deliberate choices. The grooves you have walked are deepening. The new default settings are being laid.

And while storms will still come—and they will—you will no longer meet them as a passive target. You will meet them as an active participant. With agency. With precision. With grace.

You will not always get it right. None of us do. But the measure of mastery is not in never faltering—it is in how you return. How quickly. How cleanly. How compassionately. And over time, something quiet and powerful will take root. You will trust yourself.

Not in the brittle way of bravado. But in the deep, cellular way of someone who has been tested—and who knows, from experience, that they can find their way home. That trust is rare. Precious. Contagious. And it changes everything.

This is the art you have begun. This is the leadership you are learning to embody. This is the map you now carry. Not as a paper folded in a pocket. But as a living, breathing compass within you. And when the world wobbles—and it will—you will not have to scrabble for directions. You will already know the way.

From State to Signal

We often speak of non-verbal communication as if it were an add-on—something optional, soft-skill adjacent, or vaguely poetic. But that's a category error. It's not secondary. It's not supplementary. It's ancient. Long before we formed words, we formed signals.

Mammals appeared over 200 million years ago. Primates about 55 million. Homo sapiens have walked the earth for perhaps 300,000 years—but complex, structured language? That's a very recent development. Estimates vary, but most suggest it's at most 100,000 years old—maybe just 50,000. That means for over 99% of our evolutionary journey, all meaningful communication was non-verbal.

These weren't vague vibes or ornamental gestures. They were precise, embodied transmissions: a raised hackle, a flattened ear, a

CONCLUSION TO PART I

shift in breath, a widened eye. Our nervous systems evolved not just to emit these signals—but to read them. *And we still do.*

We blush when we're embarrassed—and if we're on stage, the side of the face visible to the audience reddens most. We pale when we receive bad news. We weep in grief, in joy, in frustration—each with a different breath pattern and facial configuration. Our pupils dilate when we're attracted. Our shoulders rise when we feel exposed. Our hands freeze mid-gesture when the air shifts.

This is not performance. It's neurological conversation. My nervous system signalling yours, and yours responding—before either of us utters a word. And it's happening continuously. Before, during, and after every meeting, every pitch, every pause.

This is why we began this book not with what you say—but with how you are. Because your state—how you breathe, how you orient, how you *are*—is already setting the stage for how your words will be read.

But there's a problem. Because language is new—and flashy—it steals our attention. Our slow, reflective, symbolic brain assumes the driver's seat. Meanwhile, our older, faster systems—the emotional, the instinctual, the non-verbal—are quietly running the show, largely unsupervised.

That's the opportunity. When we educate the verbal mind—our primate brain—about what our mammalian and reptilian systems already know, we don't regress. We integrate. We gain range. We begin to lead not just from script, but from signal.

So if Part One was about **knowing your own state**, Part Two is about **projecting it cleanly**. About reading others clearly. About leading not just with what you say, but with what they feel—often before they realise they've felt it.

Let's step into that deeper conversation now—the one beneath the words, the one your body has been having all along. *It begins before language. Before logic. Before the plan.*

TECHNIQUE SUMMARIES I
TOOLS FOR STATE, STRUCTURE & SENSORY PRECISION

Ex 1. Surfacing Submodalities

1. Choose Two Instinctual States

- Pick one strong *"move towards"* state (e.g. lustful desire, rabid hunger, intense craving).
- Pick one strong *"move away from"* state (e.g. terror, rage, revulsion, grief).

Yes, these are all very primal and uncivilised but they are part of us. It's better to understand and control *them* rather than the other way around.

- Write them down without overthinking it.

2. Recall a Peak Memory for the 'Move Towards' State

- Close your eyes.

- Fully recall a vivid moment when you experienced that forward-pulling impulse at full intensity (e.g. lust, ambition, craving).
- Don't sanitise—immerse.

3. Reconstruct the Memory Using VAKOG Senses

- **Visual**: What did you see?
  - *Brightness, colour, movement, distance, clarity, size, location, still or moving image, framed or panoramic, associated (through your own eyes) or dissociated (seeing yourself in the scene)*
- **Auditory**: What did you hear?
  - *Tone, rhythm, source (internal or external), direction, volume, clarity, pitch, tempo, background sounds, dialogue, silence, music*
- **Kinaesthetic**: What did you feel in your body?
  - *Feeling, flow, location (chest, gut, limbs), breathing, temperature, pressure, texture, movement (pulsing, swirling, rising), tension or relaxation, heaviness or lightness*
- **Olfactory**: What do you smell?
  - *Scent quality (sharp, sweet, sour, musty), strength/intensity, familiarity, temperature (cool/warm), single or layered, natural or artificial, pleasant or repulsive*
- **Gustatory**: What do you taste?
  - *Flavour type (sweet, salty, sour, bitter, umami), intensity, aftertaste, texture (smooth, gritty, dry), temperature, freshness or staleness, chemical or natural*

4. Amplify the Experience

- Intensify the sensory aspects:

- Sharpen the visuals
- Raise the volume
- Deepen the body sensations
- Let your nervous system *relive* it, not just recall it.

5. Record the Submodalities

- Use the *Submodality Comparison Sheets* below to log the sensory attributes (VAKOG) in detail.

6. Repeat Steps 2–5 for the 'Move Away From' State

- Recall a vivid moment of fear, disgust, or sorrow.
- Relive it from the inside—not at arm's length.
- Log the VAKOG properties again.

7. Compare the Two Submodality Maps

- Place the two side by side.
- Don't look for what's *similar*. Look for *differences*:
- Direction of movement (rising vs. sinking)
- Colour, brightness, or sharpness
- Location and tone of inner voice
- Texture or rhythm of bodily sensation

8. Identify Structural Patterns of Encoding

- Note how your mind distinguishes between attraction and aversion using submodality shifts.
- You are *not* analysing the content—you are decoding the structure.

TECHNIQUE SUMMARIES I

Submodality Comparison Sheet

	Experience 1	Experience 2
VISUAL		
Number of images		
Motion/still		
Colour/black and white		
Bright/dim		
Focused/unfocused		
Bordered/panoramic		
Associated/dissociated		
Centre-weighted/wide angle		
Size (relative to life)		
Shape Three-dimensional/flat		
Close/distant		
Location in space		
AUDITORY		
Number of sounds/sources		
Volume		
Tone		
Tempo		
Pitch		
Pace		
Timber		
Duration		
Intensity		
Direction		
Intensity		
Direction		
Rhythm		
Harmony		
More in one ear than another		
KINESTHETIC		
Location in body		
Breathing rate		
Pulse rate		
Skin temperature		
Weight		
Pressure		
Intensity		
Tactile sensations		
OLFACTORY & GUSTATORY		
Sweet		
Sour		
Salt		
Bitter		
Aroma		
Fragrance		
Essences		
Pungence		

Submodality Comparison Sheet

	Experience 1	Experience 2
VISUAL		
Number of images		
Motion/still		
Colour/black and white		
Bright/dim		
Focused/unfocused		
Bordered/panoramic		
Associated/dissociated		
Centre-weighted/wide angle		
Size (relative to life)		
Shape Three-dimensional/flat		
Close/distant		
Location in space		
AUDITORY		
Number of sounds/sources		
Volume		
Tone		
Tempo		
Pitch		
Pace		
Timber		
Duration		
Intensity		
Direction		
Intensity		
Direction		
Rhythm		
Harmony		
More in one ear than another		
KINESTHETIC		
Location in body		
Breathing rate		
Pulse rate		
Skin temperature		
Weight		
Pressure		
Intensity		
Tactile sensations		
OLFACTORY & GUSTATORY		
Sweet		
Sour		
Salt		
Bitter		
Aroma		
Fragrance		
Essences		
Pungency		

TECHNIQUE SUMMARIES I

Submodality Comparison Sheet

	Experience 1	Experience 2
VISUAL		
Number of images		
Motion/still		
Colour/black and white		
Bright/dim		
Focused/unfocused		
Bordered/panoramic		
Associated/dissociated		
Centre-weighted/wide angle		
Size (relative to life)		
Shape Three-dimensional/flat		
Close/distant		
Location in space		
AUDITORY		
Number of sounds/sources		
Volume		
Tone		
Tempo		
Pitch		
Pace		
Timber		
Duration		
Intensity		
Direction		
Intensity		
Direction		
Rhythm		
Harmony		
More in one ear than another		
KINESTHETIC		
Location in body		
Breathing rate		
Pulse rate		
Skin temperature		
Weight		
Pressure		
Intensity		
Tactile sensations		
OLFACTORY & GUSTATORY		
Sweet		
Sour		
Salt		
Bitter		
Aroma		
Fragrance		
Essences		
Pungence		

TECHNIQUE SUMMARIES I

Submodality Comparison Sheet

	Experience 1	Experience 2
VISUAL		
Number of images		
Motion/still		
Colour/black and white		
Bright/dim		
Focused/unfocused		
Bordered/panoramic		
Associated/dissociated		
Centre-weighted/wide angle		
Size (relative to life)		
Shape Three-dimensional/flat		
Close/distant		
Location in space		
AUDITORY		
Number of sounds/sources		
Volume		
Tone		
Tempo		
Pitch		
Pace		
Timber		
Duration		
Intensity		
Direction		
Intensity		
Direction		
Rhythm		
Harmony		
More in one ear than another		
KINESTHETIC		
Location in body		
Breathing rate		
Pulse rate		
Skin temperature		
Weight		
Pressure		
Intensity		
Tactile sensations		
OLFACTORY & GUSTATORY		
Sweet		
Sour		
Salt		
Bitter		
Aroma		
Fragrance		
Essences		
Pungence		

Ex 2. Anchoring

Step 1: Identify the Desired State

Choose an internal state you want access to under pressure (e.g., calm, confidence, clarity).

Step 2: Recall a Vivid Memory

Bring to mind a specific past moment when you felt that state strongly. Make the memory sensory-rich — notice the sights, sounds, sensations, and emotions.

Step 3: Intensify the State

As the memory becomes vivid, turn up its intensity. Let yourself fully feel it — amplify the emotion as if reliving it now.

Step 4: Choose a Physical Anchor

Select a simple, distinct physical gesture (e.g., pressing thumb and middle finger together) that you don't typically use in daily life.

Step 5: Fire the Anchor at Peak State

Just as the emotional intensity peaks, apply the gesture. Hold it briefly while the feeling is strongest. Then release.

Step 6: Break State

Distract yourself — stand up, shake out your body, or think about something unrelated. This clears your mind before testing the anchor.

Step 7: Test the Anchor

Reapply the physical gesture without recalling the memory. Notice if the desired state returns. If not, repeat steps 2–6, deepening intensity each time.

Step 8: Reinforce with Repetition

Practice the anchoring regularly over several days. Each reinforcement strengthens the neural pathway.

Step 9: Deploy Under Pressure

Use the anchor in real-world moments — before a meeting, during stress, or when needing focus — to shift your state quickly and reliably.

Ex 3. Connect With Yourself

Step 1: Notice the Hijack

- Pause and acknowledge the signs of overwhelm (racing thoughts, tight muscles, emotional noise).
- Simply observe the storm—without judgment.
- This awareness disrupts autopilot and begins to slow the system.

Step 2: Drop Your Attention

- Bring your focus one inch below your bellybutton.
- Choose a colour that represents joy for you.
- Place your hand gently over that spot, imagining the colour glowing softly beneath it.

Step 3: Breathe Into Centre

- Take **three slow, honest breaths** into that spot and that colour.
- Let your tummy rise and fall naturally—no exaggeration, no show.
- This re-roots you in your body and interrupts reactive patterns.

Step 4: Recall Real Joy

- Choose a *real memory* of joy (simple, not performative—like laughter, sea air, warm soup).
- Immerse yourself in the memory:
    - See it.
    - Hear it.
    - Feel it in your body.

- Let the sensations deepen and saturate your awareness.

Step 5: Ask Your Inner Guide

- Silently ask your *Unconscious Navigator* a question:
    - "What do I need right now?"
    - "What should I know?"
- Don't force it. Let the response emerge—often indirectly (a word, image, feeling).

Step 6: Follow the Nudge

- Act on the message—gently, immediately:
- Stand up, stretch, call someone, cancel a task, take a mindful walk.
- Let the small action reconnect inner truth with outer choice.

Purpose

This isn't about 'calming down' in the shallow sense.

It's about *rebuilding trust between your internal signals and your external behaviours*—so you can lead from coherence, not chaos.

Ex 4. Finding Home

1. Pause & Notice

- Stop. Sit quietly. Don't rush in.
- Turn attention inward—listen not to the world's noise, but to your body's quiet signals (tight jaw, gut flutter, eye strain, etc.).

2. Identify Five Pressures

- Ask yourself:
  - *What are five pressures pushing at me right now?*
- Be honest. Don't curate or filter. Write them down. Bringing vague stressors into language reduces their grip.

3. Don't Battle—Observe

- You're not trying to fix these pressures immediately.
- Shift your posture toward them: not with panic, but with poise. This is reflex retraining, not emergency response.

4. Choose One Stressor

- Pick one from the list to work with.
- Imagine holding it gently, like a spider in a glass. Stable. Curious. Not hostile.

5. Recall a Moment of Calm

- Return to a felt memory of calm: a breath taken fully, a body moment felt from within.
- Visualise it vividly—add warmth, detail, and emotional tone.

6. Create an Anchor

- As you recall that calm state, press your thumb and middle finger together.
- This becomes your *physical anchor*—a subtle signal of safety.

7. Add Hilarity

- Summon a memory or person that always makes you laugh.
- Let that joy rise and change your physiology—your face, muscles, and chemistry.
- At the peak of that emotion, press thumb and finger again to *strengthen the anchor*.

8. Reintroduce the Stressor

- Bring the chosen stressor back into awareness.
- View it as if from a safe distance—calm, grounded, and observing.
- Anchor again. Breathe deeply. Visualise yourself handling it with grace, not grit.

9. Stress-Test the Anchor

- Add a small imagined disruption (e.g., a tech failure or rude colleague).
- Notice: your system doesn't panic. It adapts. Breath stays steady. Anchor again.

10. Body Scan & Integration

- Check for subtle shifts: Has your breath deepened? Shoulders softened? Inner narrative softened?

- Even small changes count—they signal nervous system recalibration.

11. Repeat with the Next Stressor

- Choose another pressure. Repeat the sequence.
- No rush. No competition. Each round deepens the reprogramming.

12. Normalise Calm as Competence

- With repetition, calm becomes a reflex—not a conscious act.
- It shows up in daily challenges, tough meetings, or under pressure—*without being summoned*.
- Use the technique before high-stakes moments: presentations, confrontations, decision points.

End Result

You've begun building *neurological self-governance*—replacing reactive patterns with a calm, rehearsed, resilient response. This isn't coping. It's upgrading your operating system.

Would you like this condensed into a printable one-pager or visual card format?

Ex 5. V/K Dissociation

Purpose:

To reduce the emotional intensity of a troubling memory by shifting from *felt experience* (kinaesthetic) to *observed perspective* (visual), allowing learning without reliving.

Step 1: Identify the Residue

- Choose a memory that still carries emotional weight (e.g. shame, fear, regret).
- It's often a specific moment—an incident that replays in the body, not just the mind.

Step 2: Recall the Event Briefly (From Inside)

- Let the memory surface just enough to confirm you're experiencing it *through your own eyes*—this is called *associated view*.
- You may feel it in your chest, throat, or stomach. This confirms it still holds kinaesthetic charge.

Step 3: Dissociate—Step Out and Watch

- Now mentally *step out* of the memory.
- Imagine watching yourself from across the room or from a neutral vantage point (like CCTV or the corner of the ceiling).
- You are no longer inside the event. You are an observer. This is the *dissociated view*.

Step 4: Adjust the Internal Movie Settings

- Modify the mental image to further weaken the emotional charge:
  - Shrink the image size.
  - Dim the colours or make it black-and-white.
  - Mute the sound or lower the volume.
  - Slow it down or freeze-frame at moments of choice or change.
  - Picture it as a film with you as the character—not the experiencer.

Step 5: Observe Without Judgement

- Watch the sequence unfold as if analysing data—not reliving shame.
- Notice details you missed: other people's body language, your own shifts in breathing or tone, how the room actually responded.
- Extract learning: *What changed? What didn't? What would you do differently now?*

Step 6: Reframe the Narrative (Optional)

- If the memory still loops, ask:
  - "What better scene could I begin with?"
- Consider editing the memory's *starting point* or *emotional tone* to reflect learning or completion, rather than rawness.
- You're not erasing the past—you're updating its *position* and *function* in your system.

Step 7: Return to Neutral

- Take a deep breath.
- Open your eyes or gently return focus to the present environment.

- Check your body: Has the tension reduced? Does the memory feel less intrusive?

Step 8: Test & Repeat as Needed

- Briefly recall the memory again, from the observer's view. It should feel more manageable.
- If residue remains, repeat the dissociation or modify the movie settings again until it shifts.

Result

You gain distance, perspective, and authorship over a once-overwhelming moment. The emotional sting fades. The memory becomes informational rather than incapacitating. And leadership presence is restored—cleanly, courageously, and consciously.

Ex 6. The Swish Pattern

1. Identify the Trigger Image

- Choose the moment that usually triggers your old unhelpful reaction.
- Make it a still image — faint, small, low-quality. Think: bad passport photo after a rainstorm.
- Let it represent the reflex you want to change (e.g., shrinking, freezing, bracing).

2. Create the Desired Image (The You-On-Purpose Frame)

- Construct a vivid image of how you want to respond instead.
- Picture yourself calm, grounded, present — not performing confidence but inhabiting it.
- Add motion and ease. You're flowing, not forcing. Poised, not pretending.

3. Set the Stage: Both Images in Mind

- Place the *old image* central and weak.
- Have the *new image* waiting just out of view — bigger, brighter, more dynamic.

4. Swish!

- Rapidly shrink the old image and fling it into the distance with a mental '*swish!*'.
- Instantly replace it with the new, stronger image snapping into full focus in front of you.

- Feel the shift. Let the posture, breath, and emotional tone of the new image arrive in your body.

5. Repeat and Speed Up

- Do it again. Then again. Five times. Ten times. Each faster than the last.
- Let your nervous system learn the swap as a reflex — automatic, effortless, rehearsed.
- Amplify the feeling with each repetition. Let it flood your body with ownership and ease.

6. Test for Stickiness

- Think of the old trigger again. Notice what image comes up first.
- If the new image appears automatically — congrats, it's installed.
- If not, repeat. Faster. With more intensity and clarity.

7. Use It in the Wild

- Next time the real-world moment strikes — the look, the tone, the corridor — don't brace.
- Swish it. Reset the frame. Let the body remember the new cue before panic takes the mic.
- No drama. No denial. Just a seamless re-cueing of who you are at your best.

Ex 7. Mountains into Molehills

Step 1: Catch the Worry

- Bring the anxious thought, image, or scenario to mind.
- Don't engage or wallow—just *notice* it.
- Allow it to take form (a still image or a mental film reel).

Step 2: Step Out of the Script

- Imagine floating a little away from it—just enough to observe it as a scene on a screen.
- See yourself *in* the scene, from a ten feet/ three metres away.

Step 3: Change the Camera Angle

- From that mental distance, notice how the emotional intensity lessens.
- Like watching a rollercoaster rather than riding it.

Step 4: Desaturate the Image

- Drain the colour from the scene. Let it go black-and-white.
- Notice how the intensity lessens even more.

Step 5: Shrink the Scene

- Mentally reduce the image's size. Shrink it to a tenth of its original size.
- Let it become small enough to fit in the palm of your hand.
- As the image shrinks, so does its hold on your nervous system.

Step 6: Soften and Fade

- Fog over the scene, so you can barely see it.
- Then become transparent—just visible, but no longer sharp.
- You are not erasing the memory, just reducing its effect your state.

Step 7: Reclaim the Pause

- Ask:
    - *Do I need to act on this?*
    - *Is there something useful here?*
- Don't rush to answer
- Notice the difference between being hijacked and having agency.

Step 8: Return to the Director's Chair

- Recognise this as a design move—not denial.
- You're editing the emotional impact, not ignoring the event.
- Practise this regularly, and over time, you'll be able to do it in real-time—before the storm swells.

Summary

This is not about suppressing emotions. It's about *regaining authorship* over your inner theatre—reducing sensory intensity and narrative entanglement so that your physiology can calm, and your choices can return. Perspective isn't a given. It's a *trainable lens*.

Ex 8. The Past is Over

Step 1: Acknowledge the Trigger

- Recognise when a past memory resurfaces with emotional force.
- Instead of pushing it away, acknowledge:
  - *This is a stored survival pattern returning for processing.*

Step 2: Shift to Observer Mode

- Picture yourself seated safely and calmly in a cinema.
- Visualise floating up to the projection booth, where you can observe yourself in the theatre below—secure, relaxed, and ready.
- You are both the *watcher* and the *watched*.

Step 3: Prepare the Memory for Editing

- On the cinema screen, bring up a *freeze frame* of the memory:
  - First, a still image *just before* the event began.
  - Then, a second image *just after* it ended—you survived, and you are here now.
- Hold these frames gently. You are not re-entering the event; you are watching its residue.

Step 4: Play the Scene Through

- Let the memory unfold in real time from *before* to *after*.
- Watch it like a film—calmly, without judgment or emotional reliving.
- Observe only the facts, knowing the outcome is already known:

- *You are still here.*

Step 5: Rewind Rapidly

- Stop the scene at the end.
- Now rewind the entire memory quickly—like a video tape glitching backwards.
- Replay the reverse sequence *five times,* fast.
  - See movements rewind, sounds reverse, tension unravel.

Step 6: Notice the Shift

- After each rewind, observe how the emotional charge begins to fade.
- You are not erasing history—you are loosening its grip.
- The memory remains, but the reactivity dissolves. You are reclaiming authorship.

Step 7: Reground in the Present

- Return your attention to your breath, your body, and the present moment.
- Remind yourself:
  - *I can remember bad things but I don't have to relive them... once was enough.*
- Feel the calm of editing—not to forget, but to integrate.

Purpose

This technique helps *recode emotional memories* by engaging the brain's natural *memory reconsolidation* process. It honours survival responses while restoring choice. It's not about denial—it's about re-authoring the story so that memory becomes insight, not injury.

Ex 9. Control Your Inner Voice

Step 1: Notice the Voice

- Pause and become aware of the inner commentary. Don't argue or resist—just observe.
- Locate it: *Where is it coming from?*
  - Behind the eyes?
  - Left or right side?
  - Centre of your head?
  - Does it hover, move, or press?

Step 2: Change the Format

- Shift the voice from sound to *visual*.
- Imagine the same words appearing as *subtitles*—white text on a black screen.
- Let the *sound* drift outwards. The words are still present but no longer *inside* you.

Step 3: Relocate the Voice in Space

- Project the voice to an *external location*, around *three metres away*.
- Let it drone on from a distance—outside your head, outside your body.
- It still speaks, but now it's just noise—not command.

Step 4: Adjust the Volume

- Treat it like an old radio.
- Gradually *turn the volume down*.
- Reduce it to a murmur... a hum... then near silence.
- You're not silencing—it's just *no longer hosted* inside you.

Step 5: Notice the Shift

- Feel the change in your nervous system:
    - A clearing.
    - A physiological *exhale*.
    - Relief—not from effort, but from *absence*.
- This is your body switching out of *defence mode* and into *restoration*.

Step 6: Choose a New Lens

- In the quiet space left behind, a new perspective emerges.
- You are now the *author*, not the audience.
- The next thought can be cleaner, closer, *truer*.
- This is not suppression—it's *signal hygiene*.
- You've reclaimed control.

Summary

This technique:

- *Interrupts* the inner loop using perception, not logic.
- *Moves* the voice spatially to reduce emotional charge.
- *Down-regulates* stress physiology by shifting attention.
- *Creates choice*—the core of leadership presence.

It's not about stopping thought. It's about changing your relationship to it. From host… to observer. From reactor… to author.

Ex 10. Turning Anxiety Around

1. Locate the Sensation

- Tune into the physical *feeling* of anxiety—not the label, but the raw bodily sensation. Ask:
    - *Where do I feel this?*
    - *How does it move?*

2. Observe the Spin or Direction

- Notice how the sensation *moves* in your body:
    - Up the centreline?
    - Downward and looping?
    - Horizontally spinning through the chest?
    - Spiralling laterally?
- Map its exact direction, path, rhythm, and intensity.

3. Reverse the Spin

- In your imagination, *spin* the sensation in the *opposite* direction.
    - Change its *colour* (e.g., green), *texture*, *pace*, or *brightness*.
- Gradually *increase the speed* of this new spin until a shift is felt.

4. Anchor the New Feeling

- While the reversed spin is active, create a physical anchor:
    - Lightly pinch your thumb and middle finger together.
- This links the calm state with a specific motor action.

5. Add a Memory of Peace

- Recall a real moment when you felt deeply *calm* or *safe*.
  - E.g., by water, in a hammock, under stars.
- Let that *embodied memory* blend with the reversed sensation.
- Feel it *wrap around you* and deepen the shift.

6. Loop the Experience

- Repeat the calm state + anchor gesture + peaceful memory *five times*.
- This strengthens the neurological link:
  - "Fire together, wire together."

7. Revisit a Mild Stress Trigger

- Bring to mind a formerly stressful (but manageable) situation.
- While *holding the anchor* and the reversed, calm state, *imagine* being in that situation again. Notice:
  - Your *physiological baseline* has changed—so your response does too.

8. Practise and Reinforce

- Use the anchor regularly, even briefly, to *pre-empt* and *inoculate* anxiety or *recover* calm.
- Over time, the technique becomes faster, more automatic, and more powerful.

Core Insight:

You are not fixed in your emotional responses. By *spinning, anchoring, and rewiring* internal sensations, you show your nervous system that there's another way to be—calm, responsive, and free.

Ex 11. Wrapped in Serenity

Phase 1: Accessing the Calm

1 Recall a moment of deep serenity

Think of a time when you felt utterly calm—safe, tranquil, and unburdened. This is not just relaxation, but full-bodied peace.

2 Re-enter the scene fully

Imagine the memory in rich, sensory detail:

- What could you see?
- What could you hear?
- How did the air feel?
- What textures or smells were present?

3 Immerse in the sensory experience

Let the memory build until it's not just visualised—it's *felt* in your body.

4 Create a physical anchor

Lightly press your *thumb and middle finger together on your right hand*. This becomes your anchor—linking the physical cue to the serene state.

Phase 2: Enhancing the State

5 Soften and enrich the scene

Adjust the memory to heighten calm:

- Warm the colours.

- Blur the edges.
- Make the sounds more melodic or distant.
- Slow any movement.
- Whisper the word *"Soften"* to yourself. Then again—quieter.

6 Repeat the anchor

Press thumb and finger again while deep in this state. Each repetition reinforces the neural link between the cue and the calm feeling.

7 Layer the memory

Repeat the full experience multiple times. Let the anchor deepen its association until calm becomes easily retrievable.

Phase 3: Rewiring for Real Life

8 Introduce mild stress imagery

Bring to mind a *low-stakes stressful scenario* (e.g., awkward conversation, pressing deadline). Just enough tension to notice.

9 Activate the anchor in the stress scene

As you hold the stressful memory, **press your anchor** and **"spin in" the calm**. Imagine your serene state infusing the tension like ink in water.

10 Increase challenge, maintain calm

Take the same scene and **raise the stakes** (more pressure, more eyes on you, shorter time).

Again, use the anchor and stay grounded. Picture yourself responding with poise, not reacting in panic.

Phase 4: Reinforcement & Mastery

11 Rehearse regularly

Practise this full process daily or weekly. The nervous system learns by rhythm and repetition. Each cycle grooves the calm response deeper.

12 Deploy on demand

In real moments of tension, **press the anchor**, **soften**, and **return** to the practised calm. Over time, the gesture becomes a reliable state shift.

Final Note:

This technique is not a trick—it's *neurological craftsmanship*. Each repetition strengthens your ability to stay composed in the midst of chaos. With practice, your anchor becomes a *portable sanctuary*—a hidden tool that steadies you when leadership gets rough.

Ex 12. Delight at Dawn
— Energising Technique for Sluggish Mornings —

1 Notice the Sluggish Start

Acknowledge the lack of energy or motivation without judgement. Don't scold yourself—recognise that your system needs *spark*, not shame.

2 Begin with Breath (Box Breathing)

- Inhale for 4 seconds
- Hold for 4 seconds
- Exhale for 4 seconds
- Hold for 4 seconds

Repeat 3–4 cycles to clear space and signal calm alertness to your nervous system.

3 Activate a 'String of Pearls' Memory

Recall a vivid, energising moment from your life—something joyful, powerful, or exhilarating.

4 Step Into the Memory Fully

- See it as a bright, vivid movie
- Turn up the colours, sharpen the sound
- Imagine yourself *inside* the scene, not just observing it
- Feel it in your body: the movement, the joy, the vitality

5 Amplify the Sensation

- Intensify the feelings—brighter visuals, louder sounds, stronger emotions

- Let the feeling spin, grow, and spread through your body like a wave of delight

6 Seal It with a Declaration

From that fully embodied state, say to yourself (silently or aloud):

"This day is mine!"

Ex 13. Soften at Sunrise
— Grounding Technique for Tense Mornings —

Step 1: Notice the Tension Early

Acknowledge the clench. If your body wakes up already bracing, it's not failing—it's preparing. Recognise it as a protective reflex.

Step 2: Begin 4-7-8 Breathing

- Inhale through the nose for **4 counts**
- Hold the breath for **7 counts**
- Exhale slowly through the mouth for **8 counts**

Repeat this **3–4 times**, gently. Let each out-breath signal safety.

Step 3: Call Forth a Memory of Competence

Think of something that makes you feel quietly capable—something you do well that roots you in calm (e.g., pruning a bonsai, making the perfect tea, organising a drawer).

Step 4: Visualise with Full Sensory Detail

See the scene in **full-colour, surround sound**. Imagine it unfolding with clarity and ease. Widen the image like a cinema screen and mentally step inside.

Step 5: Anchor the Felt Sense of Confidence

Notice how it feels in your body to be grounded and competent. Let that feeling **grow**, like roots deepening.

- **Spin** or **amplify** the sensation internally at a rhythm that gives you calm, centred energy.

Step 6: Soften the Body

Allow your body to let go—shoulders, jaw, belly. Let tension rise and release like steam from a coffee cup.

Step 7: Claim the Day with Intention

When the grounded state settles in, let this quiet thought rise through you:

"Today... belongs... to me."

TECHNIQUE SUMMARIES I

Ex 14. Get Rid of It
— A Clean-Up Routine for the Nervous System —

Step 1: Identify the Residue

• Recall a moment from your day that still bothers you—an argument, a mistake, a disappointment.

• Choose one that tends to replay in your mind at night.

Step 2: Visualise the Memory as a Short Film

• See it in your mind's eye like a movie.

• Let it freeze on the most emotionally charged frame.

Step 3: Disrupt the Visual Pattern

• **Drain the Colour**: Turn the image black and white.

• **Flicker Effect**: Rapidly flicker it between colour and black-and-white five times.

• **Shrink It**: Mentally shrink the image down to a tiny, laughably small size.

• **Repeat this sequence (flicker + shrink) five times**.

Step 4: Reverse the Sequence

• Start the memory at the *end* and play it backwards.

  ○ People walk in reverse.

  ○ Speech turns to gibberish.

  ○ Actions un-happen (e.g., sitting back into chairs).

• **Repeat the rewind sequence five times**, speeding up each time.

Step 5: Anchor a Positive State

- Recall a moment of calm, strength, or safety you've previously anchored.

- Feel that good emotion build in your body.

Step 6: Overlay the Positive While Rewinding

- Hold that positive state steady.

- While feeling good, **run the backwards movie again**.

- This fuses the altered memory with a new, empowered emotional state.

Optional Humorous Anchor (for added effect):

- Imagine the sound of a toilet flushing as you send the unwanted emotion "where it belongs."

Outcome: The memory becomes neutralised. The emotional "sting" is gone. Your nervous system is no longer reacting to outdated input. This isn't erasure—it's neurological hygiene.

Ex 15. Deep Refreshing Sleep
— Safety & Softness Routine for Bedtime —

Step 1: Begin Sooner — End the Day Before Bedtime

• Don't wait until you're under the covers to unwind.

• Before bed, reflect on the day's emotional residue.

• Briefly acknowledge any stress, embarrassment, or unresolved thoughts—then **let them go**. Don't take them to bed with you.

Step 2: Build Your Bliss List

- Create a short list of soothing, real memories—**moments when you felt deeply at ease**.
    ○ Examples: a warm drink, a shared laugh, soft rain, feeling safe.
- Write them down or picture them clearly in your mind. This becomes your emotional "bedtime story."

Step 3: Settle Into Bed Gently

- As you lie down, recall items from your Bliss List **in soft detail**.
- Use your **inner voice like a lullaby**—gentle, slow, and soothing.

Step 4: Breathe Into Stillness

- Breathe gently into your belly.
    ○ Inhale.
    ○ Exhale slowly.
- Pause briefly at the end of each out-breath.

- Imagine this pause as *the silence speaking*.
- With each breath, release tension from your jaw, shoulders, arms, and legs.

Step 5: Find and Expand Your Centre

- Place your attention just below your navel.
- Visualise a *soft, glowing candle* there.
- With each breath, let this glow *expand through your body* like dawn warming a room.

Step 6: Return to Bliss

- Pick one Bliss List memory.
- Let it open like a scene in a film. Settle into it.
- If your mind wanders to something stressful, *gently switch channels* to another Bliss memory—no fuss, no judgement.

Step 7: Practise Re-Laxation

- Remember: relaxation is a skill you return to, again and again.
- Every drift, every redirection is part of the practice—not a failure.

Step 8: Re-Enter Sleep Gently (if You Wake)

- If you wake in the night, don't rush into alertness.
- Smile softly, curl your toes slightly, and *let the body feel safe again*.
- Return to your breath and your Bliss List—like welcoming the guest back in.

This technique gently *reconditions the nervous system* to associate bedtime with safety, softness, and homecoming—rather than performance or panic.

PART TWO
NON-VERBAL LEADERSHIP

INTRODUCTION TO PART II
THE SIGNALS BENEATH SPEECH

The moment before words arrive is often when the real work begins[1]. You've seen it. A tense room falls quiet. A leader rises—not yet speaking, just breathing, standing, letting the silence stretch. And still, the room shifts. You know something is happening, even if you can't name it. The tone, the focus, the temperature of the room—all of it leans, waits, watches. The message hasn't been spoken, but it has begun.

This isn't intuition. It isn't mysticism. It's structure. Non-verbal signals—breath, posture, gaze, stillness—precede language and outlast logic. They are not 'body language' in the simplistic sense. They are the behavioural substrate upon which influence is built. When a leader's signals are incongruent—when the tone says 'calm' but the eyes dart, the breath shortens, the shoulders clench—the message frays. When the signals align, something else occurs: coherence. Trust. Gravitas.

If you've ever been told to 'look confident' or 'speak with more authority' and found those instructions less than helpful, this part of the book is for you. Because it turns out *presence isn't performed—it's practised*. And what follows will give you the tools to practise it, not as theatre, but as signal hygiene.

Let's be clear: this is not about charisma. Charisma is inconsistent. This is about congruence. About the alignment between what is shown, what is sensed, and what is said. And as we'll explore, that alignment—when it's present—can reshape not just your impact, but the very biology of the room you're in.

There is an old military saying:

> You don't rise to the occasion
> —you fall to your level of training.

The same is true of presence. When pressure strikes—when conflict escalates or uncertainty spreads—your verbal skill is not what determines your leadership. Your nervous system is. And more precisely, it's what your nervous system signals before your first word lands.

People don't just follow arguments. They follow signals. They track energy, intention, safety. This is not sentiment. It's pattern. Audiences scan for coherence before they listen for logic. Teams gauge your breath before they trust your strategy. The child watches the adult's tone before the content registers. And in every context, the question is the same: *Can I trust you?* Not trust your ideas. Trust your presence.

When people answer yes, it's rarely because of what was said. It's because of how it was delivered. And more importantly, how it was *received*. The highest forms of influence don't push—they synchronise.

What does this mean in practice? That people aren't responding to what you mean to say. They're responding to what you're signalling now.

INTRODUCTION TO PART II

You've felt this. A room where something 'felt off', even if nothing explicit occurred. A negotiation that shifted when one person broke eye contact. A leader who said all the right things—but whose body, somehow, said none of them.

Non-verbal leadership lives in that space. It is not accessory to communication. It is the architecture of it. It is what breathes meaning into words and what empties them when it's absent.

Part Three is your apprenticeship in this invisible architecture. It will teach you to track the signals you already send—your tone, your timing, your tension—and to refine them into coherence. You will learn to pace and lead nervous systems. You will learn to anchor safety without saying a word. You will learn to project calm not through force, but through regulation. And when the room wobbles, you will learn to become its fulcrum.

We will start with foundational awareness—your own breath, your posture, your gaze. These are not surface details. They are levers. Once stabilised, you'll move outward—into the signals you emit, the rapport you generate, and the states you induce. From there, you'll step into deliberate rehearsal: encoding congruent states, decoding non-verbal cues in others, and shifting the emotional temperature of interactions.

Along the way, we will ground every concept in practical, applied insight. This is not theory. This is signal design—applied to leadership, negotiation, feedback, conflict, and high-stakes communication.

You'll see how voice, breath, and stillness can change the meaning of a room. You'll learn how eye contact and pause patterns can collapse resistance or summon attention. And you'll practise techniques that tune your presence—not to perform, but to project clarity and calm in the moments that matter most.

There is no such thing as a *neutral presence*. You are always signalling. You are always shaping someone else's map.

As a leader, your signals become landmarks in the mental terrain of others. A steady breath tells your team they can exhale. A grounded voice stabilises a room. A delayed blink, a clenched jaw, a shallow inhale—these are read by others, often before your message is even understood. The question isn't whether your signals are read. It's whether they're helping or harming the message they carry.

You don't need to be the loudest voice in the room. You don't need to be the most animated. But you do need to become readable, reliable, and rhythmically resonant. You need to become a tuning fork others can align to—not because you've raised your volume, but because you've lowered your noise.

In crisis, people follow the calmest available nervous system. This part of the book will help you become that. Not as performance. Not as act. But as a deeply trained, neurologically tuned signal source. You won't be memorising techniques—you'll be installing them. So they show up when your script disappears. When the pressure spikes. When the words falter, but the signal remains.

The spoken word is powerful. But the unspoken signal is primary. And if you can master that—if you can learn to lead in silence—then you can lead in any noise that the world throws at you.

SEVEN
NON-VERBAL AWARENESS
READ THE ROOM BEFORE ANYONE SPEAKS

WITHOUT UTTERING A WORD... how much is really communicated?

A firm handshake, a subtle nod, the way someone enters a room—these silent actions reverberate far more than we often realise[1]. Indeed, the words we speak are merely the tip of the iceberg[2]. Beneath the surface lies a far richer channel of communication: the world of non-verbal cues[3]. A raised eyebrow is like the flick of a safety catch—small, silent, but often the start of everything that follows.

This elusive reality often determines the success or failure of our leadership interactions as much as the words we say[4]. This is not to suggest that words lack importance, but rather to highlight that much of our instinctual reaction to leaders comes not from what they say, but from the myriad signals they give off unconsciously[5]. As leaders, we need to understand the power of the unspoken—and harness it deliberately to lead effectively[6].

Evolutionary Roots

Why do we react so powerfully to non-verbal cues? The answer lies deep in our evolutionary past[7]. Long before the invention of language, our ancestors relied on body language and facial expressions to navigate social dynamics, signal intent, and detect threats[8].

For example, a *bid* is a small snippet of behaviour designed to reaffirm connection and, by extension, safety. Picture a quick glance from someone to which you instantly respond with a smile or a nod. Mammals give one another bids because it is part of our social engagement apparatus[9]. Reptiles do not do bids.

Imagine early humans gathered around a fire, wary of predators lurking in the shadows. A raised eyebrow. A flicker of tension across the jaw. These were the first clues to approaching danger or the intent of a rival. The ability to interpret such signals quickly was not a social advantage—it was survival.

Fast forward to the modern office or boardroom, and those ancient instincts remain. Picture someone more powerful than you, or someone you regard as an ally. You're on the other side of a busy room. You make casual eye contact and nod—but receive no reciprocal gesture. Your gut acts as though something is wrong.

Mammals evolved with a safety sense that required *sufficient* cues of safety to be triggered; an absence of danger was not enough[10]. After all, there were apex predators, poisonous creepy-crawlies, and unpredictable humans lying in wait. *Nothingness is somethingness* to our neuroception's threat detection system[11].

Sure, the threats today are no longer sabre-toothed tigers. But the social risks—losing trust, missing opportunities, appearing weak—are still very real. Our brains are hardwired to read non-verbal cues faster than words[12]. Non-reciprocation is a non-verbal cue just as much as how confidently someone carries themselves[13].

To be a leader who commands respect and trust, we must acknowledge these instinctual mechanisms and learn to control the non-verbal messages we send. It's not just what you say that matters—it's what you do and *don't* do.

CASE STORY: Bruce's Instinctual Leadership

Consider Bruce, a logistics operations lead, as he enters a critical meeting with his team. The stakes are high; the project is behind schedule, and Bruce needs to regain control. As he steps into the room—before he even speaks—a wealth of non-verbal communication is already occurring.

Bruce's confident stride, the square set of his shoulders, and his open, relaxed posture send immediate signals of authority[14]. His instinctual leadership begins the moment he walks through the door. Without saying a word, he projects competence and control. His team, sensing this, subconsciously adjusts their own posture, mirroring his energy and preparing for a productive discussion.

That's what actually happened. But imagine the counterfactual: Bruce enters the room with slouched shoulders, his gaze darting nervously around the table. He fidgets with his notes and avoids eye contact. The message is clear, even if unintended: *Bruce is uncertain.* His team, picking up on these non-verbal cues, begins to feel uneasy. Trust in his leadership erodes, and before the meeting even begins, the dynamics are set against him.

The contrast between these two scenarios highlights how much leadership is conveyed non-verbally[15]. It's not what you say—it's how you say it. And more importantly, how you carry yourself when you say it.

Reading the Eyes

If the eyes are the windows to the soul, they're also—more reliably—the windows to thought. Most people don't realise they're watching others think. But the good ones do. The leaders who don't just listen to what's said, but to what flits across the eyes in that half-second pause before the words arrive. Because thought moves first. And eyes, bless them, tend to follow.

Watch closely, and you'll begin to notice the patterns. A glance up and to the left as someone retrieves a memory—perhaps what the office looked like before the reorganisation. A flick up and right as they conjure a scenario that hasn't happened yet—possibly involving you, a deadline, and a purple giraffe in a suit. Side to side suggests sound: the ghost of a voice remembered, or one rehearsed for later. Down and left, they might be in internal conversation. Down and right? That's often where the feelings live[16].

These movements aren't conscious. They're not chosen. They're structural, not strategic. Which is what makes them so useful. In the field, they're called *Eye Accessing Cues*[17]—though that name sounds like something your uncle would mutter during a PowerPoint malfunction. You might prefer to think of them as fingerprints of thought. Fleeting. Telling. And absolutely not to be trusted on their own.

Here's the general map, based on right-handed individuals (the patterns are often mirrored in left-handed people):

Eye Direction	Likely Indication
Up and Left	Visual Recall (seeing remembered images)
Up and Right	Visual Construction (creating images)
Lateral Left	Auditory Recall (hearing remembered soun
Lateral Right	Auditory Construction (imagining new sour
Down and Left	Internal Dialogue (Auditory Digital)
Down and Right	Kinaesthetic (accessing feelings or physica

Because people aren't diagrams. Some reverse the pattern. Some mix them. Some maintain perfect, unbroken eye contact while fabricating stories worthy of a Booker Prize. The trick isn't in memorising the chart. It's in learning the person.

Start with calibration. Ask a few safe, sensory-rich questions—nothing too clever. 'What colour was your first car?' 'What was the last song you listened to?' 'What did your childhood bedroom look like?' Watch the eyes. Don't stare. Don't decode. Just observe. You're not looking for meaning. You're looking for *pattern*[3].

Once you have it, the real data begins—not from what they do, but when they don't follow their usual script. That's when things get interesting because it's the changes to the cues that indicate changes to something else.

In leadership conversations, this matters more than most realise. Ask someone about a misstep, and they look up and to the right instead of their usual recall spot—maybe they're not remembering, but constructing. Doesn't mean they're lying. Could mean they're smoothing over a detail. Could mean they're scared. Either way, that flicker gives you time. Time to soften your tone. Time to stay curious. Time to lead.

Or you're in a coaching conversation. You ask how they're coping with the pressure. They smile and say they're fine, but their eyes drop down and to the right—and don't come back up. That's emotional contact. You don't need to name it. Just stay a moment longer. Let the silence hold. Let the truth settle. You'll both come out better for it.

This isn't sleight of hand. It's depth perception. It's leading with eyes open. Most of the time, you'll use this skill like you use peripheral vision—without fanfare. Just there, keeping you aligned, warning you of the subtle turns. It helps you notice the disconnect between word and signal. Between what's declared and what's actually felt.

And that gap? That's where trust lives. That's where the real work begins. Because the best leaders don't just read the room. They read the spaces between the glances.

And the eyes?

They tell stories the mouth hasn't dared rehearse.

Projecting **Non-Verbal Cues**

The significance of non-verbal communication in leadership cannot be overstated. Our brains are tuned to pick up on subtle cues—facial expressions, posture, gestures—that influence how we perceive others. In fact, research consistently shows that up to 93% of the communication of emotions and attitudes is non-verbal[18]. If that figure sounds staggering, it's because we tend to underestimate how much of our daily interaction runs on signals we barely notice.

Let's break down some key components of non-verbal communication:

- **Body Language**: A leader's posture, gestures, and movement can signal confidence, openness, or defensiveness. Standing tall with open gestures conveys confidence and approachability; crossed arms or a slouched posture can suggest uncertainty or resistance.

- **Facial Expressions**: The human face is capable of over 10,000 expressions. Even subtle changes can drastically alter how someone is perceived. A smile can disarm tension; a furrowed brow can provoke discomfort. In shutdown or freeze states, the face may go flat and impassive—a signal missed by all but the most attuned. For leaders, expressive control is a form of social precision.
- **Eye Contact**: Direct eye contact signals attentiveness, trust, and connection. Avoiding it, even subtly, can convey disinterest, defensiveness, or insecurity.
- **Tone of Voice**: The way something is said often matters more than the words themselves. A calm, measured tone instils confidence. A tight or high-pitched voice can signal distress, regardless of content.

These cues are processed in milliseconds. And unlike spoken language, non-verbal signals are often unconscious and hard to fake. That's why congruence—making your words match your signals—is not optional. It's leadership currency[19].

Tips for Leaders

How can leaders improve their non-verbal awareness and projection? Here are some practical suggestions:

- **Awareness**: Start by watching yourself. Record a meeting. Review how you stand, gesture, look. Awareness is the first intervention[20].
- **Posture**: Shoulders back, chest open, feet grounded. Confidence begins in the spine.
- **Eye Contact**: Lock eyes when it matters. Don't scan the room while delivering key points—let them know they're seen.

- **Tone and Volume**: Speak slowly. Let your voice land. Vary your pace and volume to signal intent and emphasis.
- **Controlled Breathing**: Your nervous system is contagious[21]. If your breathing is shallow, so is your presence. Regulate yourself to regulate the room.

By consciously managing these signals, you amplify your presence. People may forget what you said. But they will remember what you signalled[22]. And that's the quiet truth of leadership: *It's not what you say. It's what you signal.*

Because so very much of leadership begins before a single word is spoken. And yet, even as we refine our non-verbal cues—our posture, tone, gaze—there's something deeper still at play. Because influence isn't only about *how* we show up. It's about *where* we show up from. In high-stakes settings, leadership isn't just what you say—it's where you stand, how you're seen, and what the room remembers.

In the next chapter, we shift from *non-verbal awareness* to *perceptual positioning*. You'll meet the Red, Yellow, and Green Hats—three core vantage points leaders move between—and discover why emotional clarity often depends not on better messaging, but better placement. You'll also meet the overlooked art of *decontamination*—how emotions linger in spaces, and how great leaders learn to change not just their stance, but their *signal geography*.

Because clarity doesn't always come from content. Sometimes, it comes from geometry[23].

EIGHT
THE GEOMETRY OF PRESENCE
USING PERCEPTION AND SPACE TO SHAPE EXPERIENCE

THE MAN SPOKE WITH CONVICTION—UNSHAKABLE, steely, and about seven minutes too long. You could see it in the way his colleagues shifted: the subtle recline, the sudden interest in watch faces, the internal sighs disguised as throat-clearing. He thought he was winning the room. In truth, he was overplaying a hand no one else believed in.

It wasn't what he said. It was where he stood. Not physically—he was perfectly centred between the whiteboard and the water jug—but perceptually. He was speaking from the only vantage point that mattered to him: his own.

You've met this person. You've been this person. So have I. And the damage isn't in the passion. It's in the blindness. In mistaking your angle on the world for the shape of the world itself.

We think of attention as a spotlight. But more often, it behaves like a hat—something you wear without noticing, that quietly filters what you see, how you hear, and what you miss[1]. And in any conversation of consequence—especially the high-stakes ones—we tend to forget that others are wearing different hats entirely.

In Chapter 3, we discussed perceptual positions as part of the leader's inner game. Now, as part of non-verbal leadership, we shall revisit them as part of the leader's outer game.

Shifting Perceptual Positions

There is no such thing as a neutral viewpoint. Only positions. And only one of them is yours. And every room you enter demands a slice of your attention. Your capacity isn't infinite. It's a pie—and how you cut it, how much you serve to the first, second, or third perceptual position, decides not just what you see, but who you can be in that moment[2].

The trouble begins when we confuse location with truth. You feel something strongly—anger, inspiration, clarity—and assume that its force makes it universal. But emotion is not evidence. It's just a signal from the place you happen to be standing[3].

In the theatre of human attention, there are three primary vantage points—or 'hats'—you can wear. They are not moral stances, just mental ones. And the quality of your leadership often depends less on the hat you prefer, and more on how quickly you can change it.

The Red Hat – Self-as-Centre

This is the view from inside your own skull. It's vivid, impassioned, and unfiltered. The Red Hat is where most people live: experiencing the world through their own thoughts, feelings, and bodily cues. It's the inner monologue of 'How am I doing?' disguised as insight. It even thinks it's being objective[4]. Useful for authenticity, self-protection, and taking decisive action. But it has blind spots the size of small countries. Wear it too long and you risk becoming the main character in a story no one else is reading.

◉ THE YELLOW HAT – Other-as-Centre

Now shift. Imagine looking out through someone else's eyes. Not to agree with them. Not to appease them. But to read them. The Yellow Hat is a kind of forensic empathy—less about shared feeling, more about patterned observation. It notices breath, tone, hesitation, the micro-shifts of posture and gaze. It asks two questions: first,

> *"What is this person actually doing?"*

and second,

> *"What can I infer they're feeling based on that?"*

Skip either step, and you're not reading them[5]—you're projecting onto them. Influence without insight is just noise.

◉ THE GREEN HAT – Observer-as-Centre[6]

Finally, pull back. Not just from yourself, not just from the other person, but from the whole dynamic. The Green Hat is the fly-on-the-wall, the balcony view, the conductor watching the orchestra rather than playing first violin. It sees timing. Power dynamics. Role-played rituals. It's the position of de-escalation, pattern recognition, and choosing when not to speak. Under pressure, the Green Hat is not just useful—it's oxygen.

Now, you might think you use all three. And perhaps, on good days, you do. But under stress? People default. They snap back to Red, anchor in Yellow, or freeze in Green. Each position has its uses. Each has its risks. The skill isn't in choosing one. It's in shifting fluidly—knowing when to feel, when to read, and when to watch.

Most people, let's be honest, wear the Red Hat so long it leaves a dent.

PICTURE A LEADERSHIP TEAM meeting on a Tuesday afternoon—budget season, morale flat, coffee lukewarm. A junior exec starts speaking with a rehearsed intensity that says

"I practised this in the car park"

Her words are technically sound. But something's off. She doesn't notice the crossed arms, the polite nods that arrive a fraction late, the dead air between sentences. She's in her Red Hat, broadcasting at full power. But the signal isn't landing. No one's tuned in.

Across the table, an older colleague watches her—not unkindly, but analytically. She notices the tremor in the voice, the miss in timing. She leans forward, slightly. Her face softens. She enters the Yellow Hat—not to fix or rescue, but to observe from inside the other's experience. She adjusts her own body posture just enough to signal:

I see you.

The speaker relaxes half a breath. A sentence lands. The room tilts. Not dramatically. Just enough.

In the corner, someone else watches both. Their notebook is closed. Their gaze lingers not on who's talking, but on who's retreating, who's pretending to nod, and who's calculating a reply. This person isn't disengaged. They're Green Hatting. Tracking the rhythm of the room like a jazz musician watching the horn section miss their cue.

And here's the kicker: all three are doing leadership. But only one of them is holding the room.

Effective communication isn't about saying the right thing. It's about standing in the right place—mentally, perceptually. Most conflict isn't caused by malice. It's caused by bad positioning[7]. You thought you were meeting them in dialogue, but you were actually wearing your Red Hat while they were pleading in Yellow. Or you dropped into Green to "be strategic" just when your team needed you to burn with Red.

The tragedy of most organisations is not misalignment of goals. It's mismatched hats in rooms full of people convinced they're being ignored. So what do you do with this?

You learn to shift. Not intellectually. Physically. Deliberately. You start noticing when your Red Hat is squeezing your temples[8]—when you're speaking as if it's just you and your truth in the room. You pause. You lean into Yellow. What's their face doing? What did they just not say? You register. You adjust. And then, if needed, you float to Green—where you can spot not just the players, but the pattern they're stuck inside.

It sounds simple. It's not. It takes practice. But it pays in influence, insight, and the subtle art of knowing when to step in and when to step back.

You won't always get it right. Some days you'll Red Hat through a meeting like a human foghorn. Other days you'll Yellow yourself into empathic paralysis. Occasionally, you'll Green Hat too hard and forget you're meant to do something. But over time, the movement itself becomes the mastery. You stop reacting from one fixed place and start responding from the most useful one.

And for the record: yes, some people talk about a fourth position. The imagined future self. The version of you watching yourself, projecting poise into the situation before it arrives. That's not fantasy.

That's rehearsal. Strategic use of imagination[9]. You'll meet it properly in Chapter 10. For now, just know it exists—and that the best leaders don't just see the room. They see themselves in it, before they even enter.

So the next time you find yourself in a tense conversation, ask: What hat am I wearing? Is it helping? And is it time to change it?

Because clarity doesn't always come from having the right answer. Sometimes, it comes from standing in the right place. In the end, you have three hats and one head. The job isn't to pick the best hat. It's to know which one you're wearing—and whether it still fits.

So YES, you've got three hats and one head—but here's the problem no one talks about: sometimes the hat isn't the issue. It's the room you're wearing it in.

Because location isn't just where you are. It's what you're carrying. And if you keep delivering difficult truths from the same spot where you apologise to your team, or defend your budget, or pretend not to be exhausted, something strange starts to happen. The room becomes noisy. Not audibly—but emotionally. People stop hearing your words and start reacting to the residue of everything that's come before.

That's where **decontamination** comes in.

Keep That Over There

At six in the morning, they walked into the kitchen expecting caffeine. What greeted them instead was the spectral tang of burnt fish curry—the kind that had seemed like a bold weeknight experiment twelve hours ago and now lingered like a mistake in judgment. Not a catastrophe. But breakfast was ruined by memory.

The offending pan had been scrubbed, the windows opened, the extractor fan wheezing through its final rites. And still, the smell clung to the air like an awkward silence.

This, they thought, is how emotions behave. You try to compartmentalise. You tell yourself last night's argument won't seep into today's team meeting. That the death you haven't fully grieved won't echo in your voice during a sales pitch. That you can transition from pain to pragmatism in the time it takes to shut a door. You can't. Because emotional debris—unlike the fish—is not easily binned[10].

We like to think we can multitask feelings. Carry grief in one pocket, optimism in the other, and reach for whichever suits the hour. But it doesn't work that way. Emotional signals, like curry, cling to the curtains. And the only remedy, sometimes, is to separate the rooms. *Decontamination* isn't a luxury. It's a form of leadership hygiene.

The Furniture of Emotion

There's a peculiar truth no one wants to admit about our homes—and by extension, our heads: *the furniture remembers*. You walk into a room and forget why you came in. But go back to the seat you left and —miracle of miracles—the purpose returns, slinking back into consciousness like a cat you didn't know had slipped out.

The absurdity is real. And the explanation is simple: memory is not stored in the mind alone. It lives in places. The chair you cried in. The hallway where you rehearsed bad news. The table where you almost quit. Every room has a memory. And most of them haven't asked your permission.

The desk where you tackle inbox avalanches? Try writing a love letter there and feel how brittle your sentences become. The dining table where you once had that soul-evacuating budget meeting?

Watch how it recoils from laughter, even years later. And your bed—your poor, overburdened bed—buried under reports and unread articles, wondering why the dreams have stopped showing up[11].

We don't just live in spaces. We store parts of ourselves inside them[12]. And when you flood a location with one kind of signal—urgency, tension, control—you teach that space to expect it. Even demand it. But here's the good news: what's been mapped can be unmapped. You can decide where things live. Not just your shoes or spreadsheets. Your emotions too.

Some leaders do the opposite, of course. They intentionally return to the same physical spot to deliver vision or gratitude, reinforcing emotional meaning in that space—what's known as *spatial anchoring*[13]. That's a different art. But in high-stakes conversations, when clarity is compromised, it's not about where you usually stand. It's about standing somewhere new.

THE COACH with Two Chairs

There's a coach I know who carries two identical chairs into every room. IKEA standard, grey fabric, nothing dramatic. But the effect is often cinematic. When a client walks in, twisted between frustration and fatigue, she doesn't ask questions. She places one chair at an angle and says,

> *'Speak your anger from here'*

The client does. Spits it out like a splinter. Then she points to the other chair.

> *'Now sit there—and speak what's underneath'*

No theories. No diagrams. Just relocation. It isn't therapy. It's upholstery with purpose[14]. Because some truths are too unwieldy to share a seat. Rage and regret don't commute well. Despair won't carpool with denial. They need their own corners. Their own chairs.

You don't have to resolve every contradiction in one sitting. You just have to stop forcing them to spoon. And here's what gets people: it's not what they say in the new chair that breaks them open. It's *where* they say it. Safety doesn't live in language. It lives in geography.

We cry when we feel the shift. Not because the words are new. But because, for once, they're not soaked in the residues of everything else.

How to Keep Your Bed Clean (Metaphorically Speaking)

Let's return to the basics. If your dining table hears too much about cost centres, don't be surprised when it stops listening to joy. No one wants to share pudding with a spreadsheet. If your bed hosts back-to-back planning sessions, expect dreams that feature PowerPoint slides and unconsummated expense reports. Some things don't belong in certain places. Not because they're bad—but because they're misfiled.

Dinner tables are for digestion—of food, of stories, maybe of mild family tension. But not of professional trauma. Nightstands are for fiction, fantasy, or nothing at all. Not industry journals. Don't be the person who burns fish in the kitchen and wonders why the bedroom stinks.

And if you still think this is abstract, think of your task list. A tidy stack of paper can feel like Everest if it contains one emotionally charged item. Remove that one—and the rest becomes liftable. The stack doesn't change. You do.

Decontamination isn't denial. It's order. It's the subtle act of letting one thing be one thing—without having to carry everything else with it.

The Magic of Looking Down

Watch a seasoned newsreader. Between stories, they glance down. Not to read—the teleprompter's been scrolling dutifully at eye level the whole time. They look down to reset. To clear the stage between stories. To mark the shift. It's not hesitation. It's hygiene. And you can do the same.

When you need to move from one emotional tone to another, give yourself a line: 'Before we begin...' or 'Let's switch gears for a moment...' It doesn't matter what you say. It matters that you acknowledge the transition.

More often, it's non-verbal. A step to the left. A pause. A downward glance that resets the frame. You're not changing topics. You're changing *location*—conceptually, somatically.

I saw a leader do this once. She stood mid-presentation, stepped three paces to her left, looked down, then raised her eyes. Her voice changed. Her posture shifted. She didn't swap slides—she swapped *signals*[15]. The room leaned in. She hadn't told them what changed. She'd shown them.

Next time you deliver hard news, don't just brace your voice. Move your feet. Let the floor carry some of the weight your throat can't[16].

Clean Rooms, Clear Minds

Back to the curry. The smell always lingers longer than the cooking. And in leadership, so do emotional residues. Tones, glances, words said in anger—these live in the fibres of our meeting rooms, our dining rooms, our inner rooms. If you want clarity, don't just find the right message. Find the right place to say it from. And sometimes, that means letting different truths live in different places.

Decontamination isn't something you announce. It's something you practise. A quiet ritual. A relocation of meaning. Because not everything belongs everywhere. Especially not inside you.

NINE
RAPPORT & PERMISSION
HOW TO CONNECT & BE ALLOWED IN

A TEAM SITS IN SILENCE. The air feels heavy, as if the next thing said might tilt the whole future. Perhaps it's a crisis meeting, or the fallout from a botched delivery, or a confrontation that's been waiting in the wings for weeks. The leader stands. Doesn't speak. Just breathes. Still. Present. Watching the room—without pushing, without withdrawing. And something begins to shift.

It's not subtle, but it is quiet. Shoulders drop. A breath escapes that no one knew they were holding. The friction in the room doesn't vanish, but it softens. Eyes move toward the leader—not out of fear or obligation, but because, somehow, the space around them feels steadier. The group hasn't been given new information. They haven't even been addressed. But the signal has changed. And that changes everything.

What is this force that can settle a room without explanation? What is this form of influence that precedes content, precedes logic, precedes the comforting clutter of plans and talking points?

It's not magic. And it's not charisma. It's *signal*.

Most people never learn to read it. Fewer still learn to use it. But we all respond to it. Because beneath the level of language, beneath belief and argument and polished persuasion, lies something older—more primitive, more persuasive. We don't just listen to people. We *feel* them first[1].

This chapter is about that feeling—and how it becomes the bedrock of trust, influence, and leadership under pressure. Before we learn to speak, we learn to scan. Before we understand a message, we understand its source. Long before we know whether we agree with someone, we've already decided whether to follow them.

And that decision, in nearly every case, comes down to one thing: whether their presence feels coherent, congruent and safe. Words might win an argument. But only signal wins a room.

What Rapport Really Is (and Isn't)

Let's name something clearly: most people have been taught to think of rapport as charm. A handshake. A shared joke. Eye contact. Maybe a bit of body language voodoo, if they've skimmed a pop-psych article or sat through an HR training. But rapport is not performance. It's not friendliness on cue. And it's certainly not a thin veneer of 'relatability' pasted over pressure.

If anything, performance kills rapport—because rapport is not what you do to someone. It's what happens between you. And that distinction changes everything. Real rapport is *alignment*. Not of opinion, but of state[2]. It's the felt sense that you and the other person are, even briefly, in rhythm. You're attuned. You're in the same moment. It's not agreement. It's coherence.

When we think of those we trust—really trust—it's rarely because they impressed us. It's because they met us. They saw us. They matched us—not in facts or values or credentials, but in presence.

They entered the room without rushing to fix or explain or dazzle. They simply arrived, tuned in, and connected. And because of that, we listened differently. Not because we were convinced, but because we were safe.

This is the core misunderstanding about rapport: it is not the by-product of likability. It is the condition that makes understanding possible. A therapist sitting with a grieving patient knows this. So does a parent calming a frightened child. And so does any leader who's walked into a room that's on the edge of breaking.

Rapport doesn't live in content. It lives in tone, timing, stillness[3]. In the subtle echo between two nervous systems that says,

> *"I see you, and I'm not rushing this"*

That's not strategy. It's *signal hygiene*. And it's not optional.

We are all sending signals, all the time. The only question is whether they support or sabotage our intent. Inconsistent tone, evasive eye contact, breath that stutters under pressure—these leak before we speak. And when what we say and what we show don't align, people don't trust our words. They trust our leakage.

Which is why rapport must not be confused with persuasion. Persuasion is downstream. Rapport is the riverbed. Without it, no message travels far. With it, you don't need to push—because your presence is already pulling people into the moment with you.

Cues First

The body speaks first. The brain speaks last[4]. It doesn't matter how elegantly your presentation is structured, how cleverly your strategy has been phrased, or how sincere your intent may be. If your signal is off, the message is lost. Or worse—mistrusted.

Think of the politician who walks onto a stage with all the right soundbites, but a flickering smile that doesn't quite reach the eyes. The voice is too polished, the gestures rehearsed. Nothing is overtly wrong, but something *feels* wrong. The audience doesn't lean in. They lean away. They may not know why—but they do know *no*. And no message, however well-crafted, can make it past that.

Now flip the example. Think of the friend who enters the room without a word, and you know—instantly—that something's happened. You read it in the walk, in the way they hold their breath, in the tension across their shoulders. You haven't been told anything. But you've received everything. *Signal precedes content.*

This isn't conjecture. It's the order of operations in every room, every relationship, every moment of influence. First, people ask themselves —unconsciously—*Can I trust you?* Only if the body answers yes do they begin to consider what you've actually said.

And what answers that question is not your résumé. It's your breath. Your gaze. Your stillness. The coherence of your tone and the tempo of your speech. If these match the moment, if they carry a kind of silent integrity, then the door opens. Not to agreement, necessarily— but to possibility.

This is why people don't simply respond to meaning. They respond to signal quality. They register—before they understand. And if your signal feels dissonant, rushed, inconsistent, no amount of good intention will repair the gap.

We are taught, especially in leadership, to craft our message. But we are rarely taught to condition the medium through which that message travels—our own state. That's like tuning a violin only after the performance has started.

And so we rush into rooms full of tension, armed with bullet points and confidence tricks, unaware that our nervous system is leaking incongruence in every direction. A shallow breath here. A darting glance there. The signal fragments. And trust—the currency of real influence—drains out faster than we can speak.

Leaders who get this right don't always speak more persuasively. But they are listened to[5]. Because people track presence before they track logic. They follow regulation before they follow direction.

Consider how this plays out in high-stakes negotiations. A skilled negotiator doesn't just listen to what the other side says. They read what isn't said—the micro-pauses, the tightening jaw, the sudden drop in vocal tone. Likewise, they know their own signal is being read in kind. They stabilise themselves before they try to stabilise the conversation. They breathe before they speak.

In this way, leadership becomes a game of first response—not to the problem, but to yourself. If you can't regulate your signal, you can't regulate your influence. And you certainly can't create rapport that's worth trusting. Here's the practical truth: people don't respond to what you mean. They respond to what you're broadcasting. Your body is already having the conversation. The only question is whether you're aware of it.

This chapter will teach you how to take control of that signal—not to manipulate others, but to become congruent in high-stakes settings. It will show you how to use breath, gaze, tone, and silence not as techniques, but as instruments of presence. And it will give you the tools to align your inner state with your outer expression, so that trust becomes not a tactic, but a by-product.

Because the most powerful messages in leadership don't start with language. They start with signal. And the best leaders are the ones who learn to speak fluently, long before they speak at all.

Rapport as Accord

Most people think connection happens when we agree. That if we want to build rapport, we need to nod, sympathise, see eye to eye. And of course, shared views make things easier—when they're genuine. But the heart of rapport doesn't live in agreement. It lives in *alignment*. And those two are not the same.

You don't have to agree with someone to connect with them. You don't even have to like them. What matters—especially in leadership—is whether you can meet them where they are, without rushing to where you'd rather they be.

This is where many leaders fall short. They confuse rapport with persuasion. They assume their job is to move people quickly: from uncertainty to clarity, from doubt to confidence, from resistance to alignment. But no one moves unless they first feel seen. No one shifts unless they feel safe.

Rapport, then, is not about dragging someone into your world. It's about stepping into theirs—without losing your footing. Not to rescue. Not to fix. But to feel the ground beneath them, so you can speak from it.

Think of the great communicators—not just speakers, but those whose presence lands before their message. They don't sprint ahead. They sync. They settle into the emotional frequency of the room and begin there. They tune themselves first, not by accident, but by attention.

This is why the old advice—'mirror the other person' or 'use matching body language'—so often feels hollow. Done mechanically, it backfires. It becomes mimicry, not alignment. And people can feel the difference.

Genuine rapport isn't a trick. It's a resonance. It emerges when your signal tells someone, without saying it outright:

> *I'm not trying to win this moment.*
> *I am being with you in this moment.*

That doesn't mean surrendering your position. It means suspending your need to correct, to convert, to close. For now.

The power of this approach is not just in its softness. It's in its sequencing. Alignment first, then movement. And when that sequence is respected, the movement often happens without force. Because people don't resist being guided—they resist being misunderstood.

A seasoned leader knows this. They don't bulldoze resistance. They pace it. They listen in a way that lets the other person hear themselves more clearly. They mirror not posture, but state. Not words, but rhythm[6]. And gradually, through that rhythm, they begin to lead.

The metaphor is musical, because the process is. You can't harmonise with a melody you haven't heard. And you can't lead a team—or a room, or a conversation—if you haven't first learned to listen to its emotional key.

This is why rapport is foundational to leadership. Because without it, everything becomes harder. Meetings take longer. Conflict sharpens. Teams withhold. Influence stalls. You can have the best ideas in the world—but if the people you lead don't feel seen, they won't hear them.

But with rapport—real rapport—the opposite occurs. Defences lower. Possibilities widen. Conversations open that didn't exist five minutes earlier. People begin to meet you not just with attention, but with willingness. And once willingness is present, the work begins in earnest.

So, if you find yourself stuck—if the conversation won't move, if the team's gone cold, if the room won't lean in—don't push the message. Check the signal. Ask yourself not "How do I convince them?" but:

> "Have I met them yet?"

Because once you have, everything else gets easier.

An Elusive Skillset

There's a moment, often unnoticed, when two people fall into rhythm. It might be in conversation, where breath synchronises and gestures align. It might happen in the quiet of a hospital room, where a doctor's posture gently mirrors a grieving relative's stance—not to comfort, exactly, but to join. Or in a negotiation, when the tempo of speech slows just enough that both sides start breathing in time.

From the outside, it looks incidental. Accidental. As though rapport has simply emerged, like mist on a cold morning. But look closer, and you'll see the shape of something much more deliberate. These are not the accidents of connection. They are the signals of someone who has learned to attune[7]. And this is the skillset that sits beneath rapport—not performance, not charm, but attunement. It begins with the simplest of acts: *noticing*.

To notice is not to watch passively. It is to pay attention with intent, without intrusion. Skilled communicators, whether in leadership or care or conflict resolution, train themselves to observe the subtlest signals. They see how a colleague shifts slightly when the conversation tightens. They hear the slight crack in someone's tone before disagreement emerges. They feel the contraction in the room when silence stretches just a second too long.

This is *sensory acuity*—a kind of high-resolution presence[8]. It's not mystical. It's perceptual. The difference between someone who walks into a room and reacts, and someone who walks into a room and reads. Reading, however, is only half the skill. The other half is responding. And here we meet two more invisible arts: *mirroring and matching*, and *pacing and leading*. Together, these are the grammar of non-verbal rapport. Subtle, seamless, and—when done with precision—undetectable to anyone but the trained eye.

Let's start with mirroring. At its worst, it's a caricature: forced, exaggerated, a pantomime of connection. But at its best, it's barely visible. A gentle alignment of tone, posture, or rhythm. Not mimicry, but echo. Like tuning a violin—not by copying the sound of another instrument, but by finding the shared note beneath both.

Bill Clinton was famous for this. He didn't just listen—he reflected. If you sped up, so did he. If you slowed down, his tone dropped with you. It wasn't manipulation. It was his way of saying, without words:

> *"I'm with you"*

Princess Diana, by contrast, had a different gift. She adjusted not just tempo, but emotional quality. With the bereaved, she softened. With children, she lightened. She didn't imitate—she aligned. This is mirroring and matching done well: not scripted, not stiff, but seamless. It tells the other person

> *"You don't have to meet me*
> *—I've already met you"*

But mirroring, on its own, isn't enough. Alignment must eventually give way to direction. And that is where *pacing and leading* enters the frame.

The principle is deceptively simple: you meet the person where they are—emotionally, physically, energetically—and, once trust is felt, you begin to guide. The sequence matters. Pacing earns permission. Leading earns change[9].

Martin Luther King Jr. did not begin with dreams. He began with suffering. He met the pain of the people where it lived—acknowledged it, named it, held it in the cadence of his voice—and only then did he invite them upward, towards hope. Had he begun with vision, he would have lost them. But because he began with truth, they followed.

In daily leadership, the same principle applies. A team under pressure will not respond to synthetic optimism. But they will respond to someone who sees their exhaustion and matches its tone before shifting the pace.

> "I know you're tired... and I know what you've carried"

Then, once they feel seen:

> "Here's why it's worth finishing strong"

This is pacing and leading—not as performance, but as pattern. First match. *Then* move.

But to pace, to mirror, to lead, you must first be attuned. You cannot fake the noticing. You cannot shortcut the presence. These skills are not tactics. They are the by-products of attention, curiosity, and humility. They are how your nervous system tells someone else's:

> *"I'm listening, even if I haven't spoken yet"*

So yes, rapport can be broken down. It has structure, rhythm, mechanics. But its power lies in how imperceptibly it operates. When done well, it disappears—not because it's absent, but because it's so natural that people stop noticing *you*, and start connecting with the moment itself.

That is the mark of a master communicator: not that they draw attention to themselves, but that they dissolve the distance between speaker and listener. And the first step in closing that distance?

Read the room. Then let the room read you.

SIGNALLING INTEGRITY UNDER PRESSURE

The test doesn't come when things are calm. It comes when the stakes rise. You know the moment. The room goes cold. A voice raises. A deadline closes in. You feel the drift—away from clarity, away from poise. Words come, yes, but they no longer lead. The message has slipped beneath the surface, and something else has taken over: the signal beneath the speech.

This is where congruence matters most. Not in the quiet rehearsal of a boardroom dry-run, but in the live current of conflict, uncertainty, or exposed emotion. It is here, in the split-second mismatch between what you say and what you show, that trust either anchors or frays.

When your tone says calm, but your breath betrays haste, people notice. When your face carries steadiness, but your blink rate triples, something doesn't land. No one may say it aloud. They may not even realise it consciously. But the signal has shifted, and the body always listens first.

This is the cost of incongruence. It's not that people won't hear you. It's that they won't believe you.

And belief—real belief—is not a product of logic. It's a product of felt coherence. That what I see, what I hear, what I sense… matches. That your signal holds under pressure. That the internal rhythm of your presence doesn't buckle when the conversation turns sharp.

This is why the most powerful leaders are not the ones with the most forceful delivery, but the most reliable signal. They are read as trustworthy not because they are perfect, but because they are consistent. Their voice, breath, and presence stay anchored when others begin to drift. They don't just transmit information. They regulate the room.

Think of the teacher who calms a restless classroom not by raising their voice, but by lowering it. Slowing their gestures. Breathing from the belly. Within minutes, the room responds—not because the content changed, but because the signal became trustworthy.

Or the senior nurse in a trauma ward. She doesn't command attention with volume or titles. She brings it with breath control, clear movement, and a gaze that signals *"Follow me."* Her congruence keeps others steady—precisely because it doesn't waver when the environment does.

The same applies to leadership at any level. When a team hits turbulence, they don't look to the loudest. They look to the most stable. And stability is not a performance—*it's a signal of state.*

This isn't about perfection. You will wobble. Everyone does. What matters is whether you notice the wobble and recover your signal before it contaminates the room.

Congruence, then, is not about being robotic. It's not about suppressing emotion or training yourself into a blank expression of faux-stability[10]. It's about integrity—between intention and expression, between message and body, between purpose and presence.

It's about being able to say to yourself, in the heat of the moment:

> Hold your breath pattern.
>
> Let the face settle.
>
> Let the message land through the body first.

And to do that not as a gimmick, but as a trained reflex. Not because you're acting, but because you're aligned. This is the discipline of leadership under pressure. Not just having something to say, but being someone who can say it—without your body betraying your message. Because we speak with *words* and connect with *presence*... but we lead with *non-verbal signals*.

And just as a single presence can change a room, a room, too, speaks back—if you know how to read it. That's where permission begins. And if you miss that signal, you may be leading no one at all.

From Rapport to Group Permission

He stood at the front of the room like a man hoping no one would notice he'd just sat in a puddle. Polite nods greeted him. A few phones slipped discreetly into laps. One woman stifled a yawn so heroic it deserved a standing ovation. This was not permission. This was tolerance, and barely that.

Permission, in group settings, is not granted by titles or slide decks. It's earned—or withheld—by the body, en masse. Like murmuration in starlings, it's subtle, synchronous, and unmistakable when you see it. When you *feel* it. And if you don't feel it, you're not leading. You're flapping your arms in a tornado and hoping to influence the wind.

Real group permission is physiological before it's philosophical. It's written in the eyes, the breath, the twitch of a foot that no longer wants to flee. When a group's ready to be led, you'll see it in their stillness. The eyelid that no longer scans the door. The hand that sets the phone down screen-first. Most tellingly, the breath drops. Down past the collarbone. Past the frantic chest. Into the belly, where real decisions live.

A room with permission breathes like a mammal sleeping near safety. When that happens, you get flow: the kind of conversational glide where one thought finishes just as another's about to surface. No herding. No dragging. Just shared movement. And that, frankly, is rare.

leaders who misunderstand this imagine influence is about command. They speak louder, gesture harder, and pace the room as if movement itself were persuasive. It isn't. Especially not when your audience is breathing like they've just been asked to relive secondary school maths.

Permission doesn't follow assertion—it follows attunement. You can't fake it. You *can* watch for it, if you know where to look. A flicker of eye contact. A chin lift. A nod that echoes something you didn't just say, but meant. And yes, a breath. If the group's breathing deeply and moving fluidly, odds are they're with you. If they're tight, staccato, and still as furniture, you're a solo act with no encore.

So, what do you do when you don't have permission? You stop performing and start noticing. Breathe the way you want them to breathe. Speak in a tone that fits the room, not your script. Align with their values—not your bullet points—and make safety felt, not just referenced. This isn't group hypnosis, though it wouldn't hurt to understand the principle. It's biological choreography. Influence begins with mutual regulation.

And if none of this lands, here's the blunt version: trying to facilitate without permission is like deploying a parachute *after* you've cratered into the earth. It's not brave. It's not strategic. It's just messy physics.

The good news? Groups want to be led. They're waiting, in fact, for someone who makes coherence possible without coercion. Watch their breath. Sync with it. And when it drops—and you drop with it—that's when the real work begins.

And so, the leader doesn't begin with words. They begin with breath. Not to speak, but to listen—to the room, to the rhythm, to the readiness. Because when the group breathes as one, leadership has already begun[11].

TEN
NON-VERBAL ACUITY
OBSERVING & PROJECTING WITH PRECISION

WHAT IS REALLY BEING SIGNALLED NON-VERBALLY?

As we explored in the previous chapter, it plays both a central and critical role in leadership.

Now, it's time to move from theory into practice. Developing non-verbal skill requires not only awareness but also the deliberate and thoughtful application of these tools in real-world situations[1].

Just as a conductor wields subtle gestures to evoke harmony from an orchestra, a leader must use their body, voice, and presence to orchestrate an environment of trust, authority, and collaboration.

CASE STORY: *A Non-Verbal Fumble*

Let's examine two scenes that illustrate the power of a leader's body language. Picture Angus, the Managing Director of a supply chain business, announcing a major company culture change initiative to one of his large distribution teams called 'Values & Behaviours'.

The shop-floor workforce is known for their irreverence to authority, which is one of the reasons for the new policy to begin with. Angus has prepared a detailed presentation, explaining the rationale and benefits of the change, a summary copy of which is placed on each chair prior to the meeting.

As he begins to speak, his non-verbal cues are telling:

- His shoulders are slightly hunched, suggesting tension or uncertainty.
- He's gripping the podium tightly, his knuckles white with strain.
- His eyes dart around the room rather than making steady eye contact.
- His voice, though he is trying to sound confident, has a slight quaver.

Despite the carefully crafted words of his presentation, Angus's non-verbal cues are broadcasting uncertainty and anxiety[2]. The workforce, picking up on these unconscious signals, begin to grumble and gesticulate about the proposed changes. They realise that they are about to have their wings clipped. As Angus continues to speak, the workforce starts to point to their handouts and discuss things amongst themselves.

This makes Angus feel disrespected and embarrassed. Once he begins to blush, he stops talking and glares at the workforce. In a shrill, high-pitched voice, Angus demands respectful silence whilst he is speaking. Of course, this makes him appear flaky and, true to reputation, the audience is watching the spectacle in quiet grinning satisfaction.

Angus picks up the pace and, with the armpits of his blue business shirt wet with sweat, he gets through to the end of the presentation. When asked if there were any questions, there are none. He thanks them for their time and permits them to return to work. Once the room is emptied, all but a few summaries are left behind on the chairs or flopped to the floor.

So, that is what actually happened. However, imagine an alternative reality, where Angus walks in with an upright, relaxed posture. He makes warm eye contact with team members as he welcomes everyone. He walks around shaking hands and acknowledging familiar faces. His gestures are open and inclusive. His voice is steady, rich and resonant. He makes a few humorous remarks at his own expense that have everyone laughing together. Even before he delves into the details of the presentation, Angus's non-verbal communication has already sent a powerful message of confidence and reassurance[3].

In both versions, the content of Angus's message is identical. But the non-verbal packaging dramatically alters how his words are received and interpreted by his team's instinctual brains. So, let's start to break down the elements of non-verbal cues and communication.

Points of Focus in Communication

Much like how sailors use the terms "port" and "starboard" to orient themselves in any direction, leaders can use distinct points of focus in communication to direct attention with precision[4]. Understanding where to direct your focus—and that of your audience—can make or break the outcome of an interaction.

Here are four key points of focus that every leader should understand:

- **One-point**: This is when the leader focuses inward, looking down at themselves or their internal experience. Think of it as the introspective mode, where you are reflecting or gathering your thoughts. Leaders often use this when they pause to consider their next words carefully.

- **Two-point**: The leader makes direct eye contact with the person they're addressing. This is where rapport is built, where trust is established. Two-point focus is especially effective in one-on-one conversations or small meetings where personal connection is essential.
- **Three-point**: Both the leader and the listener direct their attention to an external third point, such as a document or a shared visual aid. This is particularly useful for discussing complex or sensitive topics, as it allows for a collaborative, less confrontational approach. It shifts the focus from being personal to being task-oriented.
- **Four-point**: This is when the leader directs their focus to something outside the immediate conversation—perhaps into the distance or at an abstract point beyond the present moment. It's often used when discussing larger ideas, the future, or something conceptual. Leaders use four-point focus when they want to take the audience beyond the immediate and make them consider broader possibilities.

Example in Action:

Bruce is leading a discussion on a new project, 'Balancing Outbound Volumes', which is aimed at equalising the outbound volumes over several distribution centres. During the discussion, Bruce focuses on a three-point—a PowerPoint presentation to which he is gesturing to clarify the logistics.

But when the conversation shifts to the project's broader impact on the company's future, he adopts a four-point focus, gesturing outward as if to encompass larger ideas, pulling the team into a vision of what the future could hold. This shift subtly signals to the audience that they are moving from detail-oriented work to visionary thinking[5].

· · ·

PERIPHERAL AWARENESS

There's a kind of seeing that doesn't involve staring. A kind of noticing that doesn't involve looking. And it may just be the most underrated skill in the leadership playbook.

Most people think of good communication as something that travels in a straight line: I look at you, you look at me, and we speak accordingly. But in high-stakes environments—especially where emotions run hot or culture discourages too much direct eye contact—those straight lines can become traps. Eye contact becomes interrogation. Attention becomes pressure. And if you're not careful, your focused stare can cause the very defensiveness you're trying to dissolve[6].

That's where *peripheral vision* enters the scene. It's the wide-angle lens to your tight-beam torch. While foveal vision—the crisp, central part of your gaze—lets you lock onto detail, read a facial twitch or focus on a spreadsheet, it's your peripheral vision that lets you *feel* the room. Literally[7].

You're using it whenever you notice someone shifting in their chair while your eyes are still on the slides. When you sense that a joke didn't land because a corner of the room went quiet. When you pick up on rising tension—not from what's said, but from how ten pairs of shoulders seem to climb north of their necklines at the same time[8].

Peripheral awareness is how leaders read group mood without watching every face. It's how you stay socially attuned without feeling like you're playing a game of emotional *Whac-A-Mole*[9].

Let me take you to Melbourne.

Twelve trade union delegates. All men. All veterans of the industrial negotiation game. They were seated in a semi-circle around me, arms folded, expressions carved out of sandstone—stern, silent, and poised for disagreement. It was the kind of room where the air arrives already holding its breath. I was there to renegotiate operational terms after a long-standing bottleneck in shift rotation. They were there, by the looks of it, to chew on management and spit out the bones.

Now, I could have met them eye for eye—scanned the room like a CCTV camera trying to spot dissidents. That's what foveal vision tempts you to do: zero in, lock on, dominate the frame. But in a situation already strung tight, a direct gaze can function like an accelerant[10]. I didn't need a fire. I needed a signal.

So, instead, I turned to one of the delegates directly in front of me and began speaking. Calm, measured, open-palmed. All the while, I kept my peripheral field wide. I let the others blur. Not into irrelevance—but into a kind of emotional radar. I could track how the room was shifting, even as I engaged just one face[11].

The signs were almost imperceptible at first. A hand unclenching. A lean forward. A brow relaxing by a few degrees. No nods yet—this wasn't the sort of crowd that nodded—but the static was breaking up. Minute by minute, the atmosphere softened. I adjusted my tone in real time, slightly more warmth here, a longer pause there. By the time we reached the key proposals, the posture in the room had shifted from 'siege' to 'sceptical curiosity'—a major win by any industrial relations standard.

And I hadn't eyeballed half the room.

That's peripheral awareness.

It's the art of keeping your emotional antennae extended while your eyes are calmly anchored. It requires stillness, not scanning. And it works best when paired with what I call the *soft gaze*—relaxed eyes that focus gently ahead while absorbing movement and mood at the margins[12]. Like watching the sea while sensing the pull of the tide.

This isn't just useful in negotiation. It's essential in any situation where you need to *lead the group without losing the individual*.

When you're facilitating a workshop, teaching a team, or giving bad news. When you want to watch the weather without causing a storm.

Peripheral awareness is how you track the signals your mouth can't reach. It's your early warning system, your silent listening, your edge in rooms where words lie and bodies tell the truth[13]. And the best part? No one knows you're doing it. They just feel seen. Even when you're not looking.

Non-Verbal Pattern Clusters

On a spectrum of non-verbal pattern clusters, at one end there are approachable clusters and, on the other, there are credible clusters. The approachable cluster is typified with movement, such as a bobbing head, swaying body, angled posture and gesticulation; facial expressions, such as smiling and raised eyebrows; and a modulating voice pattern and upward inflexions. These behaviours connote safety and send an autonomic invitation to connect. A friendly flight attendant is the poster child for this cluster[14].

The credible cluster is typified with stillness, minimal facial expression, zero gesticulation, an upright posture, with a flat voice tone that turns down at the end of sentences. A great example of this would be an airline pilot, the poster child of which is Captain Sullenberger, who was played by Tom Hanks in the movie 'Sully'. His emotionless narrative as he pilots a plane full of passengers into the Hudson River is remarkable. It connotes safety due to perceived intelligence and competence[15].

As a thought experiment, imagine the flight attendant with the credible cluster, with complete stillness, zero facial expression and flat voice welcoming you aboard. Or a highly energised, up-and-downy voice coming over the 'tannoy' excitedly telling you about the potential for bad weather and turbulence. I'm sure that you will find them comically incongruent with their new situations.

Of course, these clusters are extreme categories; however, they do give us clues on how we can modify our own non-verbals to be congruent for our teams given the different circumstances in which we find ourselves. In circumstances that benefit from a more cool, cognitive or sober approach, dialling up our inner 'Sully' would be highly advantageous. Reviewing and evaluating an important proposition, talking to the facts of an investigation or addressing people during an emergency are all times where we benefit the listener with increased credibility.

At the same time, in circumstances requiring more energy, enthusiasm, empathy or human connection, dialling up our friendly flight attendant would better suit the moment. Meeting someone at a networking event, lightening the start of an interview or ending a meeting on an upbeat note are all examples of where we benefit the listeners with increased approachability.

Eye-Hand Coordination

If you've ever watched someone give a talk and found yourself staring not at their face, but at their flailing hands—then you already understand the problem. When the hands and the eyes are having separate conversations, the message gets lost in translation. It's like being given directions by someone who points north while saying 'go left'. You'll get somewhere. But probably not where they wanted you to go.

Now, imagine the opposite. A leader who gestures toward a slide and *looks* exactly where they're pointing. A nod. A pause. A subtle tilt of the hand and shift of the gaze. Without needing to say a word, they've told the room what matters. They've drawn a red circle round the idea—without using a pen. That's eye–hand coordination. Not a fine motor skill, but a strategic one[16].

It isn't theatre. It's alignment. When the eyes and the hand move as one, attention flows effortlessly. The audience doesn't have to think.

They just follow. And in high-stakes settings—where one glance can give away nerves, or one twitch can undo a sentence—that kind of invisible leadership counts double[17].

But don't be fooled by the simplicity. Like most good things in leadership, this isn't about being fancy. It's about being *clear*.

Two gestures matter most. They sound like minor choreographic choices. They aren't.

The first is the *bouncing hand*. Not as ridiculous as it sounds. Picture it: a soft, rhythmic movement toward a point, like offering a tray of canapés to the group. It says, 'Here it is—what do you think?' The eye follows the hand with warmth. There's an invitation in the air, even if no one's speaking yet. It's a non-verbal nudge toward openness[18]. You're not just giving information. You're opening a conversation.

The second is the *vertical hold*. Flat hand, steady, upright. No flapping, no offering. It's not asking for agreement. It's declaring. This gesture says, 'This is the decision'. And if you're doing it right, your gaze locks with it. The audience sees the hand, feels the tone, and understands that this is not a debate. It's a moment of definition[19].

The difference between the two? Atmosphere. Use the bouncing hand and people feel welcomed into the space. Use the vertical hold and people feel the weight of authority. Same body. Same message. Entirely different effect[20].

And timing matters. Do it too soon, and it looks rehearsed. Too late, and it looks hesitant. But when the gesture, the glance, and the line of speech arrive together—it lands. It *sticks*. You don't even need the PowerPoint to work.

There's something primal about it. People believe your point more when your body acts like it believes it too. That's the hidden power. When your eyes and hands speak the same language, the message goes straight in. No need for translation. No need for flair.

It just feels true.

Of course, you'll mess it up the first dozen times. That's fine. The mirror will laugh at you. So will your team, if they catch you practising. Let them. Because once you've got it down, you won't need the applause. You'll have something better: attention.

And in leadership, attention is the most expensive currency in the room[21].

Breath & Perception

The Breath Behind the Words

The voice is an instrument. But unlike the violin, which sits obediently in its case until summoned, your voice plays whether you like it or not. It plays in meetings, in silence, in moments of self-doubt, and in those dazzling, razor-edged seconds where all eyes are on you. And the bow across its strings? That's breath.

A good breath isn't dramatic. It doesn't announce itself with flared nostrils and yogic fervour. It simply arrives where it should—low, steady, invisible. When it does, something curious happens: the voice deepens. Not theatrically, not in a James Earl Jones kind of way, but with just enough gravity to make people lean in instead of drift off. A voice supported by low breath carries weight. It anchors a room without needing to raise itself.

Now flip it. High breath. Chest tight. Words emerge fast, thin, and scratchy—like they're trying to escape you. The pitch rises, the cadence stutters, and suddenly, whatever you're saying—no matter how valid—sounds like a plea rather than a plan. It doesn't matter how smart your words are. If your breath betrays you, your message walks out the back door.

This is not esoteric. It's acoustics and perception, hardwired into how humans assess each other. We don't listen to what's said first—we listen to *how* it's said. It's evolutionary paranoia in action[22]. We're all tuning forks for threat and safety, scanning tone, rhythm, and breath before we let meaning in through the front gate.

So the choice becomes strategic. Want to be seen as warm, open, ready to connect? Then let the breath drop[23]. Let it flow. Let your tone undulate with a smile not only in the mouth but in the pacing of your words. You'll sound like someone who can be trusted with delicate truths and bad coffee.

Need to signal authority, seriousness, the 'we're-not-here-to-muck-about' register? Same breath—low, deliberate—but strip the edges of inflection. Level out the melody[24]. Let the full stop land like a boot heel on concrete. Credibility isn't loud. It's still.

Of course, you're free to ignore all this. Just breathe high and fast, pitch your voice like a startled squirrel, and watch your audience wonder if they're being led by someone who's moments away from a small panic attack. You'll come across as insincere, flaky, or, at worst, hostile. Which is fine, if that's the goal. Just don't be surprised when people start backing away[25].

But if what you want is resonance—not just in sound but in impact—then begin before you speak. Start with breath. Not as a performance but as preparation. Let the breath drop. Let it settle your tone, smooth your edges, calm the air around you.

Because your non-verbals aren't accessories. They're the vehicle[26]. And your breath? It's the engine. When that engine runs hot and high, everything rattles. When it runs smooth, you can steer into any conversation—turbulent or tender—and be heard, really heard, without ever having to shout.

Leadership doesn't begin with words. It begins with presence. And presence is breath made visible.

ELEVEN
GROUP DYNAMICS
LEADING & ENGAGING UNDER PRESSURE

LEADERSHIP GOES BEYOND WORDS. It is created from gestures, silences, and the breath between sentences. Imagine a leader entering a room where tension hangs like a storm cloud. Without raising their voice or uttering more than a word, they exude calm authority. Their movements are deliberate, their pauses resonate with meaning, and their breath—steady and measured—sets the rhythm of engagement[1].

Non-verbal communication is the elusive language of influence. It wields more power than is often credited. From the depth of our breathing to the spaces between our words, non-verbal cues shape how others perceive us. These subtle signals determine whether we are trusted, respected, or dismissed[2].

In this chapter, we explore how to master the unspoken elements of communication. You'll learn to control the emotional atmosphere through breathing, punctuate your words with purposeful pauses, and align your voice with your intent. These are not mere techniques; they are tools to craft a leadership presence that inspires trust, amplifies authority, and fosters genuine connection[3].

By the end, you will see how silence, breath, and voice are not empty spaces or fleeting sounds—they are the scaffolding upon which great leaders build their influence.

CASE STORY: Karen's Negotiation Success

Let's take a closer look at Karen, a senior executive entrusted with negotiating a major contract for her firm. The stakes are high, and her counterpart—a seasoned negotiator—is known for dominating discussions with fast-paced, assertive speech. Karen feels the pressure mounting but recalls her preparation: she knows that controlling the flow of conversation without appearing confrontational will be key.

As the negotiation begins, Karen feels her pulse quicken. She instinctively wants to respond immediately to counter her opponent's aggressive tone. Instead, she pauses. She takes a slow, deliberate breath, grounding herself. The silence stretches, compelling her counterpart to lean back slightly, caught off guard by the unexpected stillness. Karen uses this pause to process the argument presented and carefully shape her response.

Karen takes a rapid *Dual-Mind Reflection*[4,*] and, using her internal dialogue, says:

> *"Stay composed. Own this silence. Let them fill it."*

She consciously relaxes her shoulders, steadying her breath. The negotiation is no longer a verbal tug-of-war but a dance of controlled energy. Her deep, measured breathing sends subtle signals of confi-

---

* **Dual-Mind Reflection**: A brief internal check-in that distinguishes between instinctive reactivity and thoughtful choice. It allows the leader to pause, notice whether their response is being driven by primal reflex (fight, flight, freeze) or deliberate cognition, and to re-centre before proceeding. This technique supports autonomic regulation and leadership presence under pressure.

dence and control[5]. She notices her counterpart beginning to slow down, mirroring her calm pace[6].

As the discussion intensifies, Karen's internal dialogue keeps her balanced:

> *"Breathe. Listen.*
> *Respond with clarity."*

She poses thoughtful, open-ended questions and waits patiently for answers. The once dominant negotiator grows more reflective, unsettled by Karen's composure. The tension in the room slowly dissolves, replaced by a steady rhythm of dialogue.

By the meeting's end, Karen has secured favourable terms for her firm. Her success wasn't rooted in aggressive tactics but in the quiet strength of deliberate pauses and controlled breathing. Her poised presence turned a potentially combative negotiation into a collaborative exchange. Karen left the room not only with a signed contract but with her reputation solidified as a negotiator who commands respect without raising her voice.

LEADERSHIP & *Breathing*

Just as pauses can control the tempo of a conversation, breathing can control the emotional energy in the room. Deep, steady breathing helps leaders manage their own stress, while simultaneously influencing the emotional state of those around them.

When probing for permission, one very effective visual cue is '**BLIP**' (*Breathing Low Indicates Permission*). We can use this insight to infer whether someone has given us permission. At the same time, when a leader breathes deeply, it sends an autonomic invitation to 'approach and connect'. It's the welcome mat on your front step. Conversely, shallow, high breathing signals an autonomic warning:

"I am danger. Stay away."

It's the 'beware of the dog' sign on your fence. Others can pick up on this—often unconsciously—and will connect or disconnect accordingly.

Let's explore two ways leaders can use breathing to their advantage:

1. **Managing Personal Stress**: When under pressure, the instinct is to breathe rapidly and shallowly, which can increase stress. By consciously breathing deeply and slowly, leaders can activate the body's parasympathetic nervous system, which promotes relaxation and reduces the effects of stress hormones like cortisol.
2. **Influencing Others**: People tend to mirror the body language and breathing patterns of those around them. When a leader breathes calmly and deeply, others' mirror neurons induce them to do the same. This can be particularly useful in tense meetings or during difficult conversations. If the leader remains calm, it helps create a more relaxed atmosphere for everyone involved.

Example: Think of a leader entering a tense meeting where emotions are running high. By focusing on their breathing—taking slow, deep breaths—they not only keep their own nerves in check but also influence the breathing patterns of their team.

As the leader speaks, the team members' bodies, noticing the calm, begin to mirror this slower, more relaxed pace. The atmosphere shifts from one of tension to one of constructive dialogue.

Silence Projects Intelligence[7]

Pausing during speech isn't just about giving yourself time to think—it also enhances how others perceive your intelligence. Pauses are often interpreted as a sign of thoughtfulness and depth. When you pause, it signals to your audience that you are considering your words carefully, which in turn makes your speech feel more deliberate and meaningful.

In fact, studies have shown that people who pause before responding are often rated as more intelligent, trustworthy, and composed. This is because a pause conveys confidence—you're not rushing to fill the silence with unnecessary words. Instead, you're allowing yourself space to breathe, reflect, and respond with clarity. But what exactly makes a pause so powerful?

It comes down to a few key elements:

1. **Visual**: During a pause, remain still with your mouth closed. Movement during a pause can signal nervousness or uncertainty. Breathing through your mouth reduces your perceived intelligence. So, hold your posture confidently, breathe through your nose, and make direct eye contact.
2. **Auditory**: Silence is golden during a pause. Don't rush to fill the space with filler words like "um" or "ah." Let the silence speak for itself.
3. **Kinaesthetic**: Stay grounded. Keep your weight evenly balanced on both feet and avoid shifting or fidgeting. Your body language should reflect that you are in control of the moment.

When done effectively, a pause can raise your perceived intelligence quotient and reinforce your authority. It gives the impression that every word you utter has been carefully considered, which in turn elevates the impact of your message.

Getting Attention Professionally

See yourself walking into a crowded room, the air buzzing with conversation. Laughter ripples through pockets of chatter, and the hum of voices fills every corner. It's time for you to give a speech, a briefing, or make an announcement. As a leader, you must first earn the attention of the group before guiding them anywhere. And this begins with how you address them.

Your opening sets the tone, letting everyone know you have something important to share. So, start strong—with a pulse of volume that is sufficient to punch through the loud rumbling hum of conversation and noise.

The bigger the group or the louder the noise, the louder the vocal pulse of volume required. The smaller the group, the quieter the noise, the softer the pulse of volume needed. In either case, you're aiming for brevity, clarity and authority; because the important thing is not what you say but the way that you say it. Indeed, it could be as simple as,

> *"Good morning!"*

Once you have their attention, stop. Let the silence linger for two or three beats. This isn't hesitation—it's strategy. A deliberate pause is like the steady draw of breath before a leap, charged with energy and anticipation. While you pause, scan the room. Look at your audience calmly and purposefully. This moment of quiet creates intrigue and signals that what comes next is worth hearing. You've caught their full attention—now allow them to approach and connect with you.

When you begin to speak, lower your voice, as though you're sharing a secret that everyone in the room needs to hear. In smaller spaces, speak just below a conversational volume; in larger ones, ensure your voice still carries—softly enough to make people lean in to listen. This shift from strong to silence to soft draws the audience closer with intent. It makes your message feel intimate and profound.

Competent vocal dynamics transform the way you connect with others. A strong voice grabs attention; a pause builds anticipation; and a whisper draws people closer, creating a powerful rhythm that prevents monotony.

This is Michael Grinder's **ABOVE (Pause) Whisper** technique, which is a beautifully crafted sequence[8]. It taps into human instinct, where changes in tone signal importance and evoke emotion.

Tense Conversations

In 2006, I stood before seven hundred and fifty employees to deliver the words they feared most: they were being made redundant. Rumours had rippled through the workforce for weeks, softening the blow only in theory. Yet, when spoken aloud, the confirmation struck hard.

To my left, a large screen displayed a summary of the plan. Blue background, deep yellow lettering—an intentional choice for clarity in the mottled light of the hall. Every phrase I spoke had been crafted with care, every pause deliberately placed to give the weight of the words room to settle.

I told them the site would close after a five-week inventory rundown. I explained that the decision was final, irreversible. For most, that very day would be their last. The remaining few would stay to wind things down. My voice was slow, measured. I spoke with a prosodic calm designed not to soothe in a patronising way, but to give them space to think, to breathe, to understand.

As I spoke, I watched it happen—that quiet moment when comprehension turns cold and heavy. Bodies stilled. Faces slackened. Eyes fixed not on me but on the slides behind me, as though hoping the text might contradict what their ears had heard.

It was easy—almost painfully so—to imagine the mental arithmetic each person was performing. Mortgage payments. School fees. Superannuations. Futures rearranged in an instant.

This was no gentle crowd. The workforce had a history of industrial action, and violence wasn't beyond possibility. We had security in place, discreet but ready. Yet, not once was it needed. No shouts, no threats. Only silence. A few low murmurs after I finished. The sound of people cautiously stepping back into a world that had just changed.

Within twenty minutes, each person had their letter, detailing entitlements and final payments. One by one, they left. Quietly. Thoughtfully.

Outside, two news vans idled, cameras poised to catch whatever anger or despair might spill out onto the pavement. Later that night, I watched the broadcast. The reporter called it "sickening." Perhaps it was, though not for the reasons they intended.

That day, I learned something critical about leadership under pressure. In volatile moments, a leader's presence can either steady the ground beneath people's feet—or shake it loose entirely.

We knew the psychological responses we might provoke—anger, fear, paralysis—and we planned meticulously to guide people through it. This wasn't about manipulation, but about responsibility. It was our duty to carry them through that moment with dignity.

PACE Yourself[9]

Leadership is not just about the words we choose but how we carry ourselves when delivering them. Preparing oneself before facing a group—especially when delivering difficult news—is a profound act of respect and courtesy to those we lead. Through thorough autoregulation, we stabilise our internal state. In doing so, we honour the emotional weight our audience must bear, ensuring that our own unregulated emotions do not spill over and burden them further. This is where the *PACE Protocol*[10] supports not just our resilience but our ethical leadership.

To stand before a group and guide them through challenging news requires more than information—it requires presence, steadiness, and empathy. Leaders must first extend the principles of the PACE Protocol inward, grounding themselves so they can responsibly guide others through moments of volatility.

PACE Yourself *to Lead Effectively*

Too often, leaders rush into difficult situations half-prepared, weighed down by doubt or distraction. This unfocused, scattered mental state is unacceptable. Instead, a deliberate internal check-in reframes the moment:

> "Have I given myself full permission to speak with compassion, precision and credibility?"

This self-questioning is not indulgence—it is responsibility. If you cannot answer in the affirmative, you need to do the 'Inner Game' work. The point of delivery is no place for impostor syndrome or public speaking anxieties. Your duty is to be autonomically regulated, able to step fully into the role of guide—ready to carry both the message and its emotional consequences. If you are struggling to get there by yourself, accept it and seek coaching and support.

This is important because, in moments of high stress, our instinct is to fight, flee, or freeze. Yet leadership demands grounded, credible, and effective response. Before and during the engagement, ask yourself:

> "Is my next action driven by instinct, intuition, or thoughtful choice?"

This simple question interrupts the automatic patterns that can derail effective communication. This pause is not hesitation, nor will it be perceived as such. Rather, it will be perceived as *self-control*. It is the conscious decision to respond with Primate purpose rather than Reptile reflex.

And, whilst leaders must learn to control themselves, leadership is not about control. It is about *connection*. However, stress severs connection and locks us in survival mode. As people mirror their leaders, we must ensure our bodies are transmitting *autonomic invitations* to approach and connect. Ask:

> "Am I feeling good with full access to my social engagement behaviours?"

This ensures that the leader has safety-primed themselves. By doing so, they are emotionally available to the group, capable of meeting them where they are and leading them forward.

Resilience is not an improvised accident. Rather, it is prepared for through practice and contemplating the future with a problem-solver's mindset.

> "What scenarios can I mentally prepare for to stay composed and present?"

This question needs to be answered thoroughly. However, most leaders and influencers fail to give it its due diligence. They believe that once they've written their speech or presentation, or pulled together their support material for a difficult discussion, that they're done. They are not.

Mentally rehearsing successful outcomes means integrating new learnings and understandings in a useful way. In the PACE Protocol, we refer to this as *embedding new strategies and insights*. These strategies can be new inner game patterns of thinking and feeling. They can be outer game observational, conversational, and behavioural patterns. They can be verbal and non-verbal patterns. Its purpose is to get the speaker's particular brain and body ready to deliver a particular message to a particular group, in a way that best maintains the accuracy of the information and the safety of all parties.

PACE Yourself to *Deliver Bad News*

So, before engaging in a challenging conversation, it's essential to centre oneself within the framework of the PACE Protocol. After ensuring that you have given yourself full permission to have a successful (if challenging) encounter, check in with your instinct/cognition status with a *Dual-Mind Reflection*.

Here is a quick and effective technique that Michael Grinder calls:

Break & Breathe Twice[11]:

1. **Break**: Snap out of the negative state into which you are going. Changing your physiology is a highly effective way of doing this—shift your position by standing up, or sitting back, or looking in another direction, etc.
2. **Breathe**: Take two deep, intentional breaths. Regain your mental clarity, your cognition, and your inner calm.

I have found this to be a very practical technique with which to assert my agency over my instinct—before, during, and after difficult encounters. I like it, first, because it's simple: you're breathing anyway, so breathing a little differently on purpose is an easy way to exercise personal agency over your instinctual autonomic nervous system. Second, in meetings, it is a quick, covert, and low-concentration technique.

Either way, the technique allows me to phase-transition easily into connect-and-socialise by applying one or more technique from my inner library.

That's what I do. Try it for yourself. If it doesn't work for you, ditch it. If it works okay, tweak it so it works better. The point isn't doing my particular technique but finding your own *'go-to' autoregulation methods*. Whatever your recipe ends up being, my state management strategy prepares me to approach a challenging conversation clear-headed and with my full social engagement functions available to me.

BASELINE CALIBRATING

As the conversation initiates, you are almost always going to begin in 'two-point' communication. As you do so, ensure you take full advantage by observing and understanding the other person's state and responses. This is done through sensory acuity—paying close attention to the sensory details of the other person's verbal and non-verbal cues—and calibrating to their state in that moment.

If this is your first encounter, this becomes your baseline for the conversation, and you can watch for variation as the discussion progresses. This allows you to track whether the other person becomes more or less *socialised, mobilised* or *immobilised*.

If you already have a baseline from prior engagements, contrast (seek for differences) between their current behaviour and their usual patterns. Are you beginning the conversation from a point where they are more or less socially engaged than their typical baseline?

As always, this includes noting visual, auditory, and kinaesthetic (VAK) signals, as well as breathing patterns. By concentrating on what is genuinely happening for the other person, you remain attuned to their instinct–cognition status[12]... and then comes the moment you've been (not) looking forward to:

Sharing the bad news.

How Not to Get Shot[13]

Delivering difficult news is one of the most challenging tasks a leader faces. Missteps can erode trust, damage relationships, and escalate tension. Michael Grinder's communication technique offers a powerful solution by guiding leaders through emotionally charged conversations with greater composure and professionalism.

This approach empowers both messenger and recipient, fostering understanding and collaboration even in tough moments.

Grinder's method comprises of three core strategies designed to prevent defensive reactions and encourage constructive dialogue:

- Shifting to *third-person phrasing*
- Using *visual communication*
- Introducing a *third point of focus*

Together, these techniques can transform how difficult conversations unfold.

Go Third-Person

In high-stakes conversations, the words we choose can either defuse tension or intensify conflict. Using third-person phrasing—particularly through the passive voice—naturally creates a calmer, more neutral tone compared to the immediacy of first- and second-person language. This shift directs attention to the situation rather than individuals, reducing personal blame and emotional charge.

For example, saying

"Respect was not maintained"

focuses on the issue, whereas:

"I feel disrespected"
"You didn't follow the procedure"

personalises the problem, often triggering defensiveness. In tense situations, this subtle linguistic shift fosters problem-solving rather than blame. However, leaders must balance the passive voice with *active, solution-oriented* statements to maintain clarity and accountability.

For example:

> "Let's find a way to ensure procedures are followed next time."

This promotes collaboration without assigning blame.

Go Visual

Humans are wired to process visual information more effectively than speech alone. Presenting challenging information visually—through letters, slides, or diagrams—empowers the recipient to absorb the message at their own pace. You control how the content is framed: plain or technical language, formal or informal tone, structured layouts, and visual aids like graphs or images.

Visuals act as emotional anchors, engaging the analytical Primate Brain and tempering the Reptilian Brain's fight-or-flight response. In *Polyvagal Theory* terms, visuals support the vagal brake, sustaining social engagement behaviours. This approach promotes clarity and retention—especially for complex or emotionally sensitive information.

Consider how a financial report, presented as a clear graph rather than dense text, softens the impact of poor performance data. When recipients can revisit the information independently, they regain agency, reducing stress and emotional reactivity.

If the recipient becomes overwhelmed, cognitive function can drop by up to 35%. Allowing them to re-engage with visual material mitigates this effect, offering space for understanding and thoughtful response.

Go Three-Point

Direct eye contact during difficult conversations can intensify emotional states, whether positive or negative. Imagine two lovers sharing a gaze across candlelight versus two rivals locked in a stare-down. This is *two-point communication*—an intense, direct energy exchange.

Introducing a *third point of focus*, such as a document or visual aid, diffuses this intensity. By redirecting attention to the information rather than the messenger, the emotional load is reduced. This stabilises the interaction, preserving cognitive clarity and emotional balance.

Orally delivering bad news forces the recipient to depend solely on the messenger, increasing stress and reducing personal agency. Repeated clarifications can lead to the messenger becoming associated with negative emotions. Providing a shared reference point—like a handout or chart—allows both parties to engage with the content without amplifying interpersonal tension.

Ultimately, by proactively priming one's own safety first and applying Grinder's *'How Not to Get Shot'*, leaders (and other messengers) remain connected, approachable, and credible. In doing so, they create the conditions for sound cognitive problem-solving and group collaboration, all of which lead to a more resilient future.

In turn, their team—or other recipients, like bosses, clients, and peers—feel more connected, engaged, and in control. Becoming competent in these strategies will not only defuse tension but also strengthen relationships and build trust. Start integrating these PACE-aligned strategies into your daily practice, and resilient team outcomes will follow.

PACE Yourself *for Future Wins*

Neuro-resilient rehearsal isn't about dreamy wishful thinking. It's about conditioning your mind and body to perform with clarity and confidence under pressure. By vividly *pre-living* a desired outcome, leaders can strengthen their emotional readiness and align their actions with their goals[14].

Consider how elite athletes prepare for high-stakes moments. Before ever stepping onto the field or into the ring, they have already *lived* the victory in their minds. They visualise every detail—the sound of the crowd, the feel of the environment, the precise movements they'll execute. This mental preparation primes their nervous system and sharpens their focus, guiding their real-world actions toward that desired outcome.

Champion boxer and cultural icon Muhammad Ali called this technique *'future history'*.

You can apply this same strategy to leadership. Before entering a challenging conversation or delivering difficult news, take time to mentally walk through the experience. Visualise yourself standing confidently, speaking with composure and empathy. See what you will see—the room, their faces, your slide show, your notes in your hand. Hear what you will hear—the chatter before you begin, your voice as you deliver the message, their voices asking questions and making comments. Feel what you will feel—the emotions, the sensations, your energy levels.

Then switch from two-point to four-point and witness yourself. See how you look and how you move; hear your vocal pattern, hear your words. Did you need to get their attention with an *ABOVE* (*pause*) *Whisper*? Was the room already deathly silent? Or did a cordial initial conversation morph into the main discussion[15]?

If it is a volatile situation:

- Are you using third-party language, depersonalising your initial statements and answers to any question?
    - What questions are likely to be asked?
    - What topics must be discussed in the passive voice?
- Did you deliver the message visually?
    - Are you using handouts or individual computer devices?
    - Is there a slide show?
- Are you engaged in a three-point conversation?
    - Standing in front of a group, referring to a slide show off to the side?
    - Sitting at a table, at 90 degrees to the listener, using your pen to step them through the information?

This process is more than visualisation—it's future pacing yourself—it's strategic mental conditioning. By rehearsing success, your mind becomes attuned to recognising opportunities and responding to challenges effectively. Your actions naturally align with your preparation, making you more adaptable and resilient.

Try this practice the next time you face a difficult task:

- **Set the Scene**: Find a quiet space and close your eyes. Imagine the setting in detail—where you'll be, who will be present, and the atmosphere in the room.
- **Engage Your Senses**: What do you see, hear, and feel in this moment? Listen to your voice—calm and steady. Let your posture be strong yet approachable.
- **Visualise Success**: Picture yourself navigating the situation smoothly. See yourself guiding others toward the best possible outcome. Hear yourself responding thoughtfully. Feel yourself grounded and congruent.
- **Anchor the Feeling**: Squeeze your thumb and index

finger—because what is fired together is wired together[16].

Let your body become a resource you can draw upon.

The PACE Protocol's future pacing is designed to embed new strategies through detailed mental rehearsal, so that your desired responses arise easily and naturally in the moment they're needed. It is another example of asserting your agency over your instincts, as you programme yourself to feel and act differently in the future.

In doing so, you are preparing thoroughly—not to chase perfection, but to ensure that a dozen small things are done well.

CLOSING REFLECTION

Leadership is often mistaken for the loudest voice in the room or the sharpest command issued. Yet, as this chapter has shown, true leadership lies in mastering the subtleties—the silent pauses, the steady breath, the poised stance. These understated elements are not ancillary to leadership; they are foundational. They shape perceptions, guide emotions, and foster trust, often without a single word being spoken.

Karen's negotiation success exemplifies how a composed breath and strategic pause can shift the dynamics of power. The deliberate control of silence, the conscious modulation of voice, and the intentional use of body language are not theatrical performances but authentic expressions of authority and empathy. They are tools that signal to others:

> *"You are safe. We can get through this together"*

In moments of high tension, it is the leader's regulated presence that can anchor a group, transforming volatility into stability. The PACE Protocol, the 'Break & Breathe Twice' technique, and the strategic use of visual and third-point communication are more than methods —they are disciplines of emotional intelligence and social mastery. They enable leaders to respond with thoughtfulness rather than react with instinct, ensuring that even the most challenging messages are delivered with dignity and clarity.

These subtle skills not only help navigate difficult situations but also elevate moments of success. They make great moments greater and bad moments better, allowing leaders to amplify celebration and soften hardship. The ability to adapt and apply these techniques across varying circumstances strengthens a leader's capacity to inspire and unify their teams.

This subtle skillset, when honed, does more than prevent miscommunication or manage conflict. It builds resilient teams, fosters emotional safety, and creates environments where people feel connected and understood. The ability to project calm, invite trust, and command attention without force is a leader's greatest strength.

We often think leadership begins with what we say. But in truth, it begins with how we breathe. Before they trust your message, they trust your signal. Before they follow your direction, they follow your state. And the group is reading you—continuously.

TWELVE
CONTAINING THE MOOD-WRECKERS
HELPING THE PERSON & SHIELDING THE GROUP

SLOWLY THEN ALL OF A SUDDEN. That's how the room is lost. Like missing the first step on a staircase you thought was there. One moment you're the conductor of a mildly dysfunctional orchestra, and the next, you're the unfortunate soloist, playing triangle in an empty room while everyone else quietly turns to someone more interesting.

That pivot—the group gaze shifting from the problem back to you—is the unspoken verdict[1]. They're saying:

> 'We've noticed. So what are you going to do about it?'

What's often misunderstood is that the issue isn't the individual's behaviour. It's the group's decision about whether you still hold the permission to manage it.

Most managers miss this. They mistake leadership for control, and control for correction[2]. So when someone interrupts, sulks, showboats, or verbally sets fire to the agenda, the manager zeroes in on the offender like a disapproving schoolteacher—forgetting that it's not a one-on-one match. It's a game of chess with thirty silent observers, all deciding whether you're still the right person to follow.

Here's the quiet rule of group dynamics: if the group looks at the disruptor, then at you, you're on notice. If you don't act, they may not either—but they will clock your silence. If, instead, they glance at each other—eye rolls, sardonic smirks, awkward shrugs—then the group is starting to form its own immune system. And that's good news. Because a self-regulating group is a resilient one. It means you've earned some margin.

Now, the temptation is always to jump in. Especially if you're wired to 'keep order' or find ambiguity itchy. But over-intervening is its own hazard. Do it too soon, and you steal the group's autonomy. Too late, and you lose their trust. Leadership, in group settings, is often a silent equation: authority equals permission plus timing, squared by tone[3].

To understand that, you have to grasp one of the oldest myths in modern management—the myth of power as a blunt instrument[4]. For decades, we taught managers to lead with the volume turned up. Bark expectations. Enforce rules. Correct behaviour with the subtlety of a kettledrum. But now we know better. Influence, not force, is the modern manager's scalpel. It's not softer. It's smarter. It doesn't erode relationships—it sharpens them[5].

Think of power and influence as sitting on a continuum. At one end is raw command. The 'do it because I said so' school of leadership. Necessary sometimes, but rarely admired. At the other is silent gravity—the kind of authority that needs no declaration. Influence is what keeps a room listening even when nothing's being said.

Of course, there are times when a direct, unapologetic use of power is essential. Bullies, for instance, don't respond to warmth and wit. They only recognise boundaries when they hit one. And some situations call for a steel edge. But the art lies in knowing when to hold the line and when to let the group do your work for you.

Most of us have a default. Some are natural kats—sharp, quick to intervene, comfortable with confrontation. Others are dogs—loyal, tolerant, slow to judge, and sometimes a bit too forgiving for their own good. Both styles have their flaws. The kat might pounce too early and kill the room's self-management. The dog might wait too long and lose the right to lead.

Knowing your lean is half the battle. Managing it? That's the war. Kats must learn the power of the pause. A breath, a beat, a check for group response before pouncing. Dogs must learn to interrupt their own kindness just enough to protect the group's frame. It's not about changing who you are—it's about choosing how you lead.

This dance doesn't start with the agenda. It begins the moment people walk into the room. Before anyone speaks, the group is already forming impressions, mapping status, scanning for safety[6]. The leader who ignores this is like a pilot who doesn't check the weather. The one who notices—and starts building bridges early—buys themselves crucial leverage for later.

You don't manage disruption in the moment. You manage it in the minutes before. With eye contact. A quiet welcome. A respectful joke. An unspoken acknowledgment that says, 'I see you—and I'll still see you when things get tense.'

Because eventually, they will.

And when they do, you want the group to look at you not with expectation or exasperation, but with trust. The kind of trust that says: you don't need to fix everything. You just need to hold the space long enough for us to fix some of it ourselves.

That's when you've stopped managing the group—and started leading it.

Timing & Judgement

CONTAINING THE MOOD-WRECKERS

Let's begin with a quiet truth most managers deny until it's too late: not every fire needs a hose.

In group settings, over-correction isn't just ineffective—it's a form of narcissism[7]. It assumes the group can't cope without you. That every raised eyebrow, every offhand comment, every sigh loud enough to qualify as a performance art piece, demands your intervention. It doesn't. Sometimes it just demands your presence.

That's harder than it sounds.

Especially if you're wired to *fix*.

Now, some leaders stalk meetings like hawks in a field mouse convention. Spot the twitch, swoop in, assert dominance. Others are more spaniel than raptor—good-natured, endlessly hopeful, waiting for the group to self-correct long past the point of rescue. Both instincts have noble roots. Both will get you publicly undressed if you lean on them too hard.

The art lies in the calibration. You must read the room like a novel written in glances[8]. The group isn't asking for constant involvement. It's asking you to hold the space with just enough tension that it doesn't unravel. And when the edge frays, to know whether to stitch it quietly... or burn the thread.

Timing, of course, is the whole game. Intervene too early, and you disempower the group. Intervene too late, and you lose the right to do so. And yes, the difference is often measured in seconds, not minutes. There's no stopwatch. Just signals. The trick is learning to spot them before the moment is gone and you're left posturing at a ghost.

Here's where knowing your style matters. We all walk into the room with a leaning. Kats—your classic 'let's get this sorted' types—tend to strike early and often. They're surgical, decisive, and just a little too excited by the sound of their own authority. Dogs—more relational, more accommodating—prefer to wait, watch, and hope. Which works marvellously until the kats in the room start muttering that no one's driving the bus.

Each type has its moment. But neither should be left to run on autopilot.

Kats must rehearse the sacred pause. One beat longer than feels comfortable. Let the group breathe. Let the tension tell its own story before stepping in. That silence is not a vacuum. It's data[9]. Dogs, meanwhile, need to practice assertive discomfort. Saying the necessary thing before it's perfectly phrased. Cutting across a spiral before it wraps around the whole meeting like cling film on a badly packed sandwich.

And what of the space before the meeting begins? That's where the real management starts. Before names are written on flipcharts or agendas read aloud, the dynamics are already forming. Alliances, anxieties, power tugs in miniature. The room is a simmering stew of anticipation and unspoken tension. You want to get ahead of it before it starts spitting oil.

This is where your eyes do more work than your mouth. Notice who enters early and claims territory. Who lingers at the doorway like they're waiting for a better offer. Who scans the room for allies, and who acts like they'd rather be anywhere else, including a root canal with no anaesthetic. These are not idle social tics. They are early indicators of who may unravel, challenge, disengage, or disrupt.

So you act. Not loudly. Not yet. A well-placed greeting. A shared joke that doesn't punch down. A nod that says: I see you—and I'll still be seeing you when things get interesting. Build that bridge before you need to cross it under fire.

And when it's time to act? Keep your intervention proportionate and your tone congruent. Don't bark when a whisper will do. And don't whisper when the group is silently screaming for you to *do something*.

It's not about knowing what to say. It's about knowing when your silence says too much.

Because in that delicate sliver between tolerance and resentment, your leadership either deepens—or evaporates entirely.

Micro-Leadership Tools

A group doesn't unravel all at once. It frays. Slowly. At the edges. In flickers of eye contact that don't land. In long silences that should have been short. In the polite boredom of people privately deciding this meeting—like so many before it—won't matter.

That's where real leadership lives. Not in grand strategy documents or laminated purpose statements, but in the handful of small moves that make the difference between a session that breathes and one that bleeds out quietly into the carpet.

These are the tools of micro-leadership[10]. Tiny, precise adjustments you make mid-session, often without words, to keep the social machinery from grinding itself into dust.

Let's begin with the least sexy skill in the room: gesture.

A frozen hand—index finger raised slightly while your eyes drop, as though holding a thought—buys you three to five seconds of uninterrupted space[11]. Used sparingly, it can pre-empt an interrupter without ever needing to name them. Used rhythmically, it becomes a metronome the group unconsciously follows[12]. It's the difference between 'wait' and *wait with dignity*.

Then there's the art of visual parking. When a point becomes repetitive, or a tangent begins to unspool into madness, write it down—physically, visibly—off to the side. Not in the spotlight, but close enough for it to feel respected. The message is simple: *We're not dismissing this. We're containing it.* And that containment gives the group permission to refocus without resentment.

Spatial anchoring works too, though it's rarely taught outside drama school or therapy[13]. Establish different locations in the room for different functions—content here, questions there, wrap-up in the centre. Your body becomes a silent signpost. Over time, the group learns that where you *stand* signals what mode you're in. It's choreography, not control.

Now, let's talk about the social currency system. Every participant in a group arrives with an invisible wallet full of 'coupons'—a finite number of social allowances to speak, joke, interrupt, or monologue before the group turns. Most people spend theirs wisely. But the chronic interrupters? The external processors? The anxious oversharers? They burn through theirs before the first break. Your job isn't to revoke their right to speak. It's to signal—clearly, gently—when the tab is closed.

And sometimes that means redirecting attention without confrontation. A sudden shift in eye line. A gesture to another speaker. Even silence, held just long enough to reset the group's rhythm, becomes its own kind of authority. Silence isn't the absence of control—it's its purest form.

Tone, too, does more work than it gets credit for[14]. Flat tone equals credibility. Upward-inflected tone equals permission-seeking. If you want the room to reflect, flatten your tone. Want them to decide? Use pause and gravity. Want them to feel safe enough to disagree? Soften just enough to make dissent feel welcome without handing over the reins.

And then there's the unglamorous magic of asking a question *while modelling the behaviour you want in response*. Want hands up before questions? Ask while raising yours. Want shorter answers? Ask with a narrowed gesture and clipped phrasing. Groups, like schoolchildren and dinner guests, mirror more than they obey[15].

What you're doing in these moments is not enforcing behaviour—it's offering rhythm. Group settings crave structure, even when they pretend otherwise. When you lead with signal, not dominance, you don't just get compliance. You get coherence.

And coherence is what keeps the session from disintegrating the moment someone checks their watch or sighs into their notebook.

The tragedy of most facilitation is that we overestimate the importance of what we say, and underestimate the power of how we move, look, and breathe while we say it[16].

Micro-leadership isn't about doing more. It's about noticing sooner.

The group is already telling you what it needs. Your task is to answer —before it asks aloud.

The Rogues Gallery

A. Asocial Operator

The asocial individual doesn't storm the group. They bypass it entirely.

No fanfare. No eye contact. No appetite for belonging. Just a silent orbit outside the gravitational pull of the team—present in body, absent in spirit. The group is gathering. Meanwhile, the asocial operator is off to one side, scrolling through their phone like it contains the secrets of the universe, or scribbling in a notebook as if they're the only one clever enough to see through the whole charade.

They aren't rude. Not exactly. Just... unavailable.

You might spot them early, the way you'd notice a chess piece in a game of Jenga—technically there, but obviously wrong for the setup.

They don't block progress so much as slow its tempo. And while others are doing the subtle dance of affiliation—mirrored gestures, small talk, nods in shared confusion—the asocial type declines the invitation to join in, as if participation were a contagious disease they're determined to avoid.

And here's where most leaders make their first mistake. They treat this detachment as benign. Maybe even respectful. 'At least they're not disrupting,' they think, with the kind of optimism normally reserved for cats waiting for the dog to change. But detachment *is* disruption—just in its purest, most elegant form. Because an asocial presence doesn't merely opt out of the group. It weakens it. It leaves a hole in the fabric of shared attention, and holes, as anyone with socks or reputations knows, tend to grow.

Worse still, it sets a tone. The asocial operator may not be actively undermining cohesion, but their indifference is contagious. Others begin to model it. Participation drops. Eye contact flutters. The group starts to fragment before it's even formed.

So what's the move?

Not confrontation. That's like trying to train a house cat with a leaf blower. They'll vanish even further into their private fortress. The trick, if it can be called that, is to connect early—before the group proper has gelled—while the rules of engagement are still being written in wet cement.

It doesn't require grand gestures. A quiet welcome. A question asked one-on-one, not because you need an answer, but because you need a bridge. A moment of eye contact held just long enough to signal: 'You matter. And you'll be missed if you ghost us.'

If done well, it grants you something invaluable: leverage.

Because once the session is in full swing and the group needs to unify, the asocial individual becomes your strategic linchpin. Not because they've suddenly become warm and fuzzy—please, let's not be ridiculous—but because you've already seeded the connection. You've made them legible. And that means you can now gently pull them into proximity with others without causing visible recoil.

Positioning helps too. Don't let them sit adrift on the edge like a rejected apostle in a modern-day Last Supper. Place them near connectors—people whose energy is naturally social, but not invasive. Then, mid-session, link the asocial operator to the group non-verbally. A glance. A nod. A gesture that pulls their comment, however minor, into shared space. These cues don't demand participation. They make it possible[17].

You won't win them over with charm. But you might earn a kind of quiet allegiance. Not loyalty, exactly—but the next best thing in a group setting: contribution without resistance.

And when they do speak—eventually, inevitably—don't gush like a primary school teacher faced with a toddler who's eaten a vegetable. Treat it as normal. As expected. Because anything more, and they'll retreat back into the dark, twitching like a hedgehog who's heard applause.

The goal isn't to socialise the asocial. It's to make them part of the social field.

Because a group isn't a group until everyone matters. Even the ones who pretend they don't want to.

B. The Stressed Reactor

Some people walk into a room and set it humming. Others walk in and make it clench.

You know the type. Before they've even spoken, something feels... brittle. The breath's too fast. The voice pitches like a boiling kettle.

Movements lack rhythm. Words arrive half-chewed or not at all. Even their body looks like it's bracing for an earthquake no one else can feel.

This is the Stressed Reactor. Not a saboteur. Not a villain. Just a walking feedback loop of unprocessed anxiety, crackling through the group like faulty wiring.

In some rooms, they're an inconvenience. In others, they're a full-blown hazard.

It depends, largely, on the group's temperament. In a kat-heavy crowd—task-focused, logic-driven, borderline robotic at times—the stressed individual is usually ignored. They're a background flicker on the radar. A twitch in the corner of the frame. Nothing to see here. Let's press on.

But throw that same person into a dog-weighted group—more affiliative, more relationship-driven, less tolerant of unease—and the whole meeting jams like an old cassette. The tension is no longer personal. It's social. The group stalls, not because they dislike the stressed person, but because they can't move forward until they're sure that person is OK. And the longer that reassurance doesn't come, the harder it becomes to get the group back in gear.

So, what does one do with someone whose very *presence* destabilises the tone of the room?

You act before it starts.

You find them early. Not in the middle of their spiral, but in the liminal space before the meeting begins—when coffee is being stirred, chairs scraped back, and people are still wearing the fragile civility of strangers. Approach quietly. Offer a smile that doesn't ask too many questions. Ask one anyway, just to locate them in time and space. Not 'Are you alright?'—that's too blunt. Try 'How are you finding the space today?' or 'What's caught your attention?' Something gentle enough to slip under the wire, but specific enough to start building trust.

Your goal is not to calm them. It's to connect. Anxiety softens in the presence of rapport, not reassurance. And if you can get there before they unravel, you'll have options later.

Now, once the group is gathered, don't ignore the tension. Don't broadcast it either. Simply narrate the obvious: 'There's a lot to take in. Some of us are getting to know each other. Some of us are getting to know the content. We'll take it one step at a time.'

That kind of line—low and credible, without the scent of corporate optimism—does more than soothe. It cues the group that uncertainty is normal. That no one's being singled out. And crucially, that you're driving.

The stressed individual won't disappear. But they'll stabilise enough to participate. And that's the real win.

If you're unlucky, though, they'll still teeter. That's when your tone becomes surgical. Slower. Lower. More grounded than gravity itself. Speak to the room, but shape your voice for the person who's shaking.

And if you're truly unlucky? If their anxiety starts to leak, visibly, into the emotional climate? That's when you lean on the relationship you seeded earlier. A glance. A grounding gesture. Something that says: *Still here. Still with you. Keep going.*

You're not just managing a disruption. You're managing a nervous system[18]. One that's broadcasting live on all frequencies. One that's begging—silently—for safety.

Get it right, and the group breathes again. Get it wrong, and you'll spend the rest of the session chasing clarity that fled when anxiety walked in.

Because groups don't move faster than their slowest nervous system[19]. And the stressed reactor—though accidental—can stall the whole show.

Your job isn't to fix them. It's to make space for them without letting the centre collapse.

It's hard. It's delicate. And it's the difference between holding the room—and losing it one breath at a time.

C. The Victim Player

If asocials ghost the group and stressed reactors radiate tension, then the victim player brings a different storm entirely—one that arrives dressed in helplessness and leaves the room gasping for air.

At first glance, they seem harmless enough. Meek, hesitant, self-effacing. But give it time, and they'll begin to unfold like a well-worn grievance letter. Their energy is sticky. Their language, fogged with blame. Everything is too much, too soon, too unfair. If you're lucky, they'll merely stall the group's progress. If you're not, they'll reroute the entire conversation toward the black hole of their own disempowerment—and dare anyone to challenge them.

Here's the thing about victims. They're not operating on the usual rules of engagement. Negotiators talk about win-win, win-lose. Victims aim for lose-lose. You suffer, they suffer, and somehow, that levels the field.

They won't say that, of course. What they'll say is: 'No one ever listens to me.' Or 'I tried, but what's the point?' Or that perennial classic: 'It's not my fault.' The performance is always slightly off-centre—just believable enough to slip under the radar, just dramatic enough to fracture the group's rhythm.

You'll see it in their posture. Slumped, but ready to recoil. Their voice, either flat or tremulous, never assertive. They might not make eye contact, but they'll make everyone else feel watched. Their favourite trick is to wait until the group has just about recovered its flow... then sigh. Loudly. The kind of sigh that should come with its own soundtrack and lighting rig.

leaders, understandably, find themselves torn. Challenge the victim, and you risk looking like the villain. Ignore them, and they drag the room into a low-level emotional hostage situation. You can almost hear the group whisper: *Someone please do something. But not me.*

What they want, more than anything, is confirmation. Not of their competence, but of their suffering. If you snap at them, they win. If you validate their helplessness, they win again. It's a rigged game—and they're the only ones holding the rulebook.

The first move is to stay side-on. Literally. Don't square up. Sit or stand at ninety degrees. Don't give them full eye contact; it only amplifies their need to perform. This isn't rudeness—it's design. You're de-escalating the emotional frame without denying the person.

Next, don't get drawn into their narrative swamp. Stay anchored in the issue. When they deflect or blame, respond with something that punctures the loop gently but firmly: 'Whether or not that's true, the issue is...' It's like clearing fog with a torch beam—just enough to find the path again.

Keep your rules visible. Victims thrive in ambiguity because it gives them plausible deniability. Clarity corners them. Not in a cruel way —just enough to show that they're not exempt from the social contract[20].

But above all, you need a strategy that's as paradoxical as they are: persistent proximity. Look for moments—brief, human ones—when the victim mask slips. It might be a dry joke, a flash of curiosity, a moment of calm when they forget to defend themselves. That's your window. Build from there. Not urgently. Not obviously. Just enough to plant the idea that participation doesn't always require suffering.

Because, strangely enough, most victim players don't want to feel this way. They just don't know what to do without the pain. It's familiar. It gets attention. It lets them win without taking responsibility.

And if you can offer something better—belonging without performance, contribution without collapse—you might just coax them out of the hole they've dug and curled up in.

But don't rush it. Hope grows slowly. And in rooms like this, it often enters sideways.

These early disruptors are mood-based[21]. They shift the emotional weather before anyone speaks. Their presence is often felt more than heard—through silence, posture, or a sigh loud enough to register on the Richter scale of group tension. But not all disruption is quiet. Some arrives dressed in words—too many, too loud, too soon.

And when that happens, it's not the atmosphere you're managing. It's the tempo. The bandwidth. The very rhythm of the group's shared attention.

In the next chapter, we meet the verbal disruptors—the ones who speak to think, speak to block, speak to dominate, or speak so often they fracture the group's patience. And we learn how to lead when language becomes the very thing that unravels the work.

THIRTEEN
DISARMING THE VERBAL HIJACKER
ENFORCING BOUNDARIES & PROTECTING THE GROUP

NOT ALL DISRUPTION IS A FEELING. Some of it is a frequency. If Chapter 12 I dealt with the *mood-based disruptors*—those who enter a room and change its temperature—then this chapter deals with the *word-based ones*. The talkers. The repeaters. The over-articulators and under-regulators. They don't sit back and stall. They jump in, fill the air, and pull the group's focus like an emotional magnet taped to a microphone.

They don't mean harm. *Usually.* But intention isn't the issue. Impact is. And unless the leader learns to respond with precision—rather than panic—these voices can dominate the airwaves while everyone else quietly tunes out.

The reason that the last chapter in 'Non-Verbal Leadership' is about disarming verbal hijackers is because, in the most part, this is not done with slick argumentation, reasoning or reframes. The lion's share of the disarming is done non-verbally - with the use of tone, eye-contact, use of the space, going visual and the other tactical non-verbal tools[1]. Yes, there is some micro-dialogue but the true impact is the use of non-verbal micro-skills

. . .

The External Auditory **Processor**

Some people think to themselves. Others insist on thinking at you.

These are the external auditory processors—those tireless narrators of their own internal monologue who, once prompted, talk like it's a form of cardiovascular exercise. They don't interrupt to disrupt. They interrupt because silence is their enemy and linear thought, a distant acquaintance. Their questions are rarely actual questions. They're spoken drafts. Warm-ups. Loops. Echoes.

And to the rest of the group? It feels like being held hostage by a podcast no one subscribed to.

At first, they seem engaged—eager, even. You say one thing; they raise a hand. You get half a slide in; they're already asking if you'll cover that other thing from three slides ahead. Then they ask again, just to make sure. Then they tell you what they think the answer is. Then they double back on their own logic mid-sentence and rephrase it three ways from Sunday. By which time, of course, no one remembers what the original point was. Least of all them.

In small doses, they're tolerable. In large ones, they're a virus in the group's tempo.

And when there are three of them? Welcome to The Talking Dead—where the session becomes a slow march through unedited commentary, and the rest of the group gradually learns to hate learning.

The trouble isn't malice. It's method. External auditories process thought out loud. They need to speak to understand[2]. Unfortunately, they often need to speak a lot.

Each group member—consciously or not—gives them a few tokens of grace. A smile. A nod. A pretend-listening face. But these tokens run out fast. The longer the auditory monopolises airtime, the more the group disengages. And the more they disengage, the more the auditory fills the silence. The result? A conversational ouroboros—eating its own tail while the leader weeps quietly inside.

So, what do you do when someone is thinking so loudly it drowns out the room?

First: satisfy, satisfy, delay. That is, answer their first question with grace. Their second with structure. Then, the third time they raise their hand—or worse, don't—hold your ground.

'That's a good question. Let's bookmark it for the Q&A.'

And keep speaking prosodically. Eyes to the group. Not back to the offender. You're redirecting flow without feeding the loop.

Second: watch the warning signs. Auditory processors don't just speak—they signal[3]. A shift in the seat. A hand grazing the face. Eyebrows lifting like early warning flags. Learn their tells, and you can intercept non-verbally. A held hand, palm down. A subtle head tilt. A 'wait' gesture that's more monk than manager. Calm, congruent, and crucially, not reactive.

Space helps. Literally. Have a spot in the room where questions happen. And a different one for content delivery. Move to the Q&A spot when you're ready to receive, and return to your content position to reclaim focus. Like stage lighting, but cheaper.

And when the group is large or low-trust? Model it. Say: 'Are there any questions?' while raising your hand. This gives auditory types a cue to pause and consider whether their contribution is valuable—or just habitual. If they still speak, so be it. But at least you've framed the ritual. You've added friction to the compulsion.

Privately, if the behaviour persists, approach with precision. Never:

'You talk too much'.

Instead:

'You've got a strong auditory processing style. In groups, that can slow things down. What helps is writing the question down and watching when others raise their hand. That'll help you track your timing'.

You're not criticising. You're offering a toolkit[4].

Done well, this lands as helpful. Done badly, it activates shame—and shame is the fastest way to double their volume[5].

The goal isn't to silence the auditories. It's to help them self-regulate. Because once they do, the room breathes again. And so do you.

They're not trying to hijack the group. They're just trying to keep up with themselves.

Help them do that, and they might just start helping the group too.

THE LOOPING REPEATER

Some disruptions arrive like thunderstorms—loud, sudden, and obvious. Others seep into the room like a leaky tap: soft, repetitive, and maddening in the way they slowly erode everyone's will to live.

Enter the looping repeater. Their contribution, at first, is perfectly acceptable. Even useful. They make a point. It lands. Heads nod. Pens scribble. We move on. Except they don't.

They bring it up again. And again. Not exactly the same words, but close enough to count as déjà vu. The phrasing shifts, the emphasis changes, but the destination remains precisely where it was the first time: firmly lodged in the leader's patience and the group's dwindling attention span.

If ignored, they'll return to it like a homing pigeon with obsessive-compulsive tendencies. If acknowledged too eagerly, they take it as licence to set up permanent camp there. Either way, it becomes a sinkhole—swallowing time, energy, and the will to collaborate.

The group, to its credit, will try. Side-glances. Stiffened posture. Subtle sighs. But if the looping continues unchecked, the room settles into a state of collective despair—a sense that we're trapped in a conversational purgatory where the only sin was showing up.

So what's actually happening here?

In many cases, the repeater isn't being difficult. They're stuck. Genuinely stuck. Their brain has latched onto a piece of information like a dog with a slipper, and now they can't let go until someone acknowledges that yes, it *is* a slipper, and yes, it *has* been seen. Multiple times. From every conceivable angle[6].

Here's how to handle it without resorting to murder or self-hypnosis.

First, give the issue a place to go. A literal one. Write it down. Not front-and-centre, but off to the side. A 'parking lot', if you must, though preferably without calling it that unless you enjoy sounding like a human whiteboard marker. Label it with their words. Say:

'Let's jot that here so we can come back to it later.'

That single gesture tells them: you've been heard. You're not being dismissed. But we are, collectively, moving on.

Second, when they loop again—and they will—gesture to what you've written. Don't meet their gaze. Don't get pulled into a dialogue. Just point. Calmly. Neutrally. As if to say:

We've stored that. The system is working. Now let's proceed.

If they persist, then it's time for a firmer nudge. Still polite. Still professional. But with a hint of steel under the velvet. Try:

'Is what you're saying different from what we've already captured?'

Then pause. Let the silence do some of the heavy lifting. If they waffle, move on. The pause is the punctuation mark that tells the group: the page is turning.

And if all else fails? Shift the medium. Go visual. Visuals don't loop. They clarify[7]. Present information in diagrams, models, or mapped language. Let the conversation move forward on the whiteboard, not just in the air. It breaks the spell. Gives the group a new reference point. And quietly signals that the loop is closed.

Looping isn't sabotage. It's a sign of conceptual glue that hasn't quite set[8]. But if you let it dry in the middle of the discussion, everything else gets stuck too.

The goal isn't to stop repetition entirely. Just to make sure it doesn't become the soundtrack to your slow, spiralling descent into group dysfunction.

THE BLOCKER

There's always one. The moment you unveil the plan—your carefully worded introduction, your clear objectives, your mild and wholly unthreatening agenda—they lean back in their chair, cross their arms like they're protecting ancient secrets, and mutter something like:

'This'll never work.'

The Blocker doesn't wait for proof. They operate on prophecy[9].

Their gift—if you can call it that—is the ability to spot flaws before they exist, discredit strategies still in nappies, and rally unspoken resistance with nothing more than a well-timed scoff.

They're not obstructive by accident. This is performance resistance. Crafted, curated, and timed to land when the room is most vulnerable to doubt. And they don't always speak first—but they speak *loudest*. Not in volume, but in impact. Because nothing derails group momentum quite like a sigh laced with sarcasm and the line,

'We tried this before. It failed then too.'

Here's the cruel irony: the Blocker is often right. Not completely. Not helpfully. But right enough to make a mess. And what they're playing for isn't insight. It's influence. The power of 'I told you so'—pre-delivered.

So, how do you get out in front of someone whose mission is to undercut the show before the curtains have even opened? *You pre-empt the sabotage.*

Don't wait for them to roll their eyes like they're auditioning for Hamlet. You get there first. You lace your introduction with humour that undercuts their shtick before they have the chance to deploy it.

Say:

'Now, I know some of us are already sharpening our objections—Hank, I'm looking at you—but let's suspend disbelief just long enough to get through the next twenty minutes.'

Delivered with a smile. A slight lean. Enough irony to amuse the room and <u>disarm the assassin</u>.

What you've done is cornered them. If they object now, they're proving you right. If they hold back, you've bought space. Either way, you've rewritten the script. This isn't humiliation. It's *inoculation*.

You've named the weather before it could rain. Some blockers prefer subtlety—a raised eyebrow here, a dismissive shrug there—but the logic remains the same: they grandstand to shape group sentiment. So if they expect to be the first voice of reason, you take that spotlight away before it's theirs to steal.

If they still press on? *Then mirror their tone, but change the direction.*

When they say:

'Management's just doing this to tick a box'

Respond with:

'And yet, here we all are—tick boxes and all. Let's see what else we can make of it.'

You're not denying their view. You're denying it sole ownership of the narrative. And if they're particularly determined—relentless, even—you may have to name the game more directly.

'I appreciate the scepticism. It's useful. It keeps us honest. But let's agree to play the first half before calling the score'

You're framing contribution without giving the Blocker veto power.

Because left unchecked, blockers don't just challenge you—they recruit. Slowly. Persuasively. They convert mild doubt into collective drag, and before long, you're not facilitating a session. You're negotiating the release of hostages.

Your best move? Beat them to the punchline. Use humour with teeth - a chiding attitude and tone. Cast their protest before they can. And keep the room facing forward. Blockers aren't born. They're grown in cultures where cynicism is currency[10]. Change the currency, and you change the dynamic. They can't resist every group. Only the ones unsure if they want to be led.

THE BULLY

Not every disruption comes wrapped in apology. Some stride into the room fully inflated, convinced the air belongs to them.

The bully doesn't interrupt to clarify or think aloud or test the logic of a process. The bully interrupts to win. To dominate. To stamp their boot print on the middle of the conversation and dare anyone to clean it up.

Most leaders, if they're honest, feel it before it starts. The room tightens when the bully speaks. Heads don't turn—they stiffen. The group becomes quieter, but not in the reflective, engaged way[11].

Quieter like hostages. Waiting to see who'll speak next and what it will cost.

And if you're waiting for the group to help you out—don't.

The bully has already short-circuited the room's safety. No one will roll their eyes, sigh, or even look irritated. Because the thing about bullies is that they watch. For weakness. For disloyalty. For signs that someone in the group might not be on their side.

So the rest of the room goes still. Not peaceful-still. Prison-yard still. Because they've all made the same calculation: *Better them than me.*

The bully, of course, interprets this silence as validation. *'No one's disagreeing,'* they'll say, entirely missing the point. No one's breathing, either.

If you confront them with the impact of their behaviour, they'll deflect like it's an Olympic sport:

'I'm just being honest.'

'People are too sensitive these days.'

Or the gold medal standard:

'I'm saying what everyone else is thinking.'

Which is only true if 'everyone else' is a small committee of rage-filled sock puppets.

Now here's the real twist. Counselling doesn't work. Not with bullies. Not in the way we like to believe it does. Because bullies aren't unaware of their effect—they're insulated from it. No feedback, no mirroring, no signal from the group ever lands. Their social radar's either broken or tuned exclusively to themselves.

So don't waste your time trying to generate insight. They won't have a revelation halfway through your tactful feedback. There will be no tearful apology. They'll just think you're weak enough to lecture, but not strong enough to stop them.

Which means you stop them. Not with cruelty. Not with drama. With clarity. The only thing that manages a bully is the thing they use themselves: power[12]. But with one key difference—you use it for the group, not against it. You intervene not to punish, but to protect.

'Let's pause there. We've heard your point, and now we're moving on.'

'I'm asking for one voice at a time. That includes everyone.'

Or, when necessary:

'This space only works if people feel safe enough to speak. That includes how we challenge, not just what we say.'

Say it in front of the group. Calmly. Unshakably. Not to embarrass, but to signal:

The rules apply here. To *everyone*[13].

This is where fairness earns its paycheque. Fairness isn't about treating everyone identically. It's about protecting the social contract. When a bully breaks it, you step in. Not privately. Not later. In the moment. Because that's when the group needs to see you mean it.

If you're inconsistent, you lose the group. If you hedge, they stop looking to you. And if you let the bully dictate the tone, the room begins to hollow out—internally, then collectively. What's left is a performance of cooperation, played out by people who've already opted out[14].

But get it right, and something changes. The group recalibrates. Shoulders drop. Eye contact returns. People remember they're allowed to think out loud without flinching.

And the bully? They might sulk. Or smirk. Or try again later with a different mask. But the power's been reshuffled. Not seized—*restored*.

Because leadership isn't about out-bullying the bully. It's about refusing to let dominance masquerade as contribution. And sometimes the greatest gift you give a group isn't inspiration. It's a room where everyone feels safe before they speak.

Recovery & Repair

Every leader eventually gets it wrong. You missed the cue. Waited too long. Stepped in too hard. Backed down when you should've held. The moment passed—and with it, your authority seemed to slip, as if dropped behind the flipchart never to be found again. It's not failure. It's the job.

Because no matter how many tactics you master, no one reads the room perfectly every time[15]. And in complex group dynamics, recovery matters more than precision. What earns you long-term permission isn't your ability to get it right. It's how you carry yourself when you don't[16].

This is where the social contract wobbles. Not broken, but strained—like a trampoline that's held too much weight in one spot. The group starts to bounce differently. They hold back. They test you. They fill the silences with suspicion. It's not mutiny, exactly. But they're no longer lending you their attention for free.

So, you begin the repair. Not with apology—that's often too much. And not with denial—that's always too little. But with acknowledgment.

Label the moment, briefly, with just enough candour to make it breathable again.

'That last section dragged a little—let's reset.' Or:

'We lost the thread for a bit there—here's where we pick it back up.'

These aren't confessions. They're recalibrations. What you're doing is narrating the shared reality the group didn't know it was allowed to mention. And in doing so, you restore the unspoken bond: we're still in this together.

If an individual was involved—especially one who disrupted, challenged, or destabilised—address it with timing, not heat. Don't let the tail wag the room. Instead, reassert group rhythm first[17]. Then, when possible, find a moment—offline, off-script—to reconnect. Not to chastise. To rehumanise.

'That bit earlier—are we OK?' is sometimes all it takes.

It's not about agreement. It's about consent to continue.

And if the disruption was yours?

- If you snapped.
- If you overreached.
- If you misread the gaze and crushed the group with a tone better suited to courtroom drama.

Then offer grace by modelling it. A shrug. A reset. A wry remark that carries no shame but signals:

> 'Yes, I noticed. And yes, we can move on.'

Because leadership doesn't require perfection. It requires coherence. The group doesn't want you flawless. They want you steady. Capable of adjusting. Willing to see what's really happening beneath the words. And able to do something about it without making the room pay for your misstep.

When you repair well, something odd happens. The group relaxes too. Not because you're back in control, but because they no longer have to carry the tension inside themselves. It's released.

That's the unspoken deal at the heart of every gathering: we'll give you our attention, if you'll carry our safety. Drop it—and we'll retreat. Restore it—and we'll return. This social contract isn't inked in rules. It's written in rhythm. Learn to hear when it skips. And learn how to start the beat again.

Leading Without Losing

Leadership in a group setting is not about knowing what to say. It's about knowing when not to flinch. It's about standing there—when the victim sighs dramatically, the bully circles, the external processor revs up again like a faulty leaf blower—and not reacting like a toddler near a wasp. Not folding. Not flaring. Just... holding.

Because while the group may have come for the content, they'll stay —or drift—for your presence. They're not watching for expertise. They're watching your spine[18].

Do you wobble when challenged? Do you talk faster when silence enters the room? Do your gestures speed up, your words thin out, your breathing vanish up into your clavicle when someone disagrees with you? They see it. They feel it. And if you're not stable, they won't feel safe.

This is what it means to lead without losing. Not dominance. Not control. Not charisma, although it never hurts. It's containment. It's composure. It's the ability to be the still point in the conversational cyclone while everyone else is fumbling for a flipchart marker and a metaphor that makes sense.

Your default style may lean kat or dog. You may prefer assertion or deference, structure or flow, command or coaxing. But if you want to lead groups—properly lead them—you'll need more than your natural lean. You'll need choice. You'll need to develop range.

That means knowing when to pause when everything in your body wants to fix. When to act before you're ready. When to say less than you know. When to look someone in the eye and say 'That's enough' like it's not up for debate. And when to welcome a half-formed, possibly ludicrous question from someone who's finally found the courage to speak.

Leadership is not about winning every moment. It's about earning the next one. Because in a group, you don't inherit authority. You lease it. In minutes. In glances. In the way you respond to tension and uncertainty without reaching for volume or validation.

You lead best when you stop trying to look like a leader[19]. When you stop managing perception and start managing energy. Space. Rhythm. Safety. And so we end the last chapter as we begin the book:

Your neurological state the atmosphere the group breathes[20]. Get that right, and the content delivers itself.

LEADERSHIP LESSONS FROM PART II
SIGNAL, SPACE & SHARED RHYTHM

Signal Awareness

1. **You broadcast before you speak.**
   - Posture, eye focus, breath rhythm, and tempo arrive first. Words follow late.
2. **Your state is read in milliseconds.**
   - Others' nervous systems register your coherence—or your panic—before logic has a chance.
3. **Attention is spatial.**
   - Leadership begins with where and how you direct focus—visually, gesturally, and through stillness.
4. **Signal congruence beats verbal skill.**
   - If your shoulders say stress and your words say "all good," the body wins.
5. **Trust is built through micro-signals.**
   - It's not one grand gesture—it's thousands of tiny, matching ones over time.

Geometry of Presence

1. **Your body shapes the emotional map of a room.**
   - Where you place yourself—and how—creates zones of power, welcome, or disconnection.
2. **Triangles build unity.**
   - When you gesture between two people, you bind them into a shared signal field.
3. **Speak to one, move the many.**
   - Precision in gesture and gaze allows your influence to scale without dilution.
4. **Movement changes status.**
   - Deliberate shifts in position, gesture, or breath recalibrate group attention and authority.
5. **Stillness is leadership gravity.**
   - When everything else is noisy, your stillness becomes the centre of the room.

Non-Verbal Rapport

1. **Rapport is rhythm, not mimicry.**
   - Breath, gesture, tone, and timing matter more than words or mirroring.
2. **Posture matching signals safety.**
   - Aligning with another's body cues the message: "You're okay."
3. **Pacing builds permission.**
   - Match first. Then guide subtly—through breath, tone, tempo—into the next state.
4. **Congruence builds trust. Mirroring builds pathway.**
   - Once you reflect what's real for them, you earn the right to shift it.
5. **Rapport is co-regulation, not manipulation.**

- You're not controlling their state. You're stabilising the bridge between yours and theirs.

DISARMING DISRUPTION

1. **Disruption is a signal, not a threat.**
   - Hijackers aren't always hostile. They're often unmet needs in search of certainty.
2. **Meet the need. Quiet the noise.**
   - Control, attention, or significance—disruption softens when the underlying hunger is addressed.
3. **Use your body, not your rebuttal.**
   - Eye contact, breath, stillness, and space calm better than arguments do.
4. **Breathe. Break. Broaden.**
   - Pause your state. Interrupt theirs. Widen the group's field of attention.
5. **Presence dissolves chaos faster than persuasion.**
   - A dysregulated system doesn't respond to logic—it responds to congruent calm.

EMBODIED LEADERSHIP

1. **You are the room's thermostat.**
   - Your nervous system sets the tone—before any strategy is voiced.
2. **The group watches your breath more than your slides.**
   - Calm, grounded breathing is leadership's most trusted signal.
3. **Quiet authority signals confidence.**
   - You don't need to shout to be followed. Stillness is the new signal of strength.

4. **In wobble, offer rhythm.**
    - Breath, gesture, tempo—these recalibrate the group more reliably than reassurance.
5. **Confidence isn't louder—it's cleaner.**
    - When your body matches your message, influence flows without effort.

Field Notes for the Real World

1. **Space is emotional.**
   - Where you place your body shapes how others place their attention—and their trust.
2. **The mouth lies. The breath doesn't.**
   - Your breathing reveals your state. Others read it before you do.
3. **Rapport isn't always comfort.**
   - Sometimes it's holding tension with integrity, not smoothing it over.
4. **Direction changes feeling.**
   - A shift in gaze, gesture, or stance reorients not just focus—but group emotion.
5. **Silence is a leadership act.**
   - It says, "I trust the space. You can too."
6. **A dysregulated room can't hear you.**
   - If the group is in threat response, your message won't land. Calm is the precondition to clarity.
7. **Your hands speak.**
   - Every gesture includes or excludes, invites or cuts off. Use them wisely.
8. **You are choreographing constantly.**
   - Steps, freezes, turns, lean-ins—they're all cues to the group's emotional syntax.
9. **Visuals reframe power.**
   - When verbal loops hijack the room, switch to diagram or object—shift focus from ego to structure.
10. **You are punctuation.**
    - Breath = comma. Stillness = full stop. Gesture = italics. Your presence is the grammar of group coherence.

CONCLUSION TO PART II
THE QUIET SIGNALS THAT LEAD

Before a decision is made, before strategy is voiced, and long before trust is earned, something quieter happens. A flicker. A breath. A moment of presence. It isn't on the agenda, but the room responds. Not to a slide deck. Not to a polished pitch. To a signal—unspoken, embodied, and very often unnoticed[1].

This is how leadership begins. Not with volume, but with coherence. And not with authority in name, but with authority in posture, in stillness, in the sense that someone is truly *here*. Present. Reading the moment. Holding the room. This is not the theatre of performance. It is something older, and deeper: an animal recognition that this person's presence *matters*[2].

That moment—the microseconds before speech—often determines what happens next. Whether tension escalates or eases. Whether a team leans in or folds their arms. Whether a conversation becomes a negotiation or a silent power struggle. It happens fast. But it is not magic. And it is not luck. It is a signal. And signals can be shaped[3].

We have spent this section exploring the craft of that shaping. Not through scripts or slogans, but through breath, tone, gaze, and stance. Through pacing a room not to dominate it, but to attune to it. Through adjusting the temperature of a moment—not with words, but with presence.

But before all that becomes strategy, it must be recognised for what it is: the most human, and the most primal, layer of leadership.

People do not respond to your title. Not at first. They respond to your nervous system[4]. They read your face, your breath, your movement, and your stillness. They respond not to what you say, but to what you signal when you're not saying anything at all.

This is why a team can trust a leader who says little but *means* everything—and distrust a smooth-talking executive whose presence rings hollow. Why a field medic can calm a panicked crowd with just her eyes and steady voice. Why a single nod, offered at the right moment, can feel like a lifeline.

If leadership is influence under pressure, then non-verbal leadership is its most reliable instrument. It begins not by convincing others of your power, but by calming their uncertainty. Not by commanding attention, but by rewarding it.

This is the silent threshold of leadership. And to cross it, you do not need charisma. You need congruence.

Before you speak, you are already leading. The only question is whether it's by design—or by default.

What You Transmit Before You Speak

Every room is a conversation before a word is spoken. People walk in with their own weather systems—some humid with worry, others breezy with ease. The leader's job is not to impose control over that emotional climate, but to stabilise it—to create a kind of internal isobar, where clarity can emerge and pressure can be read accurately.

But this is only possible if the leader has first done the quieter work: noticing their own forecast.

You walk into a high-stakes meeting. The client is waiting. Tensions are expected. Your team has rehearsed, but the margins are tight. Now, without warning, you feel it—jaw tightening, chest bracing, thoughts narrowing like a tunnel. These shifts are not decisions. They're responses. And unless caught, they will govern what comes next.

This is the hinge moment. Not when you're asked the tough question, or when the tone in the room sharpens. No—this is the earlier pivot, where your system begins to prepare. The art lies in what you do with that preparation.

If you are unaware, you will transmit exactly what you feel: tension, tightness, a flicker of fear disguised as overconfidence. You will project it in your breath, in your gaze, in the way your hands hold the table too tightly. You won't mean to. But it will be read.

Yet if you are aware—if you notice the shift, accept it without judgement, and choose to engage differently—then the transmission changes. You reclaim agency. Not over the outcome, but over the signal. You steady your own pulse not to appear calm, but to become it. And that becomes the pattern others align to[5].

This is not about controlling your state like a performer on stage. It is about owning your state as a point of signal integrity. When others feel you are congruent—internally aligned, externally grounded—they relax. Not because the risk is gone, but because the ambiguity is[6]. In that moment, you stop being one more pressure in the room. You become a point of orientation.

This is how authority is earned—not by cleverness, or title, or sheer volume, but by how fluently you can navigate your own interior weather. By how little distortion exists between what you feel, what you know, and what you show.

And it is here that the myth of control begins to collapse in favour of something more powerful: responsiveness.

The best leaders don't suppress instinct. They step above it, reshape it, and use it as raw material. They know that nerves are not failure—they are energy to be redirected. They know that the wobble in the gut is not weakness—it is the body scanning for signals. And they learn to work with these impulses, not against them[7].

Agency, then, is not about overriding your instincts. It is about making space between impulse and action. A pause wide enough for choice. A breath long enough for presence. That space—tiny, practiced, deliberate—is where leadership lives.

In that space, what you transmit before you speak becomes not just a reflection of your past patterns, but a signal of who you are becoming. And the room responds.

Trust, Timing, and the Wordless Bond

Picture two strangers seated opposite one another. Nothing has been said yet, but already an exchange has begun. A slight shift in posture. A flicker of eye contact. One breath held, another released. Before words appear, signals ripple between bodies like sonar[8]. If they attune, rapport emerges. If they jar, resistance thickens. Most never realise what happened. But leaders must.

You can speak all you like of vision, values, and intent—but in the early moments of contact, none of those register first. What registers is safety. Recognition. Whether you feel present or distracted, congruent or conflicted. In the space before speech, the body becomes the biography. You are read before you are heard.

And it is in this reading that trust is either sparked or smothered.

We are taught to think of trust as an outcome of agreement. But trust is rarely built by consensus—it's built by cadence. It lives in the timing of your nod, the patience in your pause, the warmth behind your glance. These are not minor gestures. They are the bedrock of human connection. Rapport, in its deepest form, is not built by similarity but by synchrony[9].

When a leader tunes to the room—mirrors its tempo, honours its resistance, matches its mood without pandering—they communicate something rare: I see you. I am here. I am with you, not above you. From that place, alignment becomes possible. Not because it is forced, but because the conditions for trust have been met.

We think of empathy as a soft skill. In high-stakes leadership, it is more like sonar[10]. The ability to read a room without needing it to reassure you. The capacity to sense where others are, not just where you wish they'd be. This is not about being agreeable. It is about being attuned.

It is the reason some people can say difficult things and still be followed. Their message rides on a current of trust already laid down in silence.

This is why the best communicators don't rush their message. They build a bridge first. Often with nothing but their eyes, their breath, their presence. And only once that bridge holds weight do they step across with words.

In a world saturated with noise, people no longer trust what is said. They trust what is felt. A leader who says 'I care' but transmits urgency will be read as anxious, not compassionate. A speaker who declares openness but cuts off questions is telling the truth with their tone, not their text. And so, the work of connection lies in aligning what is spoken with what is signalled.

To lead well is to become legible.

Not by simplifying yourself. But by aligning your signals—inner and outer—so that others can orient themselves by your clarity.

Because people don't follow ideas. They follow people who make them feel safe to explore those ideas.

And in the quiet seconds before you speak, that decision is already being made.

The Leader Message & Medium

There are rooms that change when someone enters. Not because they speak, not because they claim authority—but because their very presence says something. Before a word is uttered, the room calibrates. You've likely felt it. The hush that falls. The shift in posture. A sense of gravity that wasn't there before.

What you're witnessing in that moment is not performance. It's alignment. The invisible symmetry between inner state and outer signal. The body, in such cases, is no longer merely a carrier of language. It has become the language. And the leader, whether they know it or not, has become the medium[11].

This is where the real craft of non-verbal leadership takes root—not in mimicry or surface signals, but in the deeper art of embodiment. Because influence is not projected. It is transmitted. Not layered on top of who you are, but radiating from what you've aligned.

To lead in complex systems, especially under pressure, is to be watched before you are heard. The way you walk into a room. Where you pause. How long you breathe before speaking. Each moment says more than most messages ever will. And if those signals carry contradiction—if the voice says calm but the breath says panic—people won't believe the content. They'll believe the state[12].

This is not to say you must be flawless. Quite the opposite. The goal is not to perform composure, but to craft it. Not to feign certainty, but to develop a way of being that holds steady even as conditions shift. The kind of steadiness that comes not from suppression, but from rehearsal. Not from ego, but from practice. Because here's the deeper truth: your state is not just personal. It is systemic[13].

In any group, people don't just listen to the leader. They take their cues from them. Emotional states spread. Breath patterns synchronise. Tension echoes. Calm cascades. The group's capacity to stay connected under pressure begins, quite often, in the silent radius around one person. Which means: the work you do on yourself isn't private. It's contagious.

A leader who understands this doesn't just 'manage' themselves. They craft their state in advance of the room. They rehearse not just what they'll say, but how they'll breathe while saying it. They don't wait until the crisis hits to centre themselves. They arrive already centred. Already tuned. Already ready to co-regulate those around them with nothing more than a nod, a breath, a pause that reminds people they're not alone[14].

And when you do this well—when your words match your walk, when your gaze lands with both clarity and kindness—you don't just deliver a message. You become the message. You carry the strategy in your body. You model the permission others need. You signal, without saying so, that presence under pressure is possible.

That's not charisma. That's signal congruence. That's the result of inner and outer states singing the same note[15].

When those around you feel it, they don't just respond. They remember. Because your signals, like theirs, bypass conscious reasoning. They enter through the body. They lodge in memory. They become reference points people return to long after the moment has passed.

The question, then, is not simply how to 'look like' a leader. It is how to live as one—internally structured, externally aligned, and capable of transmitting stability through signal.

Because in the end, when pressure rises and plans unravel, the strategy that matters most will not be on paper. It will be in you.

TECHNIQUE SUMMARIES II
TOOLS FOR RAPPORT, REGULATION & REAL-TIME INFLUENCE

Ex 1. Eye Accessing Cue Calibration
— Increased Precision, Empathy & Influence —

1) Baseline Calibration

In relaxed casual moments, ask 3–4 sensory-rich questions:

- "What colour was your first car?"
- "What song have you played too often lately?"
- "How do you feel the project has been going?"

As they answer, quietly observe their where do they look for visual, auditory or kinaesthetic recall. This gives you their personal 'signal map'—a baseline.

2) Note the Pattern

Every person has their own default pattern. Forget the textbook chart. You're not diagnosing—you're *noticing*. After a few more questions, you'll begin to see reliable directions for:

- *Memory vs. imagination*
- *Emotion vs. logic*
- *Visual vs. auditory processing*

This is their *thinking geometry*. It's valuable for pacing, timing, and emotional leadership.

3) Apply It in Live Interactions

In a meeting or coaching moment, pay attention to eye shifts when you ask:

• "What's your take on this situation?"

• "Where do you see the risk?"

• "What would success look like here?"

Their glance patterns offer subtle clues:

• *Visual construction* → they're inventing a mental image

• *Auditory recall* → remembering someone else's voice

• *Down-right shift* → contact with feelings

This isn't about calling it out. It's about attuning by *listening with your eyes.*

4) Combine with Congruence Checks

If someone says, "I'm confident," but their tone is tight and their eyes dart downward, something's mismatched. Eye cues help detect these moments of *incongruence*—and open the door to ask:

> Can I check something?
> I'm sensing there's more going on for you.

This builds psychological safety and trust, without confrontation.

Ex 2. Shifting Perceptual Positions
— *Improving Leadership by Switching Perceptual Positions* —

1) Notice Where You're Standing Mentally

- Pause before or during a conversation.
    - Ask: *"What <u>hat</u> am I currently wearing?"*
- Become aware of your current perceptual position:
    - *Red* (1st), *Yellow* (2nd), or *Green* (3rd).

2) Recognise the Red Hat (Self-as-Centre)

- You're in your own head.
- Focused on *your* feelings, thoughts, story, and performance.
- Useful for authenticity and drive—but prone to blind spots.
- Signals: long monologues, rising emotional intensity, belief that passion = truth.

Ask:

> *"Am I assuming that because I feel it strongly, it must be true for everyone?"*

3) Shift to the Yellow Hat (Other-as-Centre)

- Imagine looking through the other person's eyes.
- Focus on reading micro-signals: tone, breath, posture, eye movement, pauses.

Two core questions:

1. *"What are they doing?"*
2. *"What does that suggest they're feeling?"*

- Don't assume agreement—observe with curiosity.

Signals: leaning in, softening expression, subtle body mirroring.

4) Zoom Out to the Green Hat (Observer-as-Centre)

- Step back from both perspectives.
- Watch the full dynamic as if from above or outside.
- Notice group energy, role patterns, rhythm, who's leading and who's losing presence.

Signals: quiet attentiveness, strategic stillness, seeing timing and power shifts.

5) **Practise Fluid Transitions**

Great leadership is not about wearing one hat all the time—it's about *shifting fluidly*.

Ask:

1. *"Is this hat still helping?"*
2. *"Is it time to shift?"*

Adjust based on what the room, the moment, or the relationship needs.

6) **Recover from Overuse or Defaulting**

When under stress, you'll default (usually to Red).

Notice the signs:

- 🔴 Red overload = dominating, over-explaining.
- 🟡 Yellow overload = empathic burnout, over-identifying.
- 🟢 Green overload = detachment, over-analysing.

Forgive the slip. Rebalance by consciously shifting hats.

7) **Rehearse Future Situations (Optional Fourth Hat)**

- Imagine walking into a future room with the *right hat already chosen*.
- Mentally rehearse how you'd behave, shift, and lead from that place.
- This is not fantasy—it's strategic emotional preparation.

Ex 3. Decontamination
— Emotional Clarity Through Spatial Clarity —

1) Acknowledge Emotional Residue

- Recognise that emotions linger like smells—especially in spaces we repeatedly use.
- Understand that shifting your *state* requires more than logic; it often requires *location*.

2) Separate Emotional Contexts by Space

- Assign different rooms or zones different emotional purposes.
    - **Bedroom for rest**, not for business planning.
    - **Dining table for connection**, not for conflict.
- If a space has been flooded with stress or grief, choose a new physical location for joy, clarity, or decision-making.

3) Use Spatial Anchoring Intentionally

- Repeat certain types of conversations in the same space to embed emotional association.
    - Deliver praise or vision consistently from the same standing point.
- Avoid emotionally cross-contaminating key locations. Some emotions need their own chair.

4) Physically Relocate Contradictory States

- When feeling emotionally conflicted, *move your body* to a different position for each emotion.
- Use *two chairs* if needed:
    - One for rage or frustration.

- Another for reflection, vulnerability, or clarity.
- Allow each emotional truth its own geography.

5) Reset Between Emotional States

- Use small rituals to mark transitions:
  - A downward glance.
  - A pause.
  - A physical step to the side.
  - A phrase like "Let's switch gears."
- These gestures reset tone and signal a shift to others.

6) Decontaminate Physical & Mental Space

- If a location holds unwanted emotional residue:
  - Step away.
  - Open a window, light a candle, or move furniture (literally or metaphorically).
- Don't layer multiple emotional narratives onto one place.
  - Clean the room.
  - Clear the mind.

7) Practise Emotional Filing

- Don't suppress emotion—*store it properly*.
- Like decluttering a drawer, give each emotion its time and place to be processed.
- Let one thing be one thing.

8) Show, Don't Announce, the Shift

- When leading, embody transitions physically rather than verbally explaining them.

- A leader's subtle movement often says more than any slide or script.

9) Honour the Geography of Emotion

- Know that safety is often *geographic*, not verbal.
- When clarity is needed, change where you sit. Or stand.
- Assign sacred emotional roles to spaces, and protect them.

Ex 4. Building Rapport & Permission
— A Stairway to Elegance —

1) Notice Without Intrusion

Train your attention on the subtlest signals—shifts in breath, posture, tone, and energy. This is *sensory acuity*, not passive observation.

Goal: Become aware of micro-signals that others miss.

2) Read the Room Before You Speak

Before acting, interpret the room's emotional tone and physiological cues. Notice whether people are guarded or open, regulated or reactive.

This is reading the room before the room reads you.

3) Mirror & Match Gently

Subtly align your breath, tone, tempo, and posture with the other person. Done well, this is an *echo*, not mimicry.

Find the shared note. Echo without imitation.

4) Pace Before You Lead

Join the person's current state fully—emotionally, verbally, energetically. Express understanding before shifting direction.

Pacing earns permission. Leading earns change.

5) Lead Through Subtle Shifts

Once you've matched their rhythm, begin introducing micro-adjustments: slower breath, softer tone, forward-leaning intent. Influence begins here.

First match. Then move.

6) *Maintain Signal Coherence*

Your non-verbal cues (breath, blink rate, tone) must *match your message*. If they don't, trust erodes—especially under pressure.

Congruence means what you say and what you show align.

7) Recover Your Signal Quickly

You will wobble. What matters is the speed and subtlety of *recalibration*—bringing voice, breath, and body back into congruence.

Notice → Settle breath → Let the message land through the body.

8) Watch for Physiological Permission

In group settings, real permission shows in the *body*: a dropped phone, an exhale, a shift in stillness. No breath sync = no influence.

Group readiness is physiological, not logical.

9) Stop Performing, Start Co-Regulating

If permission is absent, pause. Breathe how you want them to breathe. Regulate *your* state first. Influence follows shared rhythm.

Your body leads their nervous systems before your words do.

10) Lead Through Shared Breath

When the group breathes deeply and collectively, *flow* emerges. Now leadership can begin—not through command, but through coherence.

When breath drops, follow begins.

Ex 5. Points of Focus
— Mastering Attention & Presence in Any Room —

1-Point: Reflective Pause

What it is: Your gaze drops briefly downwards or inward, often to your lap, hands, or a neutral spot just in front of you.

When to use it:

- When gathering your thoughts
- Before answering a complex question
- During emotional regulation

Signal conveyed: *Thoughtfulness, care, humility*

Leadership benefit: Prevents knee-jerk replies. Creates a natural pause without appearing evasive.

Practice Tip: Pair with a slow inhale or a quiet "hmm" to signal calm deliberation.

2-Point: Eye Contact & Connection

What it is: Direct eye contact with another person or small group.

When to use it:

- In 1:1 conversations
- While making key points in small meetings
- To reassure, challenge, or validate

Signal conveyed: *Engagement, confidence, personal attention*

Leadership benefit: Builds trust and psychological safety.

Practice Tip: Soften your gaze slightly to avoid intensity. Alternate naturally between individuals in a group.

3-Point: Shared Attention

What it is: Both you and the audience shift attention to a third object—like a diagram, document, prototype, or slide.

When to use it:

- When explaining technical or sensitive material
- To defuse confrontation
- To externalise a disagreement

Signal conveyed: *Collaboration, objectivity, task-focus*

Leadership benefit: Reduces interpersonal tension by shifting the 'problem' to a shared reference point.

Practice Tip: Gesture with an open palm or pointer hand. Let your gaze follow your hand to reinforce direction.

4-Point: Visionary Framing

What it is: Your gaze lifts to the distance—upward, outward, or to a conceptual space beyond the group.

When to use it:

- While talking about the future
- To inspire or reframe the conversation
- When transitioning from tactical to strategic

Signal conveyed: *Big-picture thinking, inspiration, higher purpose*

Leadership benefit: Signals possibility and elevates the group's frame of reference.

Practice Tip: Anchor this move with a slight upward gesture, such as a sweep of the hand or open-palmed lift.

Ex 6. Non-Verbal Pattern Clusters
— *Aligning Behaviour to the Situation's Emotional Needs* —

Non-verbal pattern clusters are configurations of posture, gesture, tone, and expression that either invite connection (*Approachable*) or signal control and competence (*Credible*).

The Approachable Cluster to: *connect, disarm, reassure, or open conversation.*

- **Posture**: Relaxed, slightly angled, with some body sway
- **Facial Expression**: Smiling, eyebrows raised, animated features
- **Gestures**: Flowing, frequent, palm-up or open-handed
- **Voice Tone**: Warm, expressive, modulating, varied intonation
- **Breathing**: Low and relaxed, with visible ease
- **Inflection**: Ends of sentences curve *upward* (inviting response)

The Credible Cluster: *calm a situation, command attention, or convey expertise.*

- **Posture**: Upright, squared, still and grounded
- **Facial Expression**: Neutral or serious, little movement
- **Gestures**: Minimal, deliberate, often still or downward
- **Voice Tone**: Flat, firm, slower pace
- **Breathing**: Deep and slow, with longer pauses
- **Inflection**: Ends of sentences drop *downward* (signalling closure)

Ex 7. Peripheral Awareness Calibration
— Subtle real-time social attunement —

Why This Matters in Leadership

Foveal vision helps you drill down on one person, one point, or one task. Peripheral vision helps you read the room.

1) Relax Your Gaze

- Soften your eyes. You're not focusing on any one person or object.
- Allow your vision to "pan out," like shifting from zoom-in mode to wide angle.
- Let the *centre blur slightly* so that your awareness includes what's happening around the edges.

Try this: Gaze at a point ahead of you, but consciously notice movement, shapes, or posture changes in your side vision. Stay open, not passive.

2) Expand Your Awareness Sideways

Without turning your head, scan the emotional landscape of the room.

Look for clusters of movement, micro-gestures, or shifts in posture or breathing.

Attend not to specifics, but to the mood pattern—is the group tense? Engaged? Bored?

Mental prompt: "'What is the 'energy' (tension, interest, discomfort, connection) doing right now, and where is it moving in the room?'"

Ex 8. Eye–Hand Signalling
— Using Hands and Eyes to Guide Attention —

1) Choose Your Anchor Point

Decide *where* you want the audience's attention to go:

- A physical object (e.g., a product, flip chart, handout)
- A conceptual point in space (e.g., gesturing left to reference "the past")
- A specific person (e.g., when handing over a question)
- A slide on the screen or a particular data point

Tip: In abstract conversations, you can "anchor" invisible ideas in physical space. Pointing to the left might represent 'before', the right might represent 'future', and the centre might represent 'now'.

2) Link Gesture and Gaze

Once you've identified the anchor:

- Gesture toward it clearly with your hand.
- Let your eyes follow your hand *as it moves*, then land your gaze on the same spot.

This synchrony between hand and eye acts like a *spotlight*, showing your audience:

> *"This is what we're focusing on now"*

Common mistake:

Unless that's the effect you want, and sometimes it can be, avoid pointing somewhere while looking elsewhere. It confuses the audience and undermines the authority of your point.

Ex 9. Breath–Perception Alignment
— Shape how others perceive you with breath and vocals —

1) Reset Your System Before Speaking

- Exhale *fully* through your mouth (like sighing out tension).
- Inhale slowly through your nose into your belly (not your chest).
- You'll know it's a **diaphragmatic breath** if your stomach expands more than your chest.
- Repeat 1–2 times if needed until your heart rate slows and your voice feels deeper.

Why it matters: This resets your nervous system and primes your voice for congruent, calm delivery.

2) Match Breath and Tone to Your Intent

Approachable Mode

- Breathing: Slow, low, rhythmic.
- Tone: Smiling voice, soft cadence, varied pitch.
- Movement: Natural gestures, open body language.
- Situations: Welcoming a group, ending on an upbeat note, lightening a heavy meeting.

Sounds like:

"Let's take a look at this together." (*voice warm, upward inflection, gentle rhythm*)

Credible Mode

- *Breathing*: Low, steady, even slower than Approachable Mode.

- *Tone*: Flatter, more still; ends sentences with downward inflections.
- *Movement*: Minimal gesture, upright posture, still presence.
- *Situations*: Giving instructions, setting boundaries, speaking during high stakes.

Sounds like:

"These are the three steps we'll take next." (*voice steady, flat, downward inflection, no smile in tone*)

Avoid the High-Chest Trap

- High, shallow breathing (into your upper chest) results in:
  - Tight vocal cords
  - Higher pitch
  - Faster, choppier delivery
- This creates a voice that signals:
  - Nervousness
  - Impatience
  - Tension or even panic

Unless you're in a theatre production or running for a bus, avoid high-chest breathing in leadership contexts.

How to Self-Check

Try this quick cue before a meeting or presentation:

- Say "Good morning, everyone" twice:
  - First with a low belly breath, then
  - With a shallow high chest breath.

Notice the difference. Your body will feel it—and so will your listeners.

Ex 10. Dual-Mind Reflection
— Micro-Technique for Leadership Poise Under Pressure —

This is a rapid, internal check-in designed to help you catch yourself *before* you act or speak automatically. It enables you to distinguish between three internal drivers:

- *Instinct* — primal survival reflex (fight, flight, freeze).
- *Intuition* — pattern-based, body-informed recognition.
- *Thoughtful Choice* — calm, considered, values-aligned response.

By identifying which system is currently driving your behaviour, you can shift from reactivity to regulation, and from impulse to influence.

Why It Matters

In moments of tension or high stakes, leaders often default to instinctive reactions:

- Snapping back in meetings
- Avoiding confrontation
- Over-apologising or over-explaining

These reflexes are protective pattern but not always effective strategies. Dual-Mind Reflection inserts a cognitive 'breathing space' between stimulus and response, allowing you to regain composure, make better decisions, and project leadership presence.

1) Pause.

- Literally stop—*just for a moment.*
- Let silence stretch. Take one slow breath.

- This interrupts the autopilot pattern and signals to your system: *We are not in danger.*

2) Ask Yourself:

"Is my next move coming from instinct, intuition, or thoughtful choice?"

Tip: Intuition often whispers. Instinct shouts.

3) Re-centre.

- Drop your shoulders.
- Breathe low and slow through your nose.
- Feel your feet on the floor.
- Let your body know you are safe enough to choose—not react.

4) Respond from Grounded Intent.

- Speak or act with clarity, kindness, and credibility.
- Own your tone. Slow your voice. Anchor your posture.
- Choose language that invites connection or moves the group forward.

Pro Tips

- Use *Break & Breathe Twice* before this reflection to interrupt intense states.
- Anchor the reflection with a simple physical cue (e.g., press thumb to middle finger).
- Practise during *low-stakes* situations so it's available when it counts.

Ex 11. PACE Yourself
— Regulating Your State Before Leading Others —

1) Permission

Respectful leadership begins before you speak. It starts by honouring the emotional burden your audience may carry. This is especially vital when delivering difficult or sensitive information.

Autoregulation—calming and centring your own nervous system—is not self-indulgence. It's responsibility. If your inner turbulence leaks out, your group will feel it, even if you speak the right words.

Ask yourself:

> *"Have I given myself full permission to speak with compassion, precision and credibility?"*

If the answer is no—stop. Breathe. Rehearse. Seek help. You owe your people a leader, not a stress-reactive shell.

2) Agency

In tense moments, your body may want to fight, flee, or freeze. But leadership is not instinctual—it's intentional. Before acting, *Break & Breath Twice* and do a *Dual-Mind Reflection*.

Ask:

> *"Is my next action driven by instinct, intuition, or thoughtful choice?"*

Importantly, this pause doesn't signal hesitation. It signals control. Others perceive it as composure, not weakness.

3) Connection

Leadership is about connection—not control. And connection is somatic.

When your body sends *autonomic signals of safety*—through relaxed breathing, open gestures, and steady voice—others receive the unconscious message: *It's safe to approach.* Their nervous systems downregulate. Trust grows. Collaboration becomes possible.

Ask:

> *"Am I feeling safe, calm, and socially available?"*

This is more than a vibe check. It's a leadership duty. Because others will mirror your state, your nervous system becomes the group's emotional climate.

4) Embedding

Preparation means *mentally rehearsing difficult scenarios* before they arise—not to script your every word, but to ensure composure, clarity, and flexibility. Ask:

> *"What scenarios can I mentally prepare for to stay composed and present?"*

This rehearsal includes both *inner game strategies* (e.g., calming self-talk, re-anchoring techniques) and *outer game behaviours* (e.g., voice modulation, visual aids, gesture control).

Think of this like warming up before a difficult climb: the goal isn't to control every variable, but to prepare your body and brain to adapt, safely and skilfully.

Ex 12. Break & Breathe Twice
— Quick & Discreet Stress Pattern Interrupt —

1) The Break

Disrupt your current physiological pattern. Choose one of the following (any will do):

- Stand up if you're seated.
- Sit back or change your seat position.
- Turn your head to look in a different direction.
- Stretch your hands, rotate your shoulders, or adjust your stance.
- Shift your visual field—look out a window, at a distant object, or into a neutral space.

The goal is not to fidget but to reset your sensory channel. This interrupts the stress signal cascade.

2) Breathe *Twice*

Take two deep, intentional breaths. Each breath should be:

- *Inhaled slowly through the nose,* expanding your lower belly (not the chest).
- *Exhaled gently through the nose or mouth,* allowing your body to soften on the out-breath.

This simple double-breath lowers cortisol, slows the heart rate, and returns blood flow to the rational, problem-solving parts of the brain.

Ex 13. ABOVE (Pause) Whisper
— Mastering Vocal Modulation to Command Attention —

When to Use It

This technique is ideal when:

- You need to cut through noise in a room.
- You're opening a meeting, speech, or presentation and want instant focus.
- You're transitioning into a more serious or emotional point.
- You want to engage both the primitive and conscious attention systems in your audience.

1) ABOVE – Start with Vocal Lift

- *What to do:* Deliver your first phrase with more volume than usual—clear, strong, and deliberate.
- *Purpose:* This serves as a verbal "door knock." It tells the room, *"I have something important to say."*
- *Tip:* This is not shouting. It's projecting. Think: teacher commanding a room—not a drill sergeant barking orders.

Example:

> *"GOOD MORNING, EVERYONE"*

2) (Pause) – Hold the Silence

- *What to do:* After your strong opening, pause for 2–3 beats. Say nothing. Let the air settle.
- *Purpose:* This moment of silence does two things:
  - It allows the volume spike to echo and settle.

- It increases anticipation. Humans are wired to lean into the quiet after a burst of sound.
- *Tip*: During this pause, stay still. Breathe through your nose. Make calm, measured eye contact. Don't fill it with "um" or fidgeting.

Example:

> *[Pause]. Scan the room. Breathe.*

3) Whisper – Speak Below Conversational Volume

- *What to do*: Resume speaking in a slower, softer voice—just below your usual tone.
- *Purpose*: This draws people in. The sudden drop in volume cues the audience to lean forward and pay closer attention.
- *Tip*: Make it feel intimate, as though you're sharing something personal or important. Even in large rooms, this whisper must still be clear and deliberate, not mumbled.

Example:

> *"What I'm about to share... matters more than numbers on a screen."*

Self-Coaching Cues

ABOVE — "Did I lift my volume without shouting?"

Pause — "Did I hold still and breathe?"

Whisper — "Did my softness draw attention inward?"

Ex 14. Breathing Low Indicates Permission
— Reliable Cue of Emotional Safety —

Humans constantly emit *somatic signals* that indicate whether connection is possible. BLIP helps you read those signals in real time—particularly during conversations, presentations, or negotiations.

If someone's breathing is:

Low and diaphragmatic

→ it means "You have permission to proceed."

High and thoracic

→ it means "Pause. Permission has not been granted."

1) Interpret the Signal

- Low Breath = Permission. They feel safe, open, and capable of dialogue.
- High Breath = Pause. They may feel under threat, anxious, or emotionally closed.

2) Adjust Your Approach Accordingly

- If breathing is *low and settled*:
    - Proceed with your message.
    - Consider softening your tone or using a pause to deepen rapport.
- If breathing is *high and shallow*:
    - Slow your own breath to model calm.
    - Consider pausing, softening your presence, or changing pace.
    - Use a light, friendly tone or visual aid to re-engage their social engagement system.

Ex 15. How Not to Get Shot
— *Delivering Bad News Without Triggering Defensiveness* —

1) Go 3rd-Person

Avoid *you* and *I* statements that provoke personal blame. Use third-person or passive voice constructions that make space between the person and the problem.

- Use passive or impersonal phrasing that focuses on *what happened*, not *who's at fault*.
- Shift the attention from the person to the process or outcome.

Examples:

Instead of... "You didn't follow protocol."

Say... "Protocol wasn't followed in this instance."

Instead of... "I'm frustrated with your attitude."

Say... "The tone of the exchange became unproductive."

Instead of... "You were disrespectful."

Say... "Respect wasn't maintained in that moment."

2) Go Visual

Share important or difficult information using a **visible reference**: a document, slide, chart, or written summary. Let the eyes do some of the processing work.

- Print or display key data, instructions, or messages clearly.
- Point to or guide the visual as you explain.
- Ensure the tone and layout are neutral, not overwhelming.

Examples:

1. In redundancy meetings, present a summary handout with key dates and entitlements.
2. In performance reviews, use a shared spreadsheet or performance dashboard.
3. In disciplinary conversations, refer to a policy or timeline document, not just memory.

3) Go 3-Point

Avoid sustained direct eye contact during intense moments. Instead, introduce a third point of focus—a slide, handout, whiteboard, or object—so the emotional intensity between speaker and listener is diffused.

- Position yourself *next to* or *at 90°* to the listener while referring to a shared reference (screen, table, diagram).
- Gesture to the visual when speaking, encouraging the listener to shift their gaze there.
- Keep your voice calm and your body oriented toward the content, not the person.

Examples:

1. In a budget meeting: Sit side-by-side with the CFO, pointing together at a printed report.
2. In a team conversation: Refer to the whiteboard showing timelines and decisions.
3. In a performance discussion: Draw attention to written notes, not faces.

Ex 16. Future Pacing
— Rehearsing Success Before It Happens —

1) Set the Scene

Close your eyes. Bring to mind the *specific environment* where the real-world situation will take place.

- Where will you be? A meeting room? A stage? A Zoom call?
- Who will be there? Name faces. Imagine their presence.
- What time of day is it? What's the lighting like? The temperature?
- Are you standing? Sitting? What are you wearing?

Take 30–60 seconds to make this picture clear. Let it settle.

> "See it as clearly as a memory—even though it hasn't happened yet."

2) Engage Your Senses

Now *step inside the scene* as if you're living it. Engage all five senses:

- **Visual**: What do you see in the room? Your notes? A slide? Facial expressions?
- **Auditory**: Hear your voice—calm, precise. Hear ambient sounds—doors, chairs, breath.
- **Kinaesthetic**: What sensations do you feel? Grounded feet? A pulse of energy in your chest? The texture of the table or your clothing?

Keep your breathing steady. Let the experience feel real.

> "What is fired together, wires together. Fire the state now—so you can wire it for later."

3) Dissociate—4th Perceptual Position

Now step *out* of yourself and *observe* from a distance.

- See yourself from across the room.
- Watch how you move, speak, breathe.
- Notice your posture, eye contact, timing, tone.

This perspective allows you to calibrate. You can adjust and refine:

- Are you projecting authority without force?
- Is your rhythm congruent with your intent?
- Would you follow the person you're seeing?

This external view helps embed the identity of a composed, grounded leader.

> "If you can see it and feel it, you can become it."

4) Anticipate Challenges

Now mentally rehearse **disruptions or tension** you may face:

- A difficult question
- An emotionally reactive person
- A delay or tech failure

Don't panic—plan. See yourself responding *with calm and clarity*:

- Pausing before replying
- Using a neutral tone
- Referring to a slide or visual
- Asking a clarifying question
- Regulating your breath

This prepares your nervous system for stress inoculation.

> "If you sweat more in rehearsal, you'll bleed less in reality."

5) Anchor the State

Now, while the experience feels *most powerful*, create an *anchor*:

- Squeeze your thumb and index finger together.
- Or touch a pressure point (e.g., palm centre, wrist).
- Or say a single word in your mind like "Ready" or "Here."

This links your peak resource state to a simple cue.

Later, when you're *actually* in the real situation, use the anchor to re-access the state instantly.

> "Your body becomes your shortcut back to presence."

Practice Template (Quick Run-Through)

You can use this whenever preparing for a presentation, tough meeting, or high-stakes conversation.

It only takes 3–5 minutes:

1. *Where am I? What do I see? Who is here?*
2. *What do I hear? What do I feel in my body?*
3. *Can I see myself handling it well from the outside?*
4. *What might go wrong—and how do I stay calm?*
5. *What anchor will I use to return to this state on command?*

Ex 17. Baseline Calibration
— Notice and Navigate State Changes in Others —

1) Establish the Baseline

Your first task is to observe and *mentally note* how the other person behaves in a neutral or regulated state.

Visual Cues

- Eye contact – Direct, darting, or avoiding?
- Blink rate – Slow and steady, or rapid?
- Facial expression – Relaxed, tense, neutral, or forced?
- Body posture – Open, slouched, rigid, or defensive?
- Gestures – Fluid, still, fidgety, or repetitive?

Auditory Cues

- Tone of voice – Warm, flat, clipped, shaky?
- Pace of speech – Slow, measured, fast, or pressured?
- Volume – Soft, steady, strained, or rising?
- Word rhythm – Smooth flow or jumbled rush?

Kinaesthetic Cues

- Movement patterns – Grounded or restless? Purposeful or scattered?
- Stillness – Calm, collapsed, or frozen?
- Energy level – Centred and fluid, or rigid and tense?

Breath Cues

- Position – Deep and low, or high and shallow?
- Rhythm – Smooth and even, or irregular and clipped?
- Visibility – Can you see it in the belly, chest, or shoulders?

- Sound – Quiet and soft, or audible and strained?
- Timing – Are they breathing between phrases, or speaking breathlessly?

2) Watch for Shifts

Now that you've established a working baseline, stay alert for *deviations*—even small ones. These signal a change in state, often from safe to threatened, open to closed, or vice versa. Watch especially for signs of:

Fight-Flight: Faster speech, narrowed eyes, increased movement, shallow breath, rising shoulders, louder volume, or vocal strain.

Freeze-Shutdown: Silence, slumped posture, loss of eye contact, slow or flat tone, gaze drift, micro-expressions of defeat.

These shifts are your *indicators* that something has changed internally. Don't assume the cause. Simply notice, and *adjust*.

3) Regulate Through Your Own Signals

Once you detect a state shift, don't rush to fix it with words. Use your own *non-verbal leadership* to co-regulate. Three subtle levers to adjust:

- *Tone*: Soften your voice. Add warmth, reduce edge. Slow your cadence.
- *Pacing*: Drop your tempo. Pause. Let the silence settle.
- *Visual cues*: Soften your gaze, relax your hands, open your posture. Breathe visibly and calmly.

These micro-adjustments signal *safety* and help the other person return to their social engagement zone. You're not controlling them—you're stabilising the space between you.

Ex 18. Social Scanning
— Reading the Room Before It Speaks —

1) Arrive Early and Go Still

- Be physically present before most participants.
- Enter slowly, breathe evenly, and observe before engaging.
- Don't rush to perform 'leadership': scan the room like a naturalist in a forest.

2) Catalogue Quietly

In your mind, Observe without judgement:

- Who's anchoring the room?... Who's hiding?
- Who seems tightly wound or over-eager?

3) Greet Selectively, Not Uniformly

- With confident early arrivers, nod with respectful acknowledgment.
- For tentative lingerers, offer eye contact and a gentle verbal bridge: "Glad you made it in."
- For avoidant types, position yourself nearby briefly—say nothing, but become visible as a calm presence.

4) Seed Micro-Connections

- Use pre-session time to lightly connect with at least one person who might otherwise destabilise the group rhythm later:
- Asocial individuals → one-on-one moment that affirms their presence.
- Stressed reactors → grounding tone and a gentle check-in.

- Status-sensitive members → subtle affirmation without spotlight.

5) Adjust the Environment if Needed

- Change seating subtly if people cluster or isolate.
- Place quieter members closer to social anchors.

Practice Tips

- *Stay Peripheral.* You're not trying to dominate pre-meeting space—you're reading it like weather. Peripheral presence lets you spot patterns without becoming the centre too early.
- *Name Nothing. Notice Everything.* Don't label people aloud. Let their behaviour inform your strategy, not your assumptions.
- *Stay Available, Not Intrusive.* Offer attention, not pressure. You're showing that you're present and attuned—not trying to control.
- Signs You've Done It Well
    - The group settles more quickly once the meeting starts.
    - Early disruptors soften without needing to be "managed."
    - You feel mentally ahead of the room's mood rather than behind it.
    - You're already connected to key individuals before tension arises.

Ex 19. Frozen Hand Gesture
— Silent Authority in 3 Seconds or Less —

When to Use It

- Someone is gearing up to speak out of turn
- The conversation is spiralling or overlapping
- You need to reset focus without breaking group momentum
- You want to punctuate a key moment with silence (letting meaning land)

How to Practise It

1. **Posture First**: Ground both feet. Let your spine lengthen. Presence must precede gesture.
2. **Raise**: Lift your hand slowly—index finger up, or palm semi-open. Not military. Not limp. Just deliberate.
3. **Drop Gaze**: Look slightly downward as if collecting your thought. Avoid darting eyes—settle.
4. **Hold Still**: Count internally: "One... two... three..." Let the silence breathe.
5. **Then Move**: When the room quiets, resume with either a verbal statement or a new gesture to release the pause.

Four Common Errors

1. **Over-freezing**: Holding too long can stall the group or create awkwardness. Aim for stillness, not suspense.
2. **Incongruent Body**: Fidgeting hands or nervous feet undercut the gesture's authority.
3. **Lack of Intention**: Doing it robotically will read as confusion. Do it with purpose.
4. **Eye Contact**: Looking up or darting your gaze while freezing breaks the spell. Ground your gaze.

Ex 20. Spatial Anchoring
— Using the Room to Lead the Group —

The deliberate use of physical space to assign meaning, organise attention, and guide group behaviour.

1) Pre-Mark the Zones (Mentally or Physically)

Before the session begins, assign informal "zones" within the space. For example:

- *Front-centre* = Content delivery
- *Stage left/right* = Q&A / Open reflection
- *Centre of the room* = Discussion
- *Back of the room* = Debrief or close

2) Move with Meaning

Move intentionally. Anchor your body to each mode:

- Move forward when giving input.
- Shift sideways when facilitating others' input.
- Step back to open the floor.
- Sit or lower your stance to cue informality or emotional safety.

The body becomes a *choreographer of group intention.*

3) Repeat Until it Teaches Itself

By using the same locations for the same purposes over time, the group will begin to associate each space with a mental frame. Eventually, you won't have to *say* "Let's move into questions"—you can simply move into that zone, and they'll follow.

Ex 21. Visual Parking
— This matters. Just not right now —

This is an effective use of spacial anchoring for when a meeting participant raises a point that is:

- Off the topic currently being discussed
- Important but not urgent
- Already addressed, but they didn't hear or absorb it
- Beginning to derail or dominate the conversation

When a topic is captured *visibly*, the group sees that the point has been noticed, respected and logged for return (if time allows). This satisfies the need for psychological safety *and* group coherence.

1) Set it up early

At the start of the session, introduce the concept - 'we'll have a *Parking Lot* over here and, if something comes up that's important but off-track, I'll pop it up here so we don't lose it. This *pre-frames* the tool as helpful—not dismissive.

2) Create the space

Use a section of the whiteboard, a separate flipchart titled *"Parking Lot"*, a post-it wall, a digital note space (if online).

3) Use respectful phrasing

- "That's a great point—let's park it so we can give it proper attention later."
- "Let me jot that down so it doesn't get lost—right now we're still on [topic]."
- "I'm going to capture that over here for our return loop."

4) Write it verbatim (or close to it): keep it neutral, short, and visible. Don't paraphrase in a way that loses the speaker's original intent.

5) Refer back to it if time allows

Near the end, return to the Parking Lot and say:

> *"We parked a few things here. Let's revisit any we have time for."*
> *"This one feels unresolved—happy to follow up offline."*

Even if you don't address all items, acknowledging them honours the signal you sent by writing them down.

Three Key Don'ts

- *Don't weaponise it.* If it's used *only* to shut down dissent or awkward topics, people will notice.
- *Don't overuse it.* If everything is parked, it stops being a respectful pause and becomes a bin.
- *Don't forget it.* If you never return to the list, the group may feel manipulated.

Practice Tips

- Rehearse saying "Let's park that" with different tones—gentle, assertive, inviting.
- In hybrid or virtual settings, assign a visual scribe to capture "parked" items live in a shared doc.
- Consider categorising the parking lot: *"Future Agenda"*, *"Offline Follow-Up"*, *"Sticky Topics"*

Ex 22. Asocial Operator
— *Engaging the Silent Orbit* —

Passive withdrawal creates a vacuum that can expand. Unchecked, the asocial presence can dampen group cohesion, lower participation, and give silent permission for others to opt out too.

The Goal: Contain the Drift Early

1) Connect Before the Group Forms

When: In the pre-meeting minutes—before chairs are claimed and energy solidifies; because the early moments are *soft clay*. Once the group sets, patterns harden.

- Approach quietly, with light presence.
- Offer a non-demanding greeting:

    > "Good to have you here."
    > "Welcome—how's your day been so far?"

- Ask a low-stakes, observational question:

    > "What caught your eye on the way in?"
    > "Have you been in this space before?"

Your goal is not information. It's visibility. You're placing a gentle marker: "You matter. And I'll still see you when things heat up."

2) Use Gentle Cues to Reintegrate

Frame: Participation isn't demanded—it's enabled.

- Use eye contact, nods, or a light gesture when they speak to signal legitimacy.

- If they make a comment, briefly paraphrase it aloud so the group orients to them.

> *"Yes, as [Name] pointed out earlier…"*

Redirect questions their way indirectly:

> *"We've heard a few views—curious what's forming for others who haven't jumped in yet."*

(glance their way without forcing).

3) **Position Them Intelligently**

Insight: Seating is social architecture. It shapes engagement.

- Don't let them sit adrift—e.g., far corner, by the door, behind others.
- Place them near *connectors*—participants who are socially warm but not invasive.
- If possible, create mixed seating before they enter the room to prevent disengagement-by-default.

4) **Frame Participation as Normal**

Insight: Asocial individuals often carry internal scripts that say:

> *"If I speak, I'll be wrong, watched, or wrongfully praised."*

- When they contribute, treat it like any other input. Do not gush. Instead just say:

> *"That's helpful—let's build on that."*

Ex 23. Stressed Reactor
— Stabilising the Person Radiating Tension —

They're dysregulated. They're not difficult. Respond early to prevent emotional contagion.

Cues of Dysregulation

- Fidgeting, rapid blinking, tightly held shoulders
- Vocal tone high
- Breathing from the chest
- Posture that leans away or curls inward
- Flickers of panic in eye movement or pacing

In-Group Impact

- Others start watching them instead of engaging
- Emotional tone of group becomes cautious or tight
- Attention drifts; momentum slows
- This isn't about performance—it's about physiology.
- Their stress state is contagious.

The Goal: Connect, calm and support their social engagement behaviours

1) Connect Early—Before the Spiral

Catch them in the margins: as people are arriving, coffee is being poured, chairs are scraped. These micro-moments are your window.

- *What to do*: Approach casually. Make eye contact. Smile without pressure.
- *What to say*: Ask a soft, present-tense question.

> *"How are you finding the room today?"*

"Anything catching your eye this morning?"

This is safety signalling. You're locating them in time and space—anchoring, not interrogating.

2. Use a Grounding Tone

Once the session begins, use a prosodic vocal tone especially when you sense their system teetering.

- *Mid-range your pitch* in a similar register that you would sing a baby a gentle lullaby.
- *Slow your rhythm:* Speed induces speed. Calm induces calm.
- *Use micro-pauses:* Let silence soften your words.

3. Narrate the Environment, Not the Person

If the tension is palpable, speak to the whole group—but shape it for the one who's shaking. Describing what's *true*—not what's *wrong*.

"There's a lot to take in. Some of us are meeting for the first time. Some of us are still settling in. Let's ease into it together."

This normalises the disorientation without pointing fingers. Everyone breathes easier—including the person in crisis.

4) Stabilise Through Rapport, Not Reassurance

Reassurance often backfires—it spotlights, patronises, or confirms that something *is* wrong. Instead, maintain relationship cues. Glance with calm eyes. Nod once in support. Re-engage later with a shared comment or redirect.

Trust without intrusion. Safety without spectacle. A co-regulative bond. Rapport is silent safety. Reassurance is noisy control. Choose the former.

Ex 24. Victim Player
— *Containing & Neutralising Helplessness* —

Their behaviour is usually not conscious manipulation. It's an entrenched coping strategy rooted in a belief that suffering earns attention or safety.

Cues of Victimhood

- Slumped posture, gaze avoidance, exaggerated sighs
- Emotional heaviness that arrives in waves, especially just as the group begins to regain momentum
- Passive resistance masked as helplessness or "just being honest"
    - "No one listens to me,"
    - "I tried, but...,"
    - "It's not my fault,"
    - "I guess it doesn't matter anyway..."

Leadership Challenge

How do you maintain *group momentum and emotional safety* without either:

- Becoming the villain by calling them out too bluntly
- Enabling the behaviour by rescuing or over-validating

The aim is to hold a *firm, clear, but emotionally spacious frame*—one that doesn't collapse under the weight of their narrative, but also doesn't push them further into isolation or performance.

Practical Strategies

1. Shift posture to side-on to disarm performance tension.
   - Avoid squaring up - it can be perceived as threatening.
2. Soften eye contact to prevent escalation.
   - Use short, glancing acknowledgment rather than full, intense attention.
3. Use clarity pivots to interrupt narrative spirals
   - "Whether or not that's true, the issue we're working on now is…"
   - "That may be how it's felt. And right now, we're looking at what happens next."
4. Keep rules visible to provide structure and reduce ambiguity
   - Write group agreements on a flip-chart or slide.
   - Reference them calmly, not punitively, when needed:
     - "One of our ground rules is shared airtime. Let's stay mindful of that as we go around."
     - "We agreed to stay solution-focused. Let's come back to that now."
5. Offer measured affirmation to reinforce behaviour, not emotional display
   - Use moments of openness or humour to bridge connection.
   - When they contribute constructively, respond neutrally—not with gushing:
     - "That's a useful lens—thank you."
     - "Glad you added that in."
6. Maintain gentle proximity to encourage safety without enabling collapse
   - Stay lightly connected across the session.
   - Check in during breaks with a calm, human tone:
     - "Anything unclear so far?"

Ex 25. External Auditory Processor
— Handling the Talk-to-Think Disruptor —

They're not trying to derail the session—they're trying to catch up with themselves. But the effect on the group is the same: mental clutter, lost focus, and growing disengagement.

Goal: Redirect their energy without escalating the disruption.

1) Satisfy → Structure → Delay

Think of this as a three-question threshold. If you let them keep the floor after that, you've handed them the mic.

First Question: Answer with warmth and clarity. Make them feel heard. Say:

"That's a great question—yes, we'll touch on that in just a moment."

Second Question: Keep it brief. Use structure to hold the frame.

"We're heading there next—hang tight one more slide."

Third Question (or interruption): Hold the line. Now's the time to delay.

"Let's bookmark that for the Q&A—good catch. For now, we'll keep going."

The rhythm matters: one warm, one brisk, one boundary. You're training both them and the group to trust the flow.

2) Non-Verbal Interception

These processors *signal their intent* before they speak. If you can spot it, you can intervene *without words*. So, learn their tells. Look for fidgeting hands, eyebrow lifts, half-lifted hand, open mouth on inhale (a "pre-speak" cue).

Respond to these gestures with other gesture, not words. Use:

- A *palm-down gesture,* subtly but clearly held
- A *head tilt,* neutral but steady
- A *"monk-like" stillness*—grounded presence signals control more than any phrase

Done well, this *soothes the need to speak,* rather than suppresses it.

3) Spatial Anchoring

Use your *physical location* as part of your communication system. It sets unconscious rules for when input is invited.

Designate:

- A *Q&A spot* in the room—where you physically move when taking questions.
- A *delivery zone*—where you present, teach, or frame new ideas.

When you're *in the Q&A zone,* open posture and group-facing stance signal receptivity. When you *step back to the delivery zone,* you reclaim tempo. The group senses "Now we listen." This is choreography, not just movement. Like stage lighting—without the budget.

4) Model Participation

Sometimes the fix is *pre-emptive.* External processors speak impulsively because they don't register when space is open to them. You can model that space.

Ask a question while raising your hand.

- "Any questions before we move on?" (*hand raised as you say it*)

This momentary mirror prompts auditory processors to *pause* and reflect:

> "Do I have something of value—or am I just in my reflex?"

Even if they speak, you've now added a *filter to the process*—a moment of consideration before the impulse becomes sound.

5) Private Guidance (For Repeat Offenders)

If the behaviour continues after group-level boundaries, it's time for a 1:1.

What NOT to say:

- "You talk too much."
- "You're dominating the session."

What TO say:

> *You've got a strong auditory processing style.*
> *In groups, that can sometimes disrupt the flow—not intentionally, but it happens.*
> *A trick that often helps is writing the question down.*
> *It gives you time to shape it and lets the rhythm stay intact.*

Avoid public shaming. If you embarrass them, they won't retreat. They'll double down.

Ex 26. Looping Repeater
— When a Point Becomes a Sinkhole —

Looping isn't malice—the disruption comes not through behaviour, but through repeated content—reframed, restated, returned to—until they feel fully seen.

Leadership Goal: Acknowledge their contribution once. Prevent repetition from hijacking momentum.

The Four-Step Response Plan

1) Give It a Place (Externalise the Idea)

Loopers often need confirmation that their point has *landed*. If it remains floating in verbal space, they'll keep reintroducing it. So:

- *Write their idea down.* Use a whiteboard, a flipchart, a digital sticky note—anything visible.
- *Place it to the side,* not at the centre of attention. Use their words as much as possible so they recognise their thought.

Say:

"Let's jot that here so we can revisit it later."

This confirms they've been heard, frees them from needing to repeat and signals to the group that the issue has been contained.

2) Gesture—Don't Re-engage

Gesture calmly to the written version of their idea—what's already on the board or paper. This communicates silently:

> *We've acknowledged this.*
> *We're not ignoring you—we're storing it.*

If done consistently and with composure, this technique teaches the group that repetition won't receive new airtime. It closes the conversational loop non-verbally.

3) Question the Novelty

If the looper persists verbally, return to dialogue—but make it purposeful. Ask, slowly and with neutrality:

Is what you're saying different from what we've already captured?

Then: *pause.* Let the silence create space for them to self-reflect. This moment of hesitation interrupts automatic speech and invites metacognition (thinking about their own thinking).

- If they say *yes*, and it truly is different, treat it as a new contribution.
- If they waffle or trail off, move on. You've drawn a clear line and offered dignity without indulgence.

4. Change the Modality

Verbal repetition is often a symptom of a stuck *processing mode.* The solution? *Change the channel.*

- Go Visual:
    - Sketch a diagram or map the concept on the board.
    - Use visual metaphors, timelines, clusters—anything that gives the idea *shape.*

Loopers are often trying to process complexity. If you help them *see* it, they're less likely to keep trying to *say* it.

- This also re-engages the group—visuals reset attention.
- It creates a *shared external reference,* reducing the need for further verbal clarification.

Ex 27. Bully
— Protecting the Group from Intimidation —

The bully hijacks the conversation to control it. Their verbal dominance, undermines group safety, and asserts authority they haven't been given.

Goal: Reassert safety through clear, visible, emotionally neutral boundaries.

Cues of Victimhood

You'll know the bully by the shift in the room. The *energy drops*. People stop participating. Not because they agree—but because they're calculating risk. No one wants to be next. The bully's common phrases include:

- "Let's be honest—this won't work."
- "That's not what people *really* think."
- "I'm just saying what everyone's afraid to."

These aren't contributions. They're assertions of control dressed up as insight.

FIVE STEPS TO BULLY CONTAINMENT

1) Interrupt Calmly, Publicly and *Early*

Timing matters. The longer you wait, the more power they claim. Use clear, neutral phrases:

- "Let's pause there. We've heard your point. Now we're moving on."
- "One voice at a time. That includes everyone."

2) Use Your Body Like a Gate

- Stand still. Feet planted. Upright, shoulders relaxed but deliberate. Eye contact: steady, not hostile.
- Voice: slow, even, downward inflection.

The group doesn't just hear you—they *watch* you for a cue: *"Are we safe again?"*

3) Avoid Back-and-Forth

You're not convincing the bully—you're *protecting the group*. If the bully tries to argue, redirect without engaging:

- "We're moving on."
- "That's been noted. Let's return to the group."
- "We can follow up later—this space is for the team."

4) Reinforce Group Norms—Not Just Individual Limits

Make it about the rules, not the person:

- "Same rules apply to all of us."
- "This isn't personal—it's a shared agreement about how we work together."

5) Follow Up Only If Necessary

If the bully persists, *escalate clarity*, not confrontation:

- "I need you to help protect this space, not dominate it."
- "I won't allow this group to be made unsafe. That's non-negotiable."

Important: Bullies respond to *boundaries*, not bonding. Don't seek rapport. Seek rebalancing.

Ex 28. Recover & Reset
— When You Mess Up or Miss It —

After a disruption, misstep, or hesitation, the group's rhythm, psychological safety, and your leadership presence needs to be restored without collapsing authority or dignity.

1) Narrate the Reset

To discharges tension, normalises the disruption, and cue a fresh rhythm, offer a simple, non-blaming comment that acknowledges the moment and reorients the group.

- "That got a little tangled—let's reset."
- "We lost the thread for a bit—here's where we pick it up."
- "Bit of a detour there—back on track."

Tone: Light. Calm. Neutral. No apology, no blame. Just leadership-as-compass.

2) Re-Humanise Privately

After the group is re-centred, reconnect with the person involved (if relevant). This restores interpersonal trust and prevents lingering shame or disconnection.

- "That bit earlier—are we OK?"

(*Gentle check-in, not a correction.*)

Tip: Do this *offline* or during a break—never as public punishment. Keep it casual but sincere. You're not rehashing. You're re-humanising.

3) Own Your Misstep with Grace

If you were the cause of the wobble (e.g., you snapped, froze, or rambled), model healthy self-correction. It shows strength, not weakness. You become trustworthy by being honest and composed—not by pretending to be bulletproof.

How to do it:

- Shrug.
- Smile.
- Reset tone or posture.

Say something like:

> *"Yep, I noticed that too. Let's move forward."*
> *"Bit clunky there—thanks for sticking with me."*
> *"That one's on me. Back we go."*

Important: This is not a *confession*. It's a *calibration*. You're showing the group it's safe to falter—as long as you can regather.

Five Guiding Principles

1. Authority is rhythmic, not rigid. You can wobble—if you recover smoothly.
2. The group doesn't need you perfect. They need you steady.
3. Self-correction is not about guilt. It's about coherence.
4. The faster you name what's already felt, the faster trust resets.
5. Narrate the shared experience. When you do, the group doesn't have to carry it alone.

AFTERWORD

By now, you've reached the far edge of this first volume—and, perhaps, something steadier within yourself. What you've just read is not a manual. It's not a promise of instant results. It's a reorientation. A return to something often overlooked in the noise of leadership: the instrument of leadership itself. *You.*

If this book has done its job, it hasn't overwhelmed you with theory. It has brought you closer to signal. To pattern. To the felt intelligence that lives beneath every word you speak and every decision you make. This is not the kind of learning that ends when the chapter does.

It's the kind that starts showing up in quiet, consequential ways:

- in how you walk into a room
- in what you notice before others do
- in the breath you take before you speak

That's the leadership shift we've begun here—not one of persona, but of presence.

No doubt, pressure will return. There will be moments ahead when the air thickens and the faces turn your way. And in those moments, the work you've done here will either be available... or it won't. That's the difference between reading a book and *training yourself through it*.

If you've practised—even lightly—you've already started to encode new patterns: in how you notice tension, how you come back to breath, how you let instinct rise without letting it take the wheel. There's a quiet power in that. It doesn't announce itself. But others will feel it.

You may also have begun to sense a change in how you relate to pressure—not as something to resist or override, but as something to meet with awareness. To move with, not just through. That's the deeper resilience. Not the brittle kind that clenches through hardship, but the adaptive kind that adjusts without losing coherence. The kind that makes you trustworthy.

This volume, though first in the trilogy, is foundational because it trains the one constant in every leadership moment: *your state.*

Strategy will vary. Language will evolve. Systems will shift. But your capacity to lead others will always depend on your capacity to *hold yourself steady* when the terrain becomes unfamiliar.

The next volume will take us into that terrain. Into language—how we build meaning, shift belief, resolve distortion, and guide others with precision and story. It will explore how we speak into complexity, not with slogans, but with structures that shape how people think, decide, and relate.

But before we build a story, we must have signal. Before we influence others, we must regulate ourselves. That's the arc you've begun. From internal pattern to external presence. From reaction to rhythm. From instinct to insight.

And now you know where to begin the next time the moment rises.

Right here.

- In the body.
- In the breath.
- In the pause.

The best leaders don't fake certainty. They model steadiness. They let others borrow their clarity until the system settles. That's not something you perform. It's something you practise.

You've started that practice. And you can return to it—at will. So, as this book closes, the real work continues. In meetings. In transitions. In silence. In motion. Not as something you remember to do—but as someone you become. Not a hero. Not a fixer. Not a persona. Just a leader. Present. Signal-clear. Adaptive. Human.

Paul O'Neill

April 2025

NOTES

INTRODUCTION TO PART I

1. Porges, Stephen W. *The Polyvagal Theory: Neurophysiological Foundations of Emotions, Attachment, Communication, and Self-regulation.* W.W. Norton & Company, 2011.
2. Levine, Peter A. *Waking the Tiger: Healing Trauma.* North Atlantic Books, 1997.
3. Dana, Deb. *Anchored: How to Befriend Your Nervous System Using Polyvagal Theory.* Sounds True, 2021.
4. Van der Kolk, Bessel. *The Body Keeps the Score: Brain, Mind, and Body in the Healing of Trauma.* Penguin Books, 2014.
5. Siegel, Daniel J. *The Mindful Brain: Reflection and Attunement in the Cultivation of Well-being.* W.W. Norton & Company, 2007.
6. Dilts, Robert. *Applications of Neuro-Linguistic Programming.* Meta Publications, 1983.
7. Ogden, Pat. *Sensorimotor Psychotherapy: Interventions for Trauma and Attachment.* W.W. Norton & Company, 2015.
8. Senge, Peter. *The Fifth Discipline: The Art & Practice of The Learning Organization.* Doubleday, 1990.
9. Goleman, Daniel. *Focus: The Hidden Driver of Excellence.* Harper, 2013.

1. MAPPING THE WORLD

1. LeDoux, J. (1996). *The Emotional Brain: The Mysterious Underpinnings of Emotional Life.* Simon & Schuster.
2. Damasio, A. (1999). *The Feeling of What Happens: Body and Emotion in the Making of Consciousness.* Harcourt
3. Bandler, R., & Grinder, J. (1975). *The Structure of Magic: Volume I.* Palo Alto, CA: Science and Behavior Books
4. Merleau-Ponty, M. (1962). *Phenomenology of Perception.* Routledge & Kegan Paul
5. Lakoff, G., & Johnson, M. (1999). *Philosophy in the Flesh: The Embodied Mind and Its Challenge to Western Thought.* Basic Books.
6. LeDoux, J. (1996). *The Emotional Brain: The Mysterious Underpinnings of Emotional Life.* Simon & Schuster.
7. Barrett, L. F. (2017). *How Emotions Are Made: The Secret Life of the Brain.* Houghton Mifflin Harcourt.
8. Merleau-Ponty, M. (1962). *Phenomenology of Perception.* Routledge & Kegan Paul.

9. Porges, S. W. (2011). *The Polyvagal Theory: Neurophysiological Foundations of Emotions, Attachment, Communication, Self-Regulation*. W. W. Norton.
10. Barrett, L. F. (2017). *How Emotions Are Made: The Secret Life of the Brain*. Houghton Mifflin Harcourt.
11. Bandler, R., & Grinder, J. (1975). *The Structure of Magic: Volume I*. Palo Alto, CA: Science and Behavior Books.
12. Lakoff, G., & Johnson, M. (1999). *Philosophy in the Flesh: The Embodied Mind and Its Challenge to Western Thought*. Basic Books.
13. Bandler, R., & Grinder, J. (1975). *The Structure of Magic: Volume I*. Palo Alto, CA: Science and Behavior Books.
14. Friston, K. (2010). The free-energy principle: a unified brain theory? *Nature Reviews Neuroscience*, 11(2), 127–138.
15. Sapolsky, R. M. (2017). *Behave: The Biology of Humans at Our Best and Worst*. Penguin Press.
16. Bandler, R., & Grinder, J. (1975). *The Structure of Magic: Volume I*. Palo Alto, CA: Science and Behavior Books.
17. Lakoff, G., & Johnson, M. (1999). *Philosophy in the Flesh: The Embodied Mind and Its Challenge to Western Thought*. Basic Books.
18. Barrett, L. F. (2017). *How Emotions Are Made: The Secret Life of the Brain*. Houghton Mifflin Harcourt.
19. Damasio, A. (1999). *The Feeling of What Happens: Body and Emotion in the Making of Consciousness*. Harcourt.
20. Damasio, A. (1999). *The Feeling of What Happens: Body and Emotion in the Making of Consciousness*. Harcourt.
21. Porges, S. W. (2011). *The Polyvagal Theory: Neurophysiological Foundations of Emotions, Attachment, Communication, Self-Regulation*. W. W. Norton.
22. Friston, K. (2010). The free-energy principle: a unified brain theory? *Nature Reviews Neuroscience*, 11(2), 127–138.
23. Barrett, L. F. (2017). *How Emotions Are Made: The Secret Life of the Brain*. Houghton Mifflin Harcourt.
24. Damasio, A. (1999). *The Feeling of What Happens: Body and Emotion in the Making of Consciousness*. Harcourt.
25. Barrett, L. F. (2017). *How Emotions Are Made: The Secret Life of the Brain*. Houghton Mifflin Harcourt.
26. Sapolsky, R. M. (2017). *Behave: The Biology of Humans at Our Best and Worst*. Penguin Press.
27. Bandler, R., & Grinder, J. (1975). *The Structure of Magic: Volume I*. Palo Alto, CA: Science and Behavior Books.
28. Damasio, A. (1999). *The Feeling of What Happens: Body and Emotion in the Making of Consciousness*. Harcourt.

2. SENSING & REALITY

1. LeDoux, J. (1996). *The Emotional Brain: The Mysterious Underpinnings of Emotional Life*. Simon & Schuster.

2. Darwin, C. (1872). *The Expression of the Emotions in Man and Animals.* John Murray.
3. Dilts, R., Grinder, J., Bandler, R., & DeLozier, J. (1980). *Neuro-Linguistic Programming: Volume I.* Meta Publications.
4. Cytowic, R. E. (2002). *Synesthesia: A Union of the Senses.* MIT Press.
5. Instinct Mapping is influenced by NLP submodality techniques, which explore how sensory details structure internal experience. See Bandler, R. & MacDonald, W. (1988). *An Insider's Guide to Submodalities.*
6. Sapolsky, R. M. (2004). *Why Zebras Don't Get Ulcers.* Henry Holt and Company.
7. Andreas, S., & Faulkner, C. (1994). *NLP: The New Technology of Achievement.* William Morrow
8. Bandler, R. & Grinder, J. (1979). *Frogs into Princes: Neuro Linguistic Programming.* Real People Press.

3. CHANGING YOUR MIND

1. Grinder, J., & Bandler, R. (1976). *The Structure of Magic, Vol. I: A Book About Language and Therapy.* Science and Behavior Books.
2. Dilts, R., Epstein, T., & Dilts, G. (1991). *Tools for Dreamers: Strategies of Creativity and the Structure of Innovation.* Meta Publications
3. Andreas, C., & Andreas, S. (1987). *Change Your Mind—and Keep the Change.* Real People Press.
4. Bandler, R., & Grinder, J. (1979). *Frogs into Princes: Neuro Linguistic Programming.* Real People Press.
5. Hall, L. M., & Bodenhamer, B. G. (2003). *The User's Manual for the Brain Volume I: The Complete Manual for Neuro-Linguistic Programming Practitioner Certification.* Crown House Publishing.
6. Satir, V. (1983). *Conjoint Family Therapy.* Science and Behavior Books.
7. Bandler, R. (1985). *Using Your Brain—for a Change.* Real People Press.
8. Dilts, R. (1998). *Visionary Leadership Skills: Creating a World to Which People Want to Belong.* Meta Publications.

4. CONTROLLING YOUR EMOTIONS

1. Andreas, S., & Faulkner, C. (1994). *NLP: The New Technology of Achievement.* William Morrow.
2. Hall, L. M., & Bodenhamer, B. G. (2003). *The User's Manual for the Brain Volume I.* Crown House Publishing.
3. Siegel, D. J. (2012). *The Developing Mind: How Relationships and the Brain Interact to Shape Who We Are.* Guilford Press
4. Bandler, R., & Grinder, J. (1979). *Frogs into Princes.* Real People Press.
5. O'Connor, J., & Seymour, J. (1990). *Introducing NLP: Psychological Skills for Understanding and Influencing People.* Thorsons.

6. McGaugh, J. L. (2003). *Memory and Emotion: The Making of Lasting Memories*. Columbia University Press
7. van der Kolk, B. (2014). *The Body Keeps the Score: Brain, Mind, and Body in the Healing of Trauma*. Viking.
8. LeDoux, J. (1996). *The Emotional Brain: The Mysterious Underpinnings of Emotional Life*. Simon & Schuster.
9. Andreas, C., & Andreas, S. (1987). *Change Your Mind—and Keep the Change*. Real People Press
10. Lane, R. D., & Nadel, L. (Eds.). (2020). *Cognitive Neuroscience of Emotion*. Oxford University Press.
11. Bandler, R. (1985). *Trance-Formations: Neuro-Linguistic Programming and the Structure of Hypnosis*. Real People Press.
12. Bandler, R. (1985). *Trance-Formations: Neuro-Linguistic Programming and the Structure of Hypnosis*. Real People Press.
13. Kahneman, D. (2011). *Thinking, Fast and Slow*. Farrar, Straus and Giroux.
14. This inner dialogue restructuring method is derived from Bandler's pattern interruption techniques and the NLP "Meta Model," which deconstructs limiting language patterns. See Bandler, R. & Grinder, J. (1975). *The Structure of Magic, Vol. 1*.

    It also has parallels in narrative therapy that encourage the re-authoring of internal stories. See White, M. & Epston, D. (1990). *Narrative Means to Therapeutic Ends*.

5. COMPLETE TURN AROUNDS

1. Bandler, R. (2008). *Get the Life You Want: The Secrets to Quick and Lasting Life Change*. Health Communications. This book outlines practical NLP techniques including emotional submodality shifting
2. *This method of noticing the "spin" of anxiety and reversing it draws from Richard Bandler's "Neuro-Hypnotic Repatterning" (NHR), a technique that builds on submodality directionality to collapse or overwrite emotional patterns. See Bandler, R. (2008). *Get the Life You Want: The Secrets to Quick and Lasting Life Change*.
3. Ibid., particularly chapters on changing internal representations through movement, color, and spatial direction.
4. Bandler, R. (2008). *Get the life you want: The secrets to quick and lasting life change with neuro-linguistic programming*. Health Communications.
5. Bandler, R. (2008). *Get the Life You Want: The Secrets to Quick and Lasting Life Change with Neuro-Linguistic Programming*. Health Communications. This final marker underscores the broader application of these emotional re-patterning methods in high-stress environments
6. Hanson, Rick. *Resilient: How to Grow an Unshakable Core of Calm, Strength, and Happiness*. Harmony, 2018.

6. DAILY DISCIPLINES

1. Steve Andreas and Charles Faulkner (Eds.), *NLP: The New Technology of Achievement*, HarperCollins, 1994. See section on "Chaining Anchors."
2. Viktor E. Frankl, *Man's Search for Meaning*, Beacon Press, 2006.
3. Sinek, Simon. *Leaders Eat Last: Why Some Teams Pull Together and Others Don't*, Portfolio, 2014.
4. Fredrickson, Barbara L. "The Role of Positive Emotions in Positive Psychology: The Broaden-and-Build Theory of Positive Emotions." *American Psychologist*, vol. 56, no. 3, 2001, pp. 218–226.
5. Richard Bandler and Owen Fitzpatrick, *The Secrets of Being Happy: The Technology of Hope, Health, and Harmony*, HarperCollins, 2009.
6. Walker, Matthew. *Why We Sleep: Unlocking the Power of Sleep and Dreams*, Scribner, 2017.

INTRODUCTION TO PART II

1. Goman, C. K. (2022). *The nonverbal advantage: Secrets and science of body language at work*. Berrett-Koehler Publishers.

7. NON-VERBAL AWARENESS

1. Grinder, M. (1997). *The Elusive Obvious*. Michael Grinder & Associates
2. Bandler, R., & Grinder, J. (1975). *The Structure of Magic I: A Book About Language and Therapy*. Science and Behavior Books.
3. Grinder, M. (2008). *ENVoY: Your Personal Guide to Classroom Management*. Michael Grinder & Associates.
4. Bandler, R. (2008). *Get the Life You Want: The Secrets to Quick and Lasting Life Change*. Health Communications, Inc
5. Grinder, M. (2013). *A Healthy Classroom: The Non-Verbal Classroom Management System*. Michael Grinder & Associates.
6. Dilts, R., Grinder, J., Bandler, R., & DeLozier, J. (1980). *Neuro-Linguistic Programming: Volume I—The Study of the Structure of Subjective Experience*. Meta Publications.
7. Goleman, D. (2006). *Social Intelligence: The New Science of Human Relationships*. Bantam Books.
8. Darwin, C. (1872). *The Expression of the Emotions in Man and Animals*. John Murray.
9. Porges, S. W. (2011). *The Polyvagal Theory: Neurophysiological Foundations of Emotions, Attachment, Communication, and Self-Regulation*. W. W. Norton & Company.
10. Levine, P. A. (2010). *In an Unspoken Voice: How the Body Releases Trauma and Restores Goodness*. North Atlantic Books

11. Porges, S. W. (2021). *Polyvagal Safety: Attachment, Communication, Self-Regulation*. Norton Professional Books
12. Mehrabian, A. (1972). *Nonverbal Communication*. Aldine-Atherton
13. Bandler, R. (2009). *Richard Bandler's Guide to Trance-formation: How to Harness the Power of Hypnosis to Ignite Effortless and Lasting Change*. Health Communications, Inc
14. Grinder, M. (2003). *Charisma: The Art of Relationships*. Michael Grinder & Associates.
15. Grinder, M. (1997). *The Elusive Obvious*.
16. Bandler, R., & Grinder, J. (1979). *Frogs into Princes: Neuro-Linguistic Programming*. Real People Press.
17. Dilts, R. (1998). *Modeling with NLP*. Meta Publications.
18. Mehrabian, A., & Wiener, M. (1967). Decoding of inconsistent communications. *Journal of Personality and Social Psychology*, 6(1), 109–114.
19. Grinder, M. (2013). *A Healthy Classroom*.
20. Bandler, R. (2008). *Get the Life You Want*.
21. Bandler, R., & LaValle, M. (1996). *Persuasion Engineering*
22. Grinder, M. (2003). *Charisma*.
23. Bandler, R., & MacDonald, W. (1993). *An insider's guide to sub-modalities*. Meta Publications.

8. THE GEOMETRY OF PRESENCE

1. Bandler, R., & MacDonald, W. (1988). *Persuasion engineering*. Meta Publications.
2. Grinder, M. (2005). *The elusive obvious: The science of nonverbal communication*. Michael Grinder & Associates.
3. Grinder, J., & DeLozier, J. (1987). *Turtles all the way down: Prerequisites to personal genius*. Grinder & Associates.
4. Bandler, R., & Grinder, J. (1979). *Frogs into princes: Neuro linguistic programming*. Moab, UT: Real People Press.
5. Grinder, M. (2011). *Charisma: The art of relationships*. Michael Grinder & Associates.
6. Dilts, R. (1990). *Changing belief systems with NLP*. Meta Publications.
7. Bandler, R. (2008). *Get the life you want: The secrets to quick and lasting life change with neuro-linguistic programming*. Atria Books.
8. Bandler, R., & Thomson, G. (1982). *Magic in action*. Meta Publications.
9. Dilts, R. (1996). *Visionary leadership skills: Creating a world to which people want to belong*. Meta Publications.
10. Siegel, D. J. (2010). *The mindful therapist: A clinician's guide to mindsight and neural integration*. W. W. Norton & Company.
11. Scaer, R. C. (2005). *The trauma spectrum: Hidden wounds and human resiliency*. W. W. Norton & Company.
12. Lakoff, G., & Johnson, M. (1999). *Philosophy in the flesh: The embodied mind and its challenge to Western thought*. Basic Books.

13. Bandler, R., & La Valle, M. (1996). *NLP: The new technology of achievement.* HarperCollins
14. Grinder, M. (2003). *A healthy distrust: Rebuilding trust through nonverbal communication.* Michael Grinder & Associates.
15. Grinder, M. (2014). *The science of nonverbal communication: Silent influence.* Michael Grinder & Associates.
16. Gendlin, E. T. (1981). *Focusing.* Bantam.

9. RAPPORT & PERMISSION

1. Bandler, R., & Grinder, J. (1975). *The Structure of Magic I: A Book About Language and Therapy.* Science and Behavior Books.
2. Grinder, J., & Bandler, R. (1976). *Patterns of the Hypnotic Techniques of Milton H. Erickson, M.D.* Volume I. Meta Publications.
3. Grinder, M. (2005). *The Elusive Obvious: The Science of Nonverbal Communication.* Michael Grinder & Associates.
4. Mehrabian, A. (1971). *Silent Messages.* Wadsworth Publishing Company.
5. Grinder, M. (2013). *Charisma: The Art of Relationships.* Michael Grinder & Associates.
6. Dilts, R. (1998). *Modeling with NLP.* Meta Publications.
7. Grinder, M. (2005). *The Elusive Obvious: The Science of Nonverbal Communication.* Michael Grinder & Associates.
8. Bandler, R., & Grinder, J. (1979). *Frogs into Princes: Neuro Linguistic Programming.* Real People Press.
9. Dilts, R. (1990). *Changing Belief Systems with NLP.* Meta Publications.
10. Rogers, C. R. (1961). *On Becoming a Person: A Therapist's View of Psychotherapy.* Houghton Mifflin.
11. Grinder, M. (2013). *Charisma: The Art of Relationships.* Michael Grinder & Associates

10. NON-VERBAL ACUITY

1. Bandler, Richard & Grinder, John. *The Structure of Magic Volume I: A Book About Language and Therapy.* Science and Behavior Books, 1975. (Discusses the application of awareness and behavioural precision in communication.)
2. Mehrabian, Albert. *Silent Messages.* Wadsworth, 1971. (Pioneered research showing how incongruence in tone, gesture, and posture undermines spoken content.)
3. Grinder, Michael. *The Elusive Obvious: The Science of Nonverbal Communication.* Michael Grinder & Associates, 2011. (Covers first impressions and the leadership impact of congruent non-verbal cues.)
4. Grinder, Michael. *A Nonverbal Edge: Body Language at Work.* Michael Grinder & Associates, 2008. (Introduces one-, two-, three-, and four-point focus as non-verbal positioning strategies.)

NOTES

5. Dilts, Robert. *Leadership and Vision: NLP Strategies for Personal and Professional Success*. Meta Publications, 1996. (Explores transitions between content detail and visionary abstraction through spatial and linguistic cues.)
6. Goleman, D. (2006). *Social intelligence: The new science of human relationships*. Bantam Books.
7. Moore, D. (2017). *The body speaks: Performance and physical expression*. Methuen Drama.
8. Grinder, M. (2011). *The elusive obvious: The science of non-verbal communication*. Michael Grinder & Associates.
9. Goleman, D. (2006). *Social intelligence: The new science of human relationships*. Bantam Books.
10. Cuddy, A. (2015). *Presence: Bringing your boldest self to your biggest challenges*. Little, Brown.
11. Grinder, M. (2008). *A nonverbal edge: Body language at work*. Michael Grinder & Associates.
12. Dilts, R. (1996). *Visionary leadership skills: Creating a world to which people want to belong*. Meta Publications.
13. Mehrabian, A. (1971). *Silent messages*. Wadsworth.
14. Grinder, Michael. *Charisma: The Art of Relationships*. Michael Grinder & Associates, 2007. (Defines the approachable and credible clusters in leadership settings.)
15. Cuddy, Amy. *Presence: Bringing Your Boldest Self to Your Biggest Challenges*. Little, Brown, 2015. (Discusses body-language congruence in high-stakes presentations.)
16. Grinder, M. (2011). *The elusive obvious: The science of nonverbal communication*. Michael Grinder & Associates.
    – Discusses eye–hand congruence and how synchrony increases message clarity and attention guidance.
17. Bandler, R., & LaValle, J. (1996). *Persuasion engineering*. Real People Press.
    – Covers embodied metaphor and the power of gesture in persuasive delivery.
18. Grinder, M. (2008). *A nonverbal edge: Body language at work*. Michael Grinder & Associates.
    – Describes how bouncing gestures increase approachability and audience receptivity.
19. Grinder, M. (2017). *A healthy classroom: Using the 7 gems of nonverbal communication*. Michael Grinder & Associates.
    – Details how stillness and vertical hand gestures convey control and authority.
20. Cuddy, A. (2015). *Presence: Bringing your boldest self to your biggest challenges*. Little, Brown.
    – Explores how body posture and gesture alter perception in high-stakes communication.
21. Dilts, R. (1996). *Leadership and vision: NLP strategies for personal and professional success*. Meta Publications.

— Explains how congruence of body and message increases audience trust and attention.
22. Grinder, M. (2008). *A nonverbal edge: Body language at work.* Michael Grinder & Associates.
— Explains non-verbal signals as precognitive, instinctively processed cues in communication.
23. Dilts, R., Epstein, T., & Dilts, G. (1990). *Dynamic learning.* Meta Publications.
— Links low, diaphragmatic breathing with improved vocal tone, state regulation, and audience perception.
24. Grinder, M. (2011). *The elusive obvious: The science of nonverbal communication.* Michael Grinder & Associates.
— Discusses tone inflection, stillness, and the correlation between breath depth and perceived credibility.
25. Bandler, R., & Grinder, J. (1979). *Frogs into princes: Neuro linguistic programming.* Real People Press.
— Explores how poor state control, signalled through tone and breathing, creates incongruence and undermines authority.
26. Mehrabian, A. (1971). *Silent messages.* Wadsworth.
— Outlines how non-verbal components, including breath-fuelled tone and posture, outweigh verbal content in perceived meaning.

11. GROUP DYNAMICS

1. Grinder, M. (2003). *The Elusive Obvious.* Michael Grinder & Associates.
2. Bandler, R., & Grinder, J. (1979). *Frogs into Princes: Neuro Linguistic Programming.* Real People Press.
3. Dilts, R. (1990). *Changing Belief Systems with NLP.* Meta Publications.
4. O'Neill, P. (2025). *Dual-Mind Reflection*, The Inner Game of Leadership, Lantern & Light Press.
5. Grinder, M. (1998). *A Modest Proposal: For Resolving the Mind/Body Problem.* Michael Grinder & Associates.
6. Iacoboni, M. (2008). *Mirroring People: The New Science of How We Connect with Others.* Farrar, Straus and Giroux.
7. Anderson, C. (2016). *TED Talks: The Official TED Guide to Public Speaking.* Houghton Mifflin Harcourt.
8. Grinder, M. (2011). *Charisma: The Art of Relationships.* Michael Grinder & Associates.
9. O'Neill, P. (2025). *The PACE Yourself*, The Outer Game of Leadership, Lantern & Light Press.
10. O'Neill, P. (2025). *The PACE Protocol*, The Inner Game of Leadership, Lantern & Light Press.
11. Grinder, M. (2003). *The Elusive Obvious.* Michael Grinder & Associates.
12. Bandler, R., & Grinder, J. (1975). *The Structure of Magic: A Book about Language and Therapy.* Science and Behavior Books.

13. Grinder, M. (1998). *A Modest Proposal: For Resolving the Mind/Body Problem.* Michael Grinder & Associates.
14. Bandler, R. (1993). *Time for a Change.* Meta Publications.
15. Bandler, R. (1993). *Time for a Change.* Meta Publications.
16. Hebb, D. O. (1949). *The Organization of Behavior: A Neuropsychological Theory.* Wiley

12. CONTAINING THE MOOD-WRECKERS

1. Grinder, M. (2004). *The Elusive Obvious: The Science of Nonverbal Communication.* Michael Grinder & Associates.
2. Managers often default to corrective control due to inherited industrial-era leadership models, where order and compliance were prioritised over engagement and psychological safety

    Bandler, R., & Grinder, J. (1975). *The Structure of Magic I: A Book about Language and Therapy.* Science and Behavior Books.

    Kets de Vries, M. F. R. (2011). *The leader on the couch: A clinical approach to changing people and organizations.* Jossey-Bass.
3. The subtlety of power in group settings aligns with the research on "soft power" and distributed authority in organisational contexts.

    Nye, J. S. (2004). *Soft power: The means to success in world politics.* PublicAffairs.
4. Grinder, M. (2012). *ENVoY: Your Personal Guide to Classroom Management.* Michael Grinder & Associates.
5. Contemporary leadership increasingly relies on relational influence, resonance, and signal congruence, rather than formal authority.

    Uhl-Bien, M., Marion, R., & McKelvey, B. (2007). Complexity leadership theory: Shifting leadership from the industrial age to the knowledge era. *The Leadership Quarterly, 18*(4), 298–318.
6. Group status formation begins within seconds of interaction, as social neurobiology and perception mechanisms scan for safety and cohesion.

    Porges, S. W. (2011). *The Polyvagal Theory: Neurophysiological Foundations of Emotions, Attachment, Communication, and Self-Regulation.* W. W. Norton & Company.

    Cuddy, A. J. C., Fiske, S. T., & Glick, P. (2008). Warmth and competence as universal dimensions of social perception. *Trends in Cognitive Sciences, 12*(12), 491–493.
7. Over-control in groups can signal insecurity and reduce perceived leadership legitimacy.

    Goleman, D. (1995). *Emotional intelligence: Why it can matter more than IQ.* Bantam Books.
8. Non-verbal cues are more influential than verbal ones in group dynamics and are the primary signals through which trust and authority are assessed.

    Mehrabian, A. (1972). *Nonverbal communication.* Aldine-Atherton.

9. Silence functions as an active social cue in group settings, shaping attention and response patterns.
    Jaworski, A. (1993). *The power of silence: Social and pragmatic perspectives.* Sage.
10. Micro-interventions and embodied leadership tactics have been shown to regulate group emotion and enhance coherence.
    Ladkin, D. (2010). *Rethinking leadership: A new look at old leadership questions.* Edward Elgar Publishing.
11. Grinder, M. (2005). *Charisma: The Art of Relationships.* Michael Grinder & Associates.
12. Gesture-based interventions act as non-verbal regulators of group tempo and are closely tied to embodied cognition.
    McNeill, D. (1992). *Hand and mind: What gestures reveal about thought.* University of Chicago Press.
13. Bandler, R., & Grinder, J. (1979). *Frogs into Princes: Neuro Linguistic Programming.* Real People Press.
14. Tonality plays a core role in perceived authority, emotional congruence, and trust-building.
    Dilts, R. (1990). *Changing Belief Systems with NLP.* Meta Publications.
    Apple, M. W. (1996). *Cultural politics and education.* Teachers College Press.
15. Bandler, R. (2008). *Get the Life You Want: The Secrets to Quick and Lasting Life Change with Neuro-Linguistic Programming.* Health Communications.
16. Studies in psycholinguistics confirm that the majority of message impact in high-stakes settings derives from non-verbal channels.
    Burgoon, J. K., Guerrero, L. K., & Floyd, K. (2016). *Nonverbal communication.* Routledge.
17. Grinder, M. (2010). *A Cat in the Doghouse: 3 Steps to Conflict Prevention.* Michael Grinder & Associates.
18. Leadership involves co-regulation, a process by which the leader's physiological and behavioural signals support group stability.
    Siegel, D. J. (2012). *The Developing Mind: How Relationships and the Brain Interact to Shape Who We Are* (2nd ed.). Guilford Press.
19. The pace of group engagement is often modulated by the most dysregulated member's nervous system state.
    Porges, S. W. (2011). *The polyvagal theory: Neurophysiological foundations of emotions, attachment, communication, self-regulation.* W. W. Norton & Company.
20. Victim-based dynamics exploit ambiguity; boundary clarity is critical in disarming passive-aggressive behaviour.
    Forward, S., & Frazier, C. (2002). *Emotional blackmail: When the people in your life use fear, obligation, and guilt to manipulate you.* Harper Perennial.
21. Group affect can be shifted through pre-verbal signals; mood-setters in early stages significantly influence eventual cohesion or fragmentation.
    Barsade, S. G. (2002). The ripple effect: Emotional contagion and its influence on group behavior. *Administrative Science Quarterly, 47*(4), 644–675.

13. DISARMING THE VERBAL HIJACKER

1. Michael Grinder outlines how gesture, posture, tone, and spatial anchoring communicate authority and calm more effectively than verbal correction.

    Grinder, M. (2012). *Nonverbal communication: Control the conversation and connect with your audience without saying a word.* Michael Grinder & Associates.

2. Bandler and Grinder identified that some individuals 'think out loud' to process thought—interruptions are attempts at clarity, not sabotage.

    Bandler, R., & Grinder, J. (1975). *The structure of magic I: A book about language and therapy.* Science and Behavior Books.

3. Robert Dilts showed how eye movements, posture shifts, and facial cues reveal intent before speech begins.

    Dilts, R. (1998). *Modeling with NLP.* Meta Publications.

4. Behaviour change happens through precision, not confrontation. Andreas and Faulkner recommend redirecting through compatible strategies—like writing or delayed response—to help auditory types self-regulate.

    Andreas, S., & Faulkner, C. (1994). *NLP: The new technology of achievement.* William Morrow Paperbacks.

5. Public shame does not regulate—it escalates—it suppresses participation and increases defensive behaviour.

    Brown, B. (2012). *Daring greatly: How the courage to be vulnerable transforms the way we live, love, parent, and lead.* Gotham Books.

6. Repetition often signals cognitive fixation, not malice. James and Woodsmall describe this as a 'stuck state'—requiring redirection, not correction.

    James, T., & Woodsmall, W. (1988). *Time Line Therapy and the basis of personality.* Meta Publications.

7. Changing sensory modality shifts attention and breaks repetition. Visual mapping redirects looping by engaging external reference points.

    O'Connor, J., & McDermott, I. (1996). *Principles of NLP.* Thorsons.

8. Looping stems from the brain's Default Mode Network (DMN), which is the brain's self-referential circuit. Loopers are often stuck in internal rehearsal.

    Raichle, M. E., et al. (2001). A default mode of brain function. *Proceedings of the National Academy of Sciences,* 98(2), 676–682.

9. Most disruption is a status game, not a truth claim. Behaviours like blocking or repeating are often unconscious moves to regain social relevance.

    Berne, E. (1964). *Games people play: The basic handbook of transactional analysis.* Grove Press.

10. Blockers are often shaped by culture, not just personality. Argyris explained how defensive reasoning is rewarded in cynical cultures—Blockers are sometimes just its mouthpiece.

    Argyris, C. (1990). *Overcoming organizational defenses: Facilitating organizational learning.* Allyn & Bacon.

11. People stay quiet under dominance—not because they agree, but because they

fear exclusion. Conformity studies explain the hostage-like stillness that occurs around bullies.

Asch, S. E. (1956). Studies of independence and conformity. *Psychological Monographs*, 70(9), 1–70.

12. Bullies don't respond to insight. They respond to boundaries. Power, calmly and clearly applied, is an effective antidote to disruptive dominance.

Patterson, K., Grenny, J., McMillan, R., & Switzler, A. (2002). *Crucial conversations: Tools for talking when stakes are high*. McGraw-Hill.

13. The leader signals the group's rules by how they behave, not what they say. Goffman demonstrated that non-verbal cues set the 'frame' for interactions.

Goffman, E. (1959). *The presentation of self in everyday life*. Anchor Books.

14. Groups make judgments through emotion first, then logic. It's been shown that intuition and emotional resonance precede conscious reasoning in group moral decisions.

Haidt, J. (2012). *The righteous mind: Why good people are divided by politics and religion*. Pantheon Books.

15. Disruption often emerges from emotional dysregulation, not poor reasoning. It's been proven that decision-making is emotionally rooted—cognition fails when we ignore this layer.

Damasio, A. (1994). *Descartes' error: Emotion, reason, and the human brain*. G.P. Putnam.

16. Stress shuts down the prefrontal cortex—where logic lives—hijacking executive function. As such, calm leaders help others think clearly.

Arnsten, A. F. T. (2009). Stress signalling pathways that impair prefrontal cortex structure and function. *Nature Reviews Neuroscience*, 10(6), 410–422.

17. Recovery after disruption is a rhythmic act, not a rational one. Studies in conversational rhythm in complex systems supports the practice of narrating recovery without blame.

Shaw, P. (2002). *Changing conversations in organizations: A complexity approach to change*. Routledge.

18. Group emotion is contagious. Hatfield et al. showed that tone, breath, and facial expression are contagious—both tension and calm ripple through the room.

Hatfield, E., Cacioppo, J. T., & Rapson, R. L. (1994). *Emotional contagion*. Cambridge University Press.

19. True leadership is felt, not performed. Influence arises from presence, not from mimicking leadership tropes.

Grinder, J., & Bandler, R. (1981). *Frogs into princes: Neuro linguistic programming*. Real People Press.

20. Your nervous system sets the tone for the room. Polyvagal Theory explains how voice, face, and stillness cue others' sense of safety—especially under pressure.

Porges, S. W. (2011). *The polyvagal theory: Neurophysiological foundations of emotions, attachment, communication, and self-regulation*. W. W. Norton.

CONCLUSION TO PART II

1. Bandler, R., & Grinder, J. (1975). *The structure of magic: A book about language and therapy* (Vol. 1). Science and Behavior Books.
    Describes the implicit mapping of signals and unspoken communication patterns in human interaction.
2. Grinder, M. (2012). *The elusive obvious: The science of non-verbal communication*. Michael Grinder & Associates.
    Offers precise observations about presence, posture, and breath as primary communicative signals in leadership.
3. Dilts, R. (1990). *Changing belief systems with NLP*. Meta Publications.
    Discusses how unconscious signals and belief congruence impact rapport, trust, and behavioural change.
4. Siegel, D. J. (2010). *The mindful therapist: A clinician's guide to mindsight and neural integration*. W. W. Norton & Company.
    Explores nervous system regulation and presence in high-trust interpersonal settings.
5. Bandler, R. (2008). *Get the life you want: The secrets to quick and lasting life change with NLP*. Health Communications.
    Introduces state calibration and signal control as agency-restoring practices.
6. Goleman, D. (2006). *Social intelligence: The new science of human relationships*. Bantam.
    Describes emotional contagion, group synchrony, and pre-verbal trust signalling.
7. Grinder, J., & Bostic St. Clair, C. (2001). *Whispering in the wind*. J & C Enterprises.
    Expands the notion of "state" as a systemic and somatic phenomenon that precedes speech or strategy.
8. Dilts, R., Hallbom, T., & Smith, S. (1990). *Beliefs: Pathways to health and wellbeing*. Meta Publications.
    Covers early-stage rapport development, mirror neurons, and somatic congruence in behavioural modelling.
9. Grinder, J., & Bostic St. Clair, C. (2001). *Whispering in the wind*. J & C Enterprises.
    Expands the notion of "state" as a systemic and somatic phenomenon that precedes speech or strategy
10. Satir, V., Banmen, J., Gerber, J., & Gomori, M. (1991). *The Satir model: Family therapy and beyond*. Science and Behavior Books.
    Describes how non-verbal signalling precedes verbal alignment in trust-building.
11. Bandler, R., & LaValle, J. (1996). *Persuasion engineering*. Meta Publications.
    On embodied influence, unconscious perception of state, and communication as multilevel signalling.
12. Porges, S. W. (2011). *The polyvagal theory: Neurophysiological foundations of*

emotions, attachment, communication, and self-regulation. W. W. Norton & Company.

Demonstrates how physiological cues of safety drive social engagement and leadership resonance.

13. Dilts, R. (1998). *Modeling with NLP*. Meta Publications.

    Outlines the feedback loops between state, environment, and leadership system dynamics.

14. Grinder, M. (2005). *A healthy classroom*. Michael Grinder & Associates.

    Describes anticipatory regulation and the leader's responsibility in pre-loading calm into high-stress settings.

15. Bandler, R., & Thomson, G. (2011). *Conversations with Richard Bandler: Two NLP pioneers reveal the secrets to success*. Health Communications.

    Discusses internal alignment and signal congruence as cornerstones of reliable influence.

BIBLIOGRAPHY

Andreas, C., & Andreas, S. (1987). *Change Your Mind—and Keep the Change*. Real People Press.
Andreas, S., & Faulkner, C. (1994). *NLP: The New Technology of Achievement*. William Morrow.
Bandler, R. (1985). *Using Your Brain—for a Change*. Real People Press.
Bandler, R. (2008). *Get the Life You Want: The Secrets to Quick and Lasting Life Change with Neuro-Linguistic Programming*. Health Communications.
Bandler, R. (2009). *Richard Bandler's Guide to Trance-formation: How to Harness the Power of Hypnosis to Ignite Effortless and Lasting Change*. Health Communications.
Bandler, R., & Grinder, J. (1975). *The Structure of Magic: Volume I*. Science and Behavior Books.
Bandler, R., & Grinder, J. (1979). *Frogs into Princes: Neuro Linguistic Programming*. Real People Press.
Bandler, R., & LaValle, J. (1996). *Persuasion Engineering*. Meta Publications.
Bandler, R., & MacDonald, W. (1993). *An Insider's Guide to Sub-Modalities*. Meta Publications.
Bandler, R., & Thomson, G. (1982). *Magic in Action*. Meta Publications.
Bandler, R., & Thomson, G. (2011). *Conversations with Richard Bandler: Two NLP Pioneers Reveal the Secrets to Success*. Health Communications.
Barrett, L. F. (2017). *How Emotions Are Made: The Secret Life of the Brain*. Houghton Mifflin Harcourt.
Bateson, G. (1972). *Steps to an Ecology of Mind*. University of Chicago Press.
Beck, A. T. (1976). *Cognitive Therapy and the Emotional Disorders*. International Universities Press.
Damasio, A. (1999). *The Feeling of What Happens: Body and Emotion in the Making of Consciousness*. Harcourt.
Dana, D. (2021). *Anchored: How to Befriend Your Nervous System Using Polyvagal Theory*. Sounds True.
Darwin, C. (1872). *The Expression of the Emotions in Man and Animals*. John Murray.
Dilts, R. (1990). *Changing Belief Systems with NLP*. Meta Publications.
Dilts, R. (1996). *Visionary Leadership Skills: Creating a World to Which People Want to Belong*. Meta Publications.
Dilts, R. (1998). *Modeling with NLP*. Meta Publications.
Dilts, R. (1999). *Sleight of Mouth: The Magic of Conversational Belief Change*. Meta Publications.

Dilts, R., Epstein, T., & Dilts, G. (1991). *Tools for Dreamers: Strategies of Creativity and the Structure of Innovation*. Meta Publications.

Dilts, R., Grinder, J., Bandler, R., & DeLozier, J. (1980). *Neuro-Linguistic Programming: Volume I*. Meta Publications.

Dilts, R., Hallbom, T., & Smith, S. (1990). *Beliefs: Pathways to Health and Well-Being*. Meta Publications.

Fredrickson, B. L. (2001). The role of positive emotions in positive psychology: The broaden-and-build theory of positive emotions. *American Psychologist, 56*(3), 218–226.

Gendlin, E. T. (1981). *Focusing*. Bantam.

Goleman, D. (2006). *Social Intelligence: The New Science of Human Relationships*. Bantam.

Goman, C. K. (2022). *The Nonverbal Advantage: Secrets and Science of Body Language at Work*. Berrett-Koehler.

Grinder, J., & Bandler, R. (1976). *The Structure of Magic, Vol. I: A Book About Language and Therapy*. Science and Behavior Books.

Grinder, J., & Bandler, R. (1979). *Frogs into Princes: Neuro Linguistic Programming*. Real People Press.

Grinder, J., & DeLozier, J. (1987). *Turtles All the Way Down: Prerequisites to Personal Genius*. Grinder & Associates.

Grinder, M. (1997). *The Elusive Obvious*. Michael Grinder & Associates.

Grinder, M. (2003). *Charisma: The Art of Relationships*. Michael Grinder & Associates.

Grinder, M. (2005). *A Healthy Classroom*. Michael Grinder & Associates.

Grinder, M. (2008). *ENVoY: Your Personal Guide to Classroom Management*. Michael Grinder & Associates.

Grinder, M. (2014). *The Science of Nonverbal Communication: Silent Influence*. Michael Grinder & Associates.

Grinder, M. (2016). *The Elusive Obvious*. Michael Grinder & Associates.

Hall, L. M., & Bodenhamer, B. G. (2003). *The User's Manual for the Brain, Volume I*. Crown House Publishing.

Kahneman, D. (2011). *Thinking, Fast and Slow*. Farrar, Straus and Giroux.

Lakoff, G., & Johnson, M. (1999). *Philosophy in the Flesh: The Embodied Mind and Its Challenge to Western Thought*. Basic Books.

LeDoux, J. (1996). *The Emotional Brain: The Mysterious Underpinnings of Emotional Life*. Simon & Schuster.

Levine, P. A. (1997). *Waking the Tiger: Healing Trauma*. North Atlantic Books.

Levine, P. A. (2010). *In an Unspoken Voice: How the Body Releases Trauma and Restores Goodness*. North Atlantic Books.

Mehrabian, A. (1972). *Nonverbal Communication*. Aldine-Atherton.

Mehrabian, A., & Wiener, M. (1967). Decoding of inconsistent communications. *Journal of Personality and Social Psychology, 6*(1), 109–114.

Merleau-Ponty, M. (1962). *Phenomenology of Perception*. Routledge & Kegan Paul.

Ogden, P. (2006). *Trauma and the Body: A Sensorimotor Approach to Psychotherapy.* W. W. Norton & Company.

O'Connor, J., & Seymour, J. (1990). *Introducing NLP: Psychological Skills for Understanding and Influencing People.* Thorsons.

O'Neill, P. (2025). *Adaptive Wisdoms: Lead from the Skin In* (NLP Mastery for Leaders, Vol. 1). Lantern & Light Press.

O'Neill, P. (2025). *Back into Delight: Grief Recovery at the Speed of Life.* Lantern & Light Press.

O'Neill, P. (2025). *The Inner Game of Leadership: How Leaders Conquer Stress to Shine in Turbulence* (Neuro-Resilience Skills, Vol. 1). Lantern & Light Press.

O'Neill, P. (2025). *The Outer Game of Leadership: How to Unite and Inspire Teams in Times of Challenge and Crisis*(Neuro-Resilience Skills, Vol. 2). Lantern & Light Press.

O'Neill, P. (in press). *Logic & Language: Solve and Shift What's Stuck* (NLP Mastery for Leaders, Vol. 2). Lantern & Light Press.

O'Neill, P. (in press). *Moving As One: Align, Adapt and Lead Together* (NLP Mastery for Leaders, Vol. 3). Lantern & Light Press.

O'Neill, P. (in preparation). *The Iron Laws: Constraints That Shape Every Leader* (NLP Mastery for Leaders, Vol. 0). Lantern & Light Press.

Porges, S. W. (2011). *The Polyvagal Theory: Neurophysiological Foundations of Emotions, Attachment, Communication, and Self-Regulation.* W. W. Norton & Company.

Porges, S. W. (2017). *The Pocket Guide to the Polyvagal Theory.* W. W. Norton & Company.

Porges, S. W. (2021). *Polyvagal Safety: Attachment, Communication, Self-Regulation.* Norton Professional Books.

Rogers, C. R. (1961). *On Becoming a Person: A Therapist's View of Psychotherapy.* Houghton Mifflin.

Sapolsky, R. M. (2004). *Why Zebras Don't Get Ulcers.* Henry Holt.

Sapolsky, R. M. (2017). *Behave: The Biology of Humans at Our Best and Worst.* Penguin Press.

Scaer, R. C. (2005). *The Trauma Spectrum: Hidden Wounds and Human Resiliency.* W. W. Norton & Company.

Senge, P. M. (1990). *The Fifth Discipline: The Art and Practice of the Learning Organization.* Doubleday.

Siegel, D. J. (2007). *The Mindful Brain: Reflection and Attunement in the Cultivation of Well-Being.* W. W. Norton & Company.

Siegel, D. J. (2010). *The Mindful Therapist: A Clinician's Guide to Mindsight and Neural Integration.* W. W. Norton & Company.

Siegel, D. J. (2012). *The Developing Mind: How Relationships and the Brain Interact to Shape Who We Are.* Guilford Press.

Tosey, P., & Mathison, J. (2009). *Neuro-Linguistic Programming: A Critical Appreciation for Managers and Developers.* Palgrave Macmillan.

van der Kolk, B. (2014). *The Body Keeps the Score: Brain, Mind, and Body in the Healing of Trauma*. Viking.

Walker, M. (2017). *Why We Sleep: Unlocking the Power of Sleep and Dreams*. Scribner.

Watzlawick, P., Bavelas, J. B., & Jackson, D. D. (1967). *Pragmatics of Human Communication*. Norton.

White, M., & Epston, D. (1990). *Narrative Means to Therapeutic Ends*. Norton.

INDEX

A
ABOVE (Pause) Whisper
Agency Over Instinct
Anchoring
Asocial Operator
Attunement Before Action
Authority is Silent
Autonomic Signals

B
Baseline Calibrating
Behaviour & Reflex
Belief Change
Bids & Social Safety
BLIP
Break & Breathe Twice
Breath & Perception
Bruce Case Study

C
Coach with Two Chairs
Collapsing Anchors
Congruence
Connect With Yourself
Content–Structure–State Model
Controlling Your Inner Voice
Control Your Inner Voice

D
Deep Refreshing Sleep
Decontamination
Deletion
Delight at Dawn
Dissociation (V/K)
Distortion
Dog–Kat Spectrum
Dual-Mind Reflection

E
Embodied Cognition
Embodied Signal Influence
Experience is Structured

External Auditory Processor
Eye Accessing Cues
Eye–Hand Signalling
F
Filtering Reality
Finding Home
Frame Shift
Frozen Hand Gesture
Future Pacing
G
Generalisation
Get Rid of It
Group Development Curve
Group Fairness
Group Permission
Group Self-Regulation
H
How Not to Get Shot
I
Ignorance to Intelligence Pathway
Influence–Power Dial
Instinct Before Intellect
Internal Dialogue
K
Karen's Case Study
L
Looping Repeater
M
Mammalian Mapping Model
Mirroring & Matching
Morning Momentum
Mountains into Molehills
N
Neuroception
Neuro-Spa Reset
Non-Verbal Fumble
Non-Verbal Leadership
Non-Verbal Pattern Clusters
P
PACE Protocol
PACE Yourself
Pacing & Leading
Pause & Reflect
Perceptual Positions

Peripheral Awareness
Permission Loop
Points of Focus
Pre-Linguistic Mapping
Pre-Session Rapport
Projecting Non-Verbal Cues
R
Rapport (Non-Verbal)
Recover & Reset
Reflective Capacity
Representational Systems
S
Sensory Acuity
Shifting Perceptual Positions
Signal Hygiene
Signal Literacy
Silence Projects Intelligence
Social Scanning
Soften at Sunrise
Spatial Anchoring
Species-Specific Subjectivity
State Calibration
State–Structure–Content
String of Pearls
Stressed Reactor
Surfacing Submodalities
Swish Pattern
Synesthetic Crossings
T
The Past is Over
Turning Anxiety Around
U
Universal Model
V
VAKOG
Victim Player
Visual Parking
Visual–Kinaesthetic Dissociation
Voice Tone
W
Wrapped in Serenity

ACKNOWLEDGMENTS

My sincere thanks to **Francinne Kaye Gacilo**, whose sharp eye and creative mind brought this book to life in more ways than one.

As a digital media specialist with a flair for graphic design, Francinne not only proofread the manuscript with care but also contributed a series of interior graphics that added clarity, elegance, and visual depth to the pages.

Her work helped turn concepts into compelling visuals, and for that, I'm deeply grateful.

ABOUT THE AUTHOR

Paul O'Neill is trusted by professionals in business, heavy industry, medical and mental health, and elite sports as consultant, coach and guide. For more than twenty-five years, he's been doing exactly that: guiding individuals, teams and entire organisations through the thickets of change, chaos and contradiction with a calm intensity that refuses to settle for surface solutions.

His leadership record spans continents and industries, yet his work never follows a formula. That's the point. Real transformation, he insists, can't be imposed or standardised. It must be built, brick by deliberate brick, in the language, rhythm, and logic of those who live it.

Clients across Australia, New Zealand, the UK, North America, and South Africa describe him as 'visionary', 'invaluable', 'a lifelong friend' - though the word most often repeated is 'transformational'. Not because Paul performs miracles, but because he hands the tools over. He trains people to recognise patterns, to respond to pressure with composure, to build resilience that sticks - not just in the individual nervous system, but in the culture of entire teams.

Paul's training and coaching in neuro-resilience skills, verbal and non-verbal skills, group dynamics, complex problem-solving, stakeholder engagement and adaptive strategic leadership has helped professionals across sectors rewrite their stories - by both negating the harsh effect change can have on the leaders, as well as by navigating their group through it differently. He's known for making the complex understandable, for challenging the status quo with warmth and rigour, and for turning the work of change into something deeply human and fiercely practical.

He remains, above all else, a practitioner. Someone who steps in, shoulder to shoulder, as a guide; and he stays until the work is done.

If you've reached the edge of what you know and understand, Paul is someone you want in the room.

ALSO BY PAUL O'NEILL

Back into Delight

Letters to a Young Teacher

The Iron Laws

Grounded, Bonded & Flowing

Neuro-Resilience Skills series

Vol. 1: The Inner Game of Leadership

Vol 2: The Outer Game of Leadership

NLP Mastery for Leaders series

Vol 1: Adaptive Wisdoms

Vol 2: Logic & Language

Vol 3: Moving As One

Six Pillars of Successful Executives

Pillar 1: Personal Resilience

Pillar 2: Non-Verbal Cues

Pillar 3: Pristine Problem Solving

Pillar 4: Impactful Speaking

Pillar 5: Engagement Excellence

Pillar 6: Strategic Resilience

www.ingramcontent.com/pod-product-compliance
Lightning Source LLC
Chambersburg PA
CBHW061725070526
44583CB00024B/3005